**ARCTIC NAVAL COMBAT IN
SUPPORT OF GROUND OPERATIONS**

Arctic Naval Combat in Support of Ground Operations

Soviet Naval Support of the Petsamo-Kirkenes Operation, October 1944

Translated and annotated from the original Soviet official history with additional supporting material on large-scale Arctic combat

Directorate of the Naval Press of the People's Commissariat of the Navy of the USSR

Translated and annotated by MAJOR (RETIRED) JAMES F. GEBHARDT
Edited by LIEUTENANT-COLONEL (RETIRED) LESTER W. GRAU, PHD
Maps by LIEUTENANT-COLONEL CHARLES K. BARTLES, PHD

UNIVERSITY OF ALASKA PRESS *Fairbanks*

© 2025 by University Press of Colorado

Published by University of Alaska Press
An imprint of University Press of Colorado
1580 North Logan Street, Suite 660
PMB 39883
Denver, Colorado 80203-1942

All rights reserved

 The University Press of Colorado is a proud member of Association of University Presses.

The University Press of Colorado is a cooperative publishing enterprise supported, in part, by Adams State University, Colorado School of Mines, Colorado State University, Fort Lewis College, Metropolitan State University of Denver, University of Alaska Fairbanks, University of Colorado, University of Denver, University of Northern Colorado, University of Wyoming, Utah State University, and Western Colorado University.

ISBN: 978-1-64642-790-1 (hardcover)
ISBN: 978-1-64642-791-8 (ebook)
https://doi.org/10.5876/9781646427918

Cataloging-in-Publication data for this title is available online at the Library of Congress

All maps in this work are in the public domain.

Cover photo: Ships of the Northern Fleet with paratroopers on the way to Petsamo, Finland. October 1944. Alamy/World History Archive

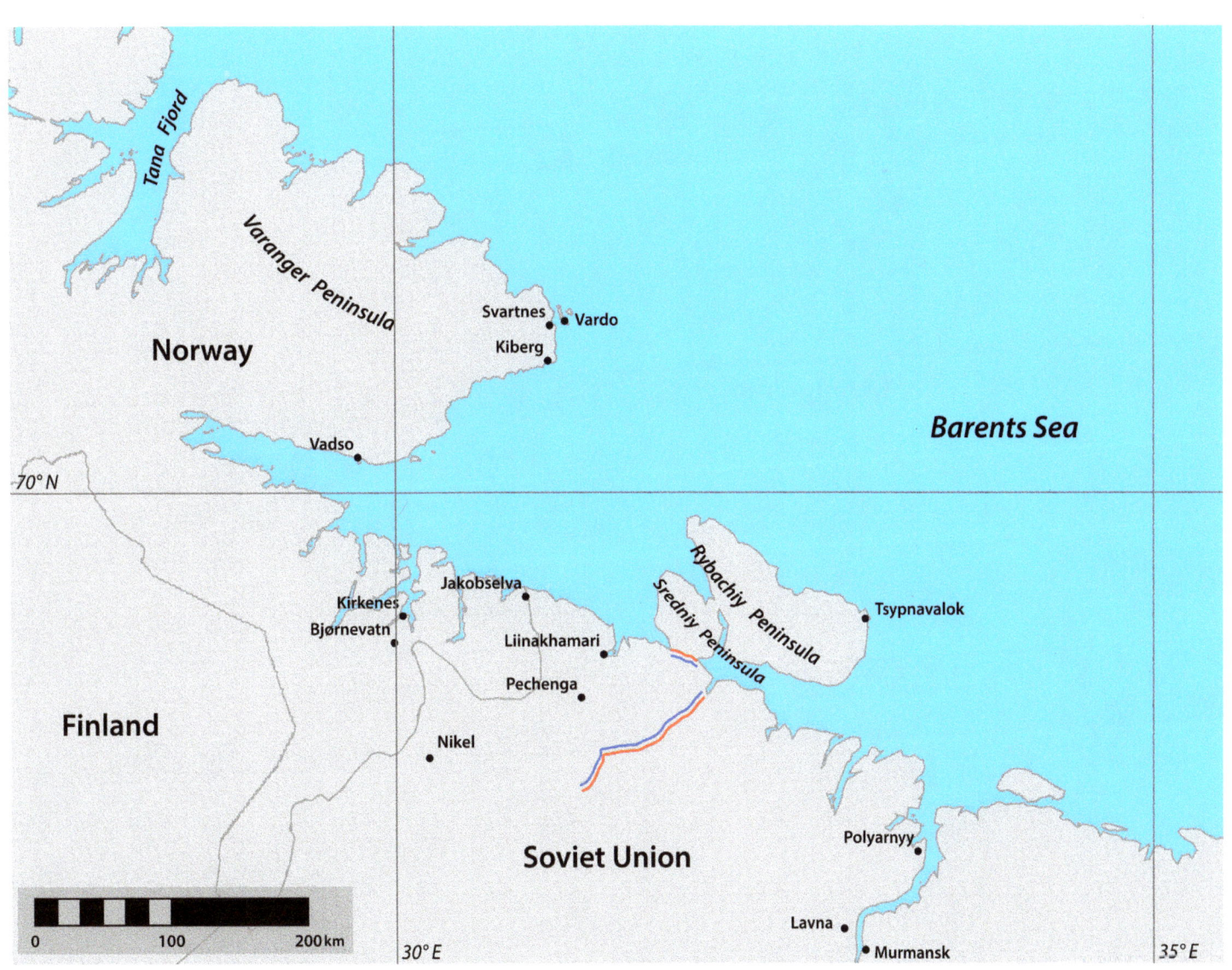

FIGURE 0.1. Map showing areas of conflict described in this book

Contents

Foreword
David M. Glantz, Colonel, US Army, Retired ix

Manuscript Editor's Preface
Lester W. Grau xi

Original Title Page xiii

Translator's Foreword
James Gebhardt xv

List of Abbreviations Used in This Study
James Gebhardt xix

Preface xxi

Order of the Supreme High Command,
15 October 1944 xxiii

Order of the Supreme High Command,
1 November 1944 xxv

CHAPTER I. Frontline Situation of the
Forces of the Northern Defensive Region
on the Coast of Varangerfjord and Sredniy
and Rybachyy Peninsulas 3

CHAPTER II. Commander's Concept and
Operational Plan 10

    1. Concept of the Operation and Plan of Actions
of the Forces of the Karelian *Front* 10

    2. Missions of the Northern Fleet 11

CHAPTER III. Decision of the Commander, Northern
Fleet, and Plan of Joint Operations with the Karelian
Front for the Liberation of the Soviet Far North 12

    1. The Decision and Operational Plan
on Land 12

    2. Decision for Actions at Sea 14

    3. Decision for Actions from the Air 14

    4. Organization of Command and Composition
of Forces 15

CHAPTER IV. Preparation for Execution of the
Assigned Mission 17

    1. Staff Work During the Preparation for
the Operation 17

    2. Preparation of Units and Ships for
the Amphibious Landing 20

    3. Hydrometeorological Support 22

4. Navigational-Hydrographic Support   22
   5. Preparation of Units Designated for Breakthrough of the Defenses   24
   6. Preparation of Aviation   25
   7. Logistic and Medical Support   25
   8. Preparation of Military Transportation Units for the Operation   29

CHAPTER V. Execution of the Assigned Missions   31
   1. Actions of the Forces of the Karelian *Front*   31
   2. The Landing of Amphibious Assault Forces by Northern Fleet Vessels   33
      a. Amphibious Landing on the Southern Coast of Maattivuono Bay   33
      b. Actions of the Composite Reconnaissance Detachment   39
      c. Actions of the Demonstration Landing   42
      d. The Amphibious Landing in Liinakhamari Port on the Night of 12–13 October   43
      e. Amphibious Assault for the Capture of the Batteries Covering the Entrance to Petsamovuono Inlet   50
      f. Landing of Amphibious Forces on the Southern Coast of Varangerfjord   50
   3. Breakthrough of Enemy Defenses and Pursuit by Northern Defensive Region Units   52
   4. Actions Against Sea Lines of Communication   61
      a. Actions of the Surface Squadron   62
      b. Actions of Red Banner Torpedo Cutter Brigade   64
      c. Actions of Red Banner Submarine Brigade   67
      d. Actions of the Northern Fleet Air Forces   76
   5. Execution of the Mission to Transport Forces by Sea   82
   6. Execution of the Logistic Support Mission   83
   7. Execution of the Medical Support Mission   85

CHAPTER VI. Organization of Command and Control for Combat and the Accomplishment of Coordination   87
   1. The Fleet Commander's Decision as a Basis for the Organization of Combat Command and Control   87
   2. Development of the Decision   88
   3. Combat Documents   88
      a. Operational *Maskirovka* for This Operation   89
   4. Organization of Combat Command and Control   89
   5. The Organization of Coordination   91
   6. Command and Control During Combat   92
   7. Organization and Work of Communications Units   95
      a. Mutual Recognition   97

General Lessons   98

Conclusion   101

Glossary of Abbreviations Used in Appendixes   103

APPENDIX 1: Order of the Commander, Northern Fleet   107

APPENDIX 2: Combat Directive No. 0052/*op* of Commander, Northern Fleet (for Operation "West")   109

APPENDIX 3: Combat Order No. 0014/*op*, Headquarters Northern Defensive Region *SF*   115

APPENDIX 4: Results of Submarine Attacks   121

TRANSLATOR'S APPENDIX 1: Excerpted from Study No. 38, *Intelligence Support of the Northern Fleet in the Great Patriotic War (1941–1945)*   123

TRANSLATOR'S APPENDIX 2: Excerpted from *Frontovyye bydni Rybachevo* (Frontline life on the Rybachyy Peninsula) by I. P. Barchenko-Emelyanov and *Litsom k litsu: Vospominaniya morskogo razvedchika* (Face to face: Recollections of a naval scout) by Viktor Leonov   133

TRANSLATOR'S APPENDIX 3: Higgins and Vosper Patrol Torpedo Boat Deliveries to Northern Fleet Through Lend-Lease, 1943–1945   147

Recommended Bibliography   153

About the Translator   155

About the Contributors   157

Foreword

David M. Glantz, Colonel, US Army, Retired

The author of this book, Jim Gebhardt, spent his life in selfless military service defending his country, pursuing peace and a keener understanding between the United States and the Soviet Union during the waning stages of the Cold War, and promoting peaceful relations between the United States and Russian Federation in the wake of the Cold War. As such he played a key role among the small group of military researchers promoting a better understanding of combat on Germany's Eastern Front during World War II and the role played by the Soviet Armed Forces in the achievement of victory over Hitler's Third Reich. Jim worked for me when I was the director of the Soviet Military Studies Office in Fort Leavenworth. Our mission was to study the Soviet military, develop personal contacts with Soviet officers and soldiers and write about them for the US Army. Jim was a gifted scholar and Russian linguist whom I relied on for quality research based on an understanding of the Soviet/Russian military.

Born on 2 April 1948 and raised in Grand Forks, North Dakota, Jim graduated from Grand Forks Central High School in 1966, enlisted in the US Army, and spent three years as a M60 machine gunner and member of a Long Rang Reconnaissance Patrol (LRRP) in South Vietnam and stateside at Fort Dix as a Drill Sergeant and range instructor, finishing his enlistment as a staff sergeant in the summer of 1969.

Jim moved to Idaho, joined the Army Reserve and, later, the Idaho National Guard. Working nights, he enrolled at the University of Idaho and joined the Reserve Officers Training Course (ROTC) at the university. He married his wife, Debbie, in December 1970 and stood by her for 51 years until his death on 5 December 2021. After graduating from the university cum laude with a BA in political science in May 1974, he was commissioned as a second lieutenant in the armor branch. The US Army then granted him a fellowship to attend graduate school at the University of Washington in Seattle, where he earned an MA degree in history in June 1976.

During his 17 years of commissioned service, Jim graduated from the Armor Officers Basic Course, the Infantry Officer Advanced Course, and the Command and General Staff College (CGSC). He became a Soviet Foreign Area Officer in 1983 and graduated from the Defense Language Institute's Russian language course and the United States Army Russian Institute (USARI) in Garmisch, West Germany. Equipped with this superb education, Jim served as a military historian, author, and open-source analyst at the CGSC, the Soviet Army Studies Office (SASO), and its successor, the Foreign Military Studies Office (FMSO). His last active-duty tour was as an escort officer for Soviet military, scientific and diplomatic personnel conducting arms control inspections. He was stationed at Travis Air Force Base supervising US military linguists supporting the USA-USSR bilateral treaty protocol inspections.

Following his retirement in January 1992, Jim and his family returned to Leavenworth, Kansas, where he worked to support the US Army and US State Department. In 2005, he became a Department of the Army civilian (DAC) employee and worked at Combined Arms Center's (CAC) Center for Army Lessons Learned until leukemia forced his retirement in 2014.

As a skilled, dogged, and dedicated historian, selfless person, and prolific writer, Jim wrote *The Petsamo-Kirkenes Operation: Soviet Breakthrough and Pursuit in the Arctic, October 1944–March 1, 2011*, his first major work, published as Leavenworth Paper No. 17 by the Combat Studies Institute (CSI) in 1989. I sat on the "murder board" at the US Army CGSC's Combat Studies Institute, which approved his groundbreaking work. This book is a follow-up to that work, which is available as a free download at https://apps.dtic.mil/sti/citations/ADA322750.

In addition, Jim translated and published 7 memoirs of Red Army soldiers and 17 user- and technical-level manuals for Soviet small arms. Many of these memoirs were a result of Jim's personal friendship and visits with the Soviet soldiers in Russia who authored them. By skillfully revealing deliberately "forgotten" or ignored aspects of the Soviet-German War, these works likely contributed to the Russian Federation's subsequent important decision to open its military archives to public view.

Manuscript Editor's Preface

Lester W. Grau

There have only been two major air-sea-ground operations fought in the high latitudes. The US Aleutian Islands Campaign (June 1942–August 1943) involved some 144,000 Americans and Canadians against some 8,500 Japanese. It was fought in the sub-Arctic. The Petsamo-Kirkenes Operation (October 1944) involved some 133,500 Soviets and some 45,000 Germans and Quisling Norwegians.[1] It is the only large-scale ground-naval and air operation ever fought in the Arctic. This book is important to serious students of Arctic combat and large-scale multiservice military operations, since it provides the starting point.

I first met Jim Gebhardt when I was teaching Soviet Army tactics at the US Army Command and General Staff College (CGSC) in the late 1980s. Both Jim and I were US Army Soviet Foreign Area Officers. As such, we were both graduates of a year's full-time Russian-language training at the Defense Language School in Monterey, California, and the two-year full-time postgraduate US Army Russian Institute in Garmisch-Partenkirchen, West Germany, where the courses were taught in Russian by Russian émigrés. I had a Moscow tour and multiple trips to the Soviet Union (and later Russia). Jim had multiple visits there as well. At that time, there was a concentrated effort to bring the Soviet and US Army into better understanding and cooperation with each other, and we were part of that effort. While I was at the staff college, I was on a review board of Jim's *The Petsamo-Kirkenes Operation: Soviet Breakthrough and Pursuit in the Arctic, October 1944* (https://apps.dtic.mil/sti/citations/ADA322750). Jim walked the ground, and did extensive fieldwork and scholarly research to complete this study.[2] It remains the seminal document on large-scale Arctic ground combat and is the companion piece to this volume. Jim and I worked together at the Soviet Army Studies Office (later the Foreign Military Studies Office), where we both studied the Soviet/Russian military using Russian-language

---

1 Vidkun Quisling was a Norwegian military officer, politician, and Nazi collaborator who headed the Norwegian government during the German WWII occupation of Norway.—Editor

2 List of materials used in this book: (1) documents of the Northern Fleet headquarters concerning preparation and conduct of the operation for the liberation of the Soviet far north; (2) accounts of the Northern Fleet headquarters concerning the conduct of the operation; (3) accounts of headquarters of formations that participated in the operation that liberated the Soviet far north; (4) combat reports of submarine commanders concerning actions on the enemy's lines of communication; and (5) intelligence summaries of the Red Army General Staff.

open sources. Jim and I lived and worked in Leavenworth, Kansas, and remained friends until his death on 5 December 2021. He had translated this work, but he needed the maps drawn on computer. Dr. Bartles and I finished his book as a farewell homage to Jim. Jim's wife, Debbie, has been most helpful in completing the work.

Jim and I were both infantrymen in South Vietnam and career soldiers. Dr. Bartles is a veteran of Iraq and Afghanistan who has studied in Russia and served in Uzbekistan, Kyrgyzstan, and Kazakhstan. He is a lieutenant colonel in the Army Reserve and a Russian linguist. We work closely together at the Foreign Military Studies Office. We dedicate this volume to the memory of Jim. It is Jim's last book—and essential to current military appreciation of the Arctic.

There is more to this book than the Soviet naval official study. Jim has added three of his own appendixes.

Translator's appendix 1 is a translated extract from the 1950 Soviet *Intelligence Support of the Northern Fleet in the Great Patriotic War (1941–1945)*.

Translator's appendix 2 is a close combat account of two different Soviet Naval Commando teams involved in the same fight for Cape Krestovyy. The third translator's appendix is a listing of the Lend-Lease Higgins and Vosper patrol torpedo boats and large submarine chasers, which were provided to the Soviet Union by the United States and United Kingdom and played a major role in this Soviet victory. The manuscript editor did not have access to Russian-language copies of Jim's appendixes; however, Jim's Russian translation of the base manuscript is first rate as expected. Jim, thank you for excellent service to the nation and your efforts to improve the understanding and scholarship of World War II in the Arctic and the Soviet armed forces of that time. We miss you.

Main Staff of the Naval Forces of the USSR

~~SECRET~~
Declassified 21 July 1989
Copy No. 942

COLLECTION OF MATERIALS
ON THE
EXPERIENCE OF COMBAT ACTIVITIES OF THE
NAVAL FORCES OF THE USSR
NO. 27

The Northern Fleet in the Operation for the Liberation
of the Soviet Far North

[The Petsamo-Kirkenes Operation]

(7–31 October 1944)

TRANSLATED AND ANNOTATED BY

MAJOR JAMES F. GEBHARDT, US ARMY, RETIRED

Directorate of the Naval Press of the People's Commissariat of the Navy of the USSR

MOSCOW   1945   LENINGRAD

Translator's Foreword

James Gebhardt

This study, titled in English *The Northern Fleet in the Operation for the Liberation of the Soviet Far North (7–31 October 1944)*, is no. 27 from the 40-volume *Collection of Materials Concerning the Experience of Combat Operations of the Naval Forces of the Union of SSR*. It is particularly unique in that it contains a section at the front naming the commanders whose units received honorific titles to recognize their participation in the operation. Where it was possible based on other sources, I have identified those units in brackets following the commanders' names. The Russian-language text also contains 27 figures, of which the figures (originally numbered) 1.1, 1.2, 3.1, and 4.1 have been omitted from this translation because they are black-and-white photographs that do not reproduce suitably from the microfiche source document.

The observant reader will also note the significant number of footnotes that appear in this translation. Those that are followed by "Soviet Editor" appear in the original source document. Those that are followed by "Translator" were added for explanation of Russian terms, brief descriptions of German and Soviet aircraft and of USA-provided Lend-Lease aircraft and vessels, and brief biographies of the several Heroes of the Soviet Union who are identified in the text.

The study contains its original appendixes, which consist of plans and orders, a glossary of the myriad acronyms used in those plans and orders, and additional appendixes that are labeled "Translator's appendixes," which I unilaterally decided should be included in this publication for amplification of the main body text.

A second study, no. 38 in the same series, titled in English *Intelligence Support of the Northern Fleet in the Great Patriotic War (1941–1945)*, is also available. Included in its 90+ pages of text is a 13-page section (chapter 6) titled "Intelligence Support to the Northern Fleet in the Pechenga [Petsamo] Operation." Because of its relevance to the main body of this publication, and the difficulty the reader would have both to find and translate it, I have included this chapter as translator's appendix 1.

Translator's appendix 2 contains text from two sources—both participants in the raid on Cape Krestovyy on the night of 12 October 1944. The first section is from the memoir the overall commander of the raiding force, Naval Infantry Captain Ivan Barchenko-Emelyanov, who commanded the reconnaissance element of the Northern Defensive Region (NDR); the second is from the memoir of Viktor Leonov, who commanded the Reconnaissance Detachment of the Northern Fleet and was subordinated to Barchenko-Emelyanov for this raid. Each segment is approximately 12 pages in length and describes the movement from shore to the objective and the combat on the objective.

Translator's appendix 3 contains ship lists of the patrol torpedo (PT) boats, which in Russian are referred to as torpedo cutters (*TKA—torpednyy kater*), both Higgins and Vosper, which were manufactured in the United States and delivered to the Soviet Union in the Lend-Lease program, and also large submarine chasers (*BO—bolshoy okhotnik za podvodnykh lodak* [large hunter for submarines]).[3] These craft were used in several amphibious assault landing operations as well as attacks on German vessels approaching and leaving the Kirkenes–Varanger Peninsula area during the operation.

The Higgins boats (designated "A-2" in Soviet use) were the product of the Higgins Industry facility in New Orleans, Louisiana. A total of 52 boats were provided to the Soviet Navy, 20 of which were shipped by convoy to Murmansk in March, April, and December 1943 and January and February 1944. The remaining boats were shipped to Vladivostok (15 boats) and Petropavlovsk-Kamchatka (17 boats) in October 1945.

The Vosper boats (based on a licensed British design and designated "A-1" in Soviet use) were built at three shipyards: Fiff's Shipyard in New York, Annapolis Yacht in Maryland, and Herreshoff–Bristol in Rhode Island. A total of 92 Vosper boats were shipped by convoy to the Soviet Union: 43 to Murmansk, 17 to Arkhangelsk (of which 14 were crated), 18 to Vladivostok, 10 to Petropavlosk-Kamchatka, and two to Nikolaevsk-on-Amur. These boats were shipped by sea convoy (as cargo) from both East and West Coast ports beginning in March 1944 and concluding in late 1945, after the end of hostilities in the Far East.

The remaining boats shipped to Arkhangelsk and Murmansk were moved by canal and internal river and rail routes to the Baltic Fleet in Leningrad and the Black Sea Fleet at its bases along the coast of Georgia SSR. The crated boats that had been delivered to Arkhangelsk were moved by the White Sea Canal and railroad to Leningrad, where they were assembled and put into service in the Baltic Fleet.

The second Lend-Lease vessel type that experienced broad employment in the Petsamo-Kirkenes Operation was the wooden-hulled large subchaser. The Soviet Union received a total of 78 large subchasers, many of which were assigned to Northern Fleet. These vessels came from shipyards in several states along the East Coast and rivers that feed it, the Great Lakes region, and a few on the West Coast. In this operation, they were frequently used to deliver naval infantrymen crowded in large numbers on the deck of the vessel from embarkation point to an amphibious landing site on German-held shores. After the cessation of combat actions in the waters northwest of Murmansk, some of these submarine chasers were involved in minesweeping to clear naval mines laid by both sides.

Bear in mind that for both types of vessels, whatever their tactical employment purpose, their armament and, in the case of the torpedo boats, high-octane fuel requirements, also had to be fulfilled by Lend-Lease deliveries. This was not a simple task, given the distance convoys had to travel and the en route dangers they faced from German submarines and aircraft, especially when closing on Soviet ports in the far north.

The Lend-Lease, American-manufactured aircraft types mentioned in this study include the Curtiss P-40 in both *Tomahawk* and *Kittyhawk* fighter-bomber variants, the Bell P-39 *Airacobra*, and the Douglas A-20 *Boston* (generally named "Havoc" in US sources). For the sake of brevity, I have footnoted the technical descriptions of these aircraft only on first mention.

While on occasion, official postwar Soviet sources do mention Lend-Lease materiel deliveries, these descriptions tend to be statistical comparisons of US deliveries to Soviet domestic production. They rarely describe the use or significance of Lend-Lease materiel at the operational or tactical level. This study may be unique in this regard as well, in that it names the three indicated aircraft types frequently throughout the narrative.

For readers who lack knowledge of technical and tactical data for specific German and Soviet aircraft types used in World War II, I have also provided descriptions in footnotes at their first mention in the text.

Those who have additional interest in the study of this operation can examine my own work *The Petsamo-*

---

3 The source for this brief overview of these vessels, their origins, destinations, Soviet Navy hull numbers, and technical data is S. S. Berezhnoy, *Flot SSSR: Korabli i Suda Lendliza* (Navy of the USSR: Vessels and ships of Lend-Lease) (Saint Petersburg: "Belen," 1994).—Translator

Kirkenes Operation: Soviet Breakthrough and Pursuit in the Arctic, October 1944 (Washington, DC: Government Printing Office, 1990), no. 17 in the Leavenworth Papers series. It was written and published under the auspices of the Combat Studies Institute, US Army Command and General Staff College, Fort Leavenworth, Kansas, and can be found easily on the Internet under my name or simply "Petsamo-Kirkenes Operation."

List of Abbreviations Used in This Study

James Gebhardt

AMG-1. aviatsionnaya minna (naval aviation mine, 250 kg.)
BDB. bystraya desantnaya barzha (rapid amphibious barge)
BO. bolshoy okhotnik (large subchaser)
DA-TK. dumovaya apparatura—torpednyy kater (torpedo cutter smoke apparatus)
EM. esminets (destroyer)
FAB-100. fugasnaya aviatsionnaya bomba (high-explosive aviation bomb, 100 kilograms)
GVMG. glavnoy voenno-morskoy gospital (main naval hospital)
GMSh. glavnyy morskoy shtab (Main Naval Staff)
KATShch. kater tralshchik (minesweeping cutter)
LK. linyy korabl (ship of the line—battleship or cruiser)
M. minets (destroyer escort)
MDSh. morskuya dumovaya shashka (naval smoke charge)
MO. malyy okhotnik (small subchaser)
NKVMF. narodnyy komissariat VMF (People's Commissariat of the Navy)
PEP. peredovoy evakuatsionnyy punkt (forward evacuation point)
PL. podvodnaya lodka (submarine)

PMB. plavuchnaya meditsinskaya barzha (floating hospital barge)
PPG. peredovoy polevoy gospital (forward field hospital)
PVO. protivovozdushnaya oborona (andi-air defense)
SAB. svetyashchaya aviatsionnaya bomba (aircraft illumination bombs)
SKA. storozhevoy kater (patrol cutter)
SKR. storozhevoy korabl (patrol vessel)
TKA. torpednyy kater (torpedo cutter)
TR. транспорт (transport)
TShch. tralshchik (minesweeper)
VMF. voyenno-morskoy flot (military-naval fleet or simply Navy)
VMG. voyenno-morskoy gospital (naval hospital)
VPU. vspomogatelnyy punkt upravleniya (auxiliary command post)
VSON. voyennoye sudno osobovo naznacheniya (special purpose auxiliary craft)
ZM. zagraditel minnyy (minelayer)
STAVKA. The staff of the Supreme High Command, a Moscow-based national command entity, which controlled military operations of the entire Soviet Armed forces under Stalin's direct supervision.

Preface

Main Naval Staff VMF

DEPARTMENT OF THE OPERATIONS DIRECTORATE FOR STUDY AND GENERALIZATION OF WAR EXPERIENCE

The Main Staff of the Naval Forces of the USSR, through the Department for the Study and Generalization of War Experience, continues the publication of collections of materials on the experience of the combat actions of the Soviet Navy.

The purpose of this collection is to convey to the officer component of the Navy the combat experience of the *VMF* [*voyenno-morskoy flot*, military—naval fleet, or simply Navy] in the Great Patriotic War.

The Main Naval Staff considers that, in isolated cases, the incompleteness of existing materials may lead in itself to insufficiently complete examination of selected questions but, at the same time, considers it inappropriate to avoid study and generalization of the experience of combat operations until exhaustive data is collected.

The following issues are discussed in these collections:

1. preparation, organization, conduct, and support of naval and joint operations with the Red Army;
2. combat actions of vessels, and of aviation, artillery, infantry, and special units of the *VMF*;
3. command and control of operations and combat;
4. the most essential measures for organizational and logistic support of combat actions of the *VMF*.

In this manner, this collection generalizes the experience primarily of the operational employment and support of the *VMF*. Issues of tactics and combat training are examined in bulletins of the Directorate of Combat Training of the *GMSh* [*glavnyy morskoy shtab*, Main Naval Staff] *VMF*, and equipment issues are contained in bulletins of corresponding special directorates of the *NKVMF* [*narodnyy komissariat VMF*, People's Commissariat of the Navy].

A fundamental task of the collection is the examination of issues of fleet (flotilla) combat activities in order to extract the necessary lessons from immediate combat experience, to show the causes that made possible or interfered with combat success, as well as the study of those new methods of conducting activities that arose in the course of the war and proved themselves on the sea and in joint operations of the fleet with ground forces.

During this examination of separate operations and combat engagements, special attention will be given to issues of coordination of forces and combat command

and control, on which depends much of the success for accomplishing any combat mission.

Materials for these collections are taken from the following sources:

1. accounts of combat activities of fleets (flotillas) and major *VMF* commands, periodic and pertaining to specific operations, submitted to the Main Naval Staff;
2. Main Naval Staff documents;
3. articles written by *VMF* officers.

The collection is a classified document, in as much as it expresses the most recent combat experience of active fleets (flotillas), along with classified data on the organization and armaments of the Soviet Navy. Utilization and protection of these collections are governed by the regulations that pertain to classified documents.

Articles and letters containing new data pertaining to the conclusions of earlier published works should be forwarded through classified channels of headquarters of major commands and institutions in accordance with established procedures to the following address: Moscow, Main Naval Staff *VMF*, Chief of the Department for Study and Generalization of War Experience.

"The Collection of Materials on the Experience of Combat Activities of the Naval Forces of the USSR, [Study] No. 27" describes the actions of the Northern Fleet and the Karelian *Front*[4] in conducting a joint operation to liberate Pechenga oblast and the Soviet far north.

The operation for the liberation of the Soviet far north was conducted in October 1944 and is an example of operational cooperation between ground and naval forces as they executed coordinated, massive strikes against the Germans.

Especially characteristic of this operation were the staffs' meticulous work during its preparation and execution and the high degree of military mastery demonstrated by both ground and sea commanders as they executed their combat missions.

This collection was compiled from materials of the Northern Fleet staff and from the staffs of principal formations that participated in the operation by Colonel K. N. Belokopytov, along with Captain Second Rank D. A. Vershinin, Captain-Lieutenant N. B. Korak, and Major K. M. Masaltsev, who outline the actions of the fleet on the enemy's sea lines of communication.

---

4 In the Soviet Army of this era, a *front* was the command and structural equivalent of an Allied Army Group. It was composed of numbered armies, corps, divisions, and so on, and in most cases commanded by a four-star general officer.—Translator

Order of the Supreme High Command
to
Army General MERETSKOV
Admiral GOLOVKO

The forces of the **Karelian** *Front* broke through the strongly reinforced German defenses northwest of **Murmansk**, and today, 15 October, in coordination with the ships and assault units of the Northern Fleet, captured the town **Petsamo (Pechenga)**—an important German naval base and powerful strongpoint of the German defenses in the far north.

The forces of the following commanders performed exceptionally well during the breakthrough and the capture of **Petsamo**: Lieutenant General **Shcherbakov** [14th Army]; Major General **Mikulskiy** [99th Rifle Corps]; Colonel **Solovev** [126th Light Rifle Corps]; Major General **Zhukov** [127th Light Rifle Corps]; Colonel **Kalinovskiy**; Major General **Khudalov** [10th Guards Rifle Division]; Major General **Korotkov** [14th Rifle Division]; Major General **Panin** [45th Rifle Division]; Colonel **Koshchienko**; Major General **Sopenko** [368th Rifle Division]; Colonel **Kaverin** [Third Separate Naval Rifle Brigade]; Colonel **Lysenko**; Lieutenant Colonel **Blak** [70th Separate Naval Rifle Brigade]; Colonel **Amvrosov**; Colonel **Rossiychenko**; Colonel **Krylov**; Colonel **Rassokhin** [12th Naval Infantry Brigade]; Major **Timofeev**; Captain **Barchenko** [Northern Defensive Region Reconnaissance Detachment]; naval officers Rear Admiral **Mikhaylov** [amphibious landing forces, 9 October landing], Rear Admiral **Fokin** [Northern Fleet Surface Squadron]; Captain First Rank **Klevenskiy** [Large Subchaser Brigade]; Captain First Rank **Kuzmin** [Northern Fleet Torpedo Cutter Brigade]; Captain First Rank **Kolyshkin** [Northern Fleet Submarine Brigade]; Captain Second Rank **Alekseev** [third landing detachment, 9 October landing]; Captain Third Rank **Zyuzin** [first landing detachment, 9 October landing; landing force for 12 October landing]; Captain Third Rank **Fedorov**; Captain Second Rank **Korsunovich** [second landing detachment, 12 October landing]; artillery officers Lieutenant General of Artillery **Degtyarev**; Lieutenant General of Artillery **Voyevodin**; Major General of Artillery **Panitkin**; Colonel **Khramov**; Colonel **Nebozhenko**; Lieutenant Colonel **Grigorev**; Colonel **Sobolev**; Lieutenant Colonel **Strokker**; aviators Lieutenant General of Aviation **Sokolov** [Seventh Air Army, Karelian *Front*]; Major General of Aviation **Preobrazhenskiy** [Northern Fleet Air Forces]; Major General of Aviation **Kidalinskiy** [Fifth Mine-Torpedo Aviation Regiment (Navy)]; Major General of Aviation **Petrukhin** [Sixth Fighter Aviation Division (Navy)]; Colonel **Zhatkov**; Colonel **Minaev**; Colonel **Pushkarev**; Colonel **Laryushkin**; Colonel **Kalugin**; Colonel **Udonin**; Colonel **Pogreshaev** [122nd Air Defense Fighter Aviation Division]; Colonel **Finogenov**; tank officers Lieutenant General of Armored Forces **Kononov**; Colonel **Sokolov** [senior staff officer, Karelian *Front* Directorate of Tank and Mechanized Forces]; Colonel **Yurenkov**; Lieutenant Colonel **Arshenevskiy**; Lieutenant Colonel **Terentev**; Lieutenant Colonel **Suchkov** [89th Separate Tank Regiment]; Lieutenant Colonel **Torchilin**; engineer officers Lieutenant General of Engineer Forces **Khrenov** [Karelian *Front* Chief of Engineer Forces]; Colonel **Leychik**; Lieutenant Colonel **Arshba**; Lieutenant Colonel **Zakharov**; communications officers Lieutenant General of Signal Forces **Dobykin**; Colonel **Yekimov**; Captain Second Rank **Polozok**; Major of State Security **Gavrilov**.

In recognition of the victory that they have gained, the troop formations, ships, and fleet units that were most outstanding in the battles for **Petsamo (Pechenga)** are designated to bear the title **Pechenga** and authorized to be awarded decorations.

Today, 15 October, at 2100, the capital of our Motherland, **Moscow**, in the name of the Motherland, salutes with 20 artillery salvoes fired by 224 guns the glorious troops of the Karelian *Front* and the vessels and units of the Northern Fleet who captured **Petsamo**.

I express my thanks to the leaders of our forces, vessels, and units that participated in the battles for the liberation of **Petsamo** for their outstanding combat actions.

Eternal glory to the heroes who fell in battles for the freedom and independence of our Motherland!

Death to the German invaders!

SUPREME HIGH COMMAND MARSHAL
OF THE SOVIET UNION J. STALIN

15 OCTOBER 1944

Order of the Supreme High Command

to

Marshal of the Soviet Union MERETSKOV
Admiral GOLOVKO

Today, 1 November, the forces of the **Karelian** *Front*, in coordination with the formations and ships of the **Northern Fleet**, attacking in the difficult conditions of the far north, have completed the total liberation of **Pechenga (Petsamo)** oblast from the German invaders.

The forces of the following commanders performed exceptionally well during the battles for the liberation of **Pechenga** oblast: Lieutenant General **Shcherbakov** [14th Army]; Major General **Absalyamov** [31st Rifle Corps]; Major General **Mikulskiy** [99th Rifle Corps]; Major General **Korotkov** [14th Rifle Division]; Major General **Zhukov** [127th Light Rifle Corps]; Colonel **Solovev** [126th Light Rifle Corps]; Colonel **Grebenkin**; Major General **Panin** [45th Rifle Division]; Colonel **Kaverin** [Third Separate Naval Rifle Brigade]; Colonel **Koshchienko**; Colonel **Lysenko**; Colonel **Kalinovskiy**; Major General **Khudalov** [10th Guards Rifle Division]; Lieutenant Colonel **Blak** [70th Separate Naval Rifle Brigade]; Colonel **Amvrosov**; Major General **Sopenko** [368th Rifle Division]; Colonel **Startsev**; Colonel **Nikandrov**; Colonel **Yevmenov**; Colonel **Krylov**; Colonel **Rassokhin** [12th Naval Infantry Brigade]; Major General **Dubovtsev** [Northern Defensive Region]; Major General of Coastal Service **Kustov**; naval officers Rear Admiral **Mikhaylov** [amphibious landing forces, 9 October landing]; Rear Admiral **Fokin** [Northern Fleet Surface Squadron]; Captain First Rank **Kuzmin** [Northern Fleet Torpedo Cutter Brigade]; Captain First Rank **Klevenskiy** [Large Subchaser Brigade]; Captain First Rank **Kolyshkin** [Northern Fleet Submarine Brigade]; Captain Second Rank **Alekseev** [third landing detachment, 9 October landing]; Captain Third Rank **Zyuzin** [first landing detachment, 9 October landing; landing force for 12 October landing]; Captain Third Rank **Fedorov**; Captain Second Rank **Korsunovich** [second landing detachment, 12 October landing]; artillery officers Lieutenant General of Artillery **Degtyarev**; Major General of Artillery **Panitkin**; Lieutenant General of Artillery **Voyevodin**; Colonel **Yaroslavtsev**; Colonel **Grigorev**; Colonel **Bandyukevich**; Colonel **Manyakin**; Colonel **Likhut**; Colonel **Khramov**; Lieutenant Colonel **Goldykhov**; Lieutenant Colonel **Fetisov**; Lieutenant Colonel **Yeresko**; Lieutenant Colonel **Shapiro**; Lieutenant Colonel **Shepel**; Lieutenant Colonel **Zubarev**; Lieutenant Colonel **Krovosheev**; Major **Golubev**; Major **Yedemskiy**; Major **Vakurov**; Colonel **Bozhkov**; Colonel **Ukhanov**; Lieutenant Colonel **Yusov**; Colonel **Perlov**; Lieutenant Colonel **Berezin**; Major **Doludenko**; Lieutenant Colonel **Titovchev**; Lieutenant Colonel **Kozlov**; Lieutenant Colonel **Rogovoy**; Colonel **Sobolev**; tank officers Lieutenant General of Armored Forces **Kononov**; Colonel **Sokolov**; Colonel **Yurenkov**; Lieutenant Colonel **Suchkov**; Lieutenant Colonel **Terent'ev**; Lieutenant Colonel **Arshenevskiy**; Lieutenant Colonel **Torchilin**; Lieutenant Colonel **Leshchenko**; Lieutenant Colonel **Korshunov**; aviators Lieutenant General of Aviation **Sokolov** [Seventh Air Army, Karelian *Front*]; Major General of Aviation **Preobrazhenskiy** [Northern Fleet Air Forces]; Major General of Aviation **Kidalinskiy** [Fifth Mine-Torpedo Aviation Regiment (Navy)]; Major General of Aviation **Petrukhin** [Sixth Fighter Aviation Division (Navy)]; Colonel **Zhatkov**; Colonel **Udonin**; Colonel **Laryushkin**; Colonel **Finogenov**; Colonel **Kalugin**; Colonel **Minaev**; Colonel **Pushkarev**; Colonel **Pogreshaev**; Lieutenant Colonel **Litvinov**; engineer officers Lieutenant General of Engineer Forces **Khrenov** [Karelian *Front* Chief of Engineer Forces]; Colonel **Leychik**; Colonel **Arshba**; Lieutenant Colonel **Zakharov**; communications officers Lieutenant General of Signal Forces **Dobykin**; Colonel **Yekimov**; Major of State Security **Gavrilov**; Captain Second Rank **Polozok**.

In recognition of the victory that they have gained, the formations and units of the Karelian *Front*, and the formations and ships of the Northern Fleet that were most outstanding in the battles for the liberation of **Pechenga** oblast are authorized to be awarded decorations.

Today, 1 November, at 2100, the capital of our Motherland, Moscow, in the name of the Motherland salutes with 20 artillery salvoes fired by 224 guns the glorious troops of the Karelian *Front* and the sailors of the Northern Fleet who liberated **Pechenga** oblast.

I express my thanks to the leaders of our forces and also to the formations and vessels of the Northern Fleet that participated in the battles for the liberation of **Pechenga** oblast for their outstanding combat actions.

Eternal glory to the heroes who fell in battles for the freedom and independence of our Motherland!

Death to the German invaders!

SUPREME HIGH COMMAND
MARSHAL OF THE SOVIET UNION J. STALIN
1 NOVEMBER 1944

ARCTIC NAVAL COMBAT IN SUPPORT OF GROUND OPERATIONS

CHAPTER I

Frontline Situation of the Forces of the Northern Defensive Region on the Coast of Varangerfjord and Sredniy and Rybachyy Peninsulas

On the isthmus of Sredniy Peninsula, in front of the Northern Defensive Region sector, the Germans occupied a defensive line they had established in August 1941. This line stretched from the southern shore of Maattivuono Bay along Mustatunturi Range to the heights marked 122.0 and 109.0 on the map, and then to Kutovaya Inlet. The enemy's defensive line was a system of contiguous company defensive positions composed of platoon strongpoints.

These platoon strongpoints consisted of two or three permanent and 10–12 temporary or open firing positions, interconnected with a dense network of full-profile trenches and joined with a command post and troop dugouts in the rear. Between the firing positions, the trenches had embrasures to accommodate rifles and machine guns. The enemy had as many as 200 permanent and up to 800 temporary or open-type firing positions on the isthmus. The defensive line was up to three kilometers deep.

In most cases, the troop dugouts were constructed deep in the rock faces and were well protected against artillery fires. Many bomb shelters and tunnels had been dug into the rocks.

Blocking the approaches to the strongpoints were two or three rows of barbed wire, mines, explosive demolitions, and flame throwers. The barbed wire was set up like a fence on wooden posts or stakes, as rolls of concertina wire, or simply scattered about. Fastened to the barbed wire were special cartridges and signal rockets that flared upward when the wire was touched, signaling danger.

Deep in the German defensive line were separate centers of resistance and barrier systems covered by fire (minefields, barbed wire, obstacles). The heavily broken terrain consisted of naked, rock-strewn elevations, with many lakes, streams, and creeks between them, which greatly hindered the movement of dismounted infantry. The terrain extended upward out of the water to an elevation of 449 meters above sea level (Tsherdekaisi). The movement of artillery, tanks, and carts was possible only along specific roads. In some sectors, such as Lake Suormusyarvi to Porovaara, the Mustatunturi Range had only a single improved dirt road, four meters wide at the most, with turnouts for the passing of approaching traffic.

The enemy's defenses on the commanding heights at the isthmus of Sredniy Peninsula permitted German units to see throughout the entire depth of Northern Defensive Region units in the Ivari-Kutovaya sector. Units defending the shorelines of Maattivuono and

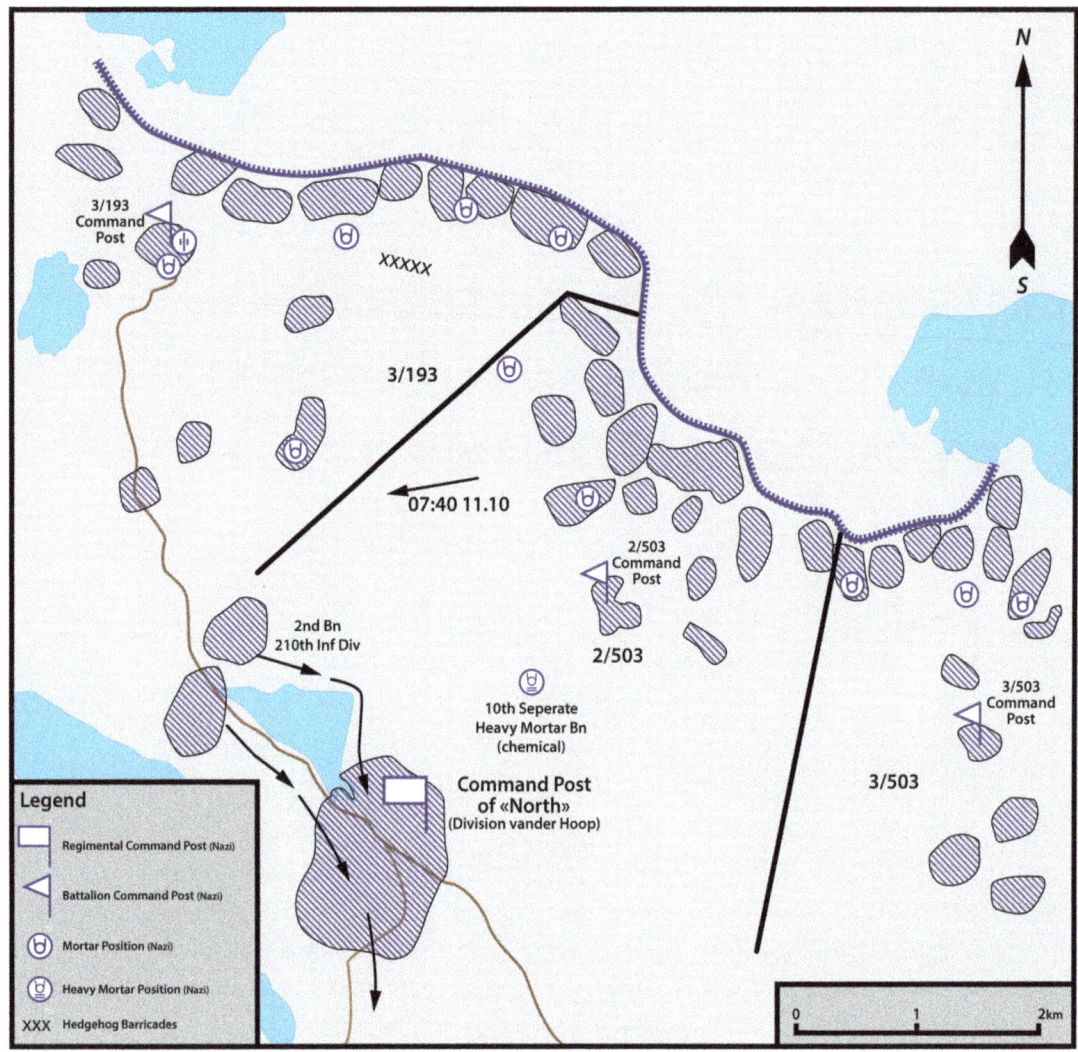

FIGURE 1.1. Disposition of Enemy Defenses on the isthmus of the peninsula

Motovskiy Bays covered the flanks of the enemy's isthmus positions.

The enemy defensive line along the coastline of Maattivuono Bay consisted of separate strongpoints guarded by field posts, between which patrols moved. The coastline of Motovskiy Bay was defended by strongpoint garrisons dispersed along a broad front ("Mogilniy," "Inzel-zee," "Oberhof," "Reuter-alm," "Landerbucht," "Zeenge").

Four shore batteries of calibers 150 and 210 mm, and several antiship and antiaircraft batteries of calibers 20–88 mm defended the approach to Petsamovuono Inlet.

Artillery and machine-gun firing positions made from rock- and steel-reinforced concrete and older model armored tank turrets were situated on the coastline near the port of Liinakhamari. Barbed wire obstacles and demolitions were installed at places along the waterline.

By the beginning of the operation, the Germans had the following units defending the southern coastline of Maattivuono Bay, the isthmus of Sredniy Peninsula, and the coastline of Motovskiy Bay: 503rd Airfield Infantry Brigade, 193rd Infantry Brigade (two-battalion composition), 10th Separate Heavy Mortar Battalion and 68th Self-propelled Battalion, 517th Heavy Coastal Artillery Battalion, 504th Heavy Artillery Battalion, and two batteries of 75 mm guns of 111th Mountain Artillery Regiment. These units had been stationed in the same sector for almost three years, knew the terrain exceptionally well, and were well armed and supplied.

The enemy had the following assets in front of Northern Defensive Region units on 5 October 1944: 8,860 troops, 114 heavy machine guns, 258 light machine guns, 72 grenade launchers, 18 flame devices, 18 mortars 105–120 mm, 38 mortars 81–82 mm, 30 mortars 50

FIGURE 1.2. Disposition of force and scheme of maneuver decided by the Northern Fleet commander

mm, four guns 210 mm, 24 guns 130–155 mm, 48 guns 20–88 mm, and an unknown quantity of special projectile launchers.

The enemy had their densest defenses on the isthmus of Sredniy Peninsula, where the following features were noted in a single kilometer of front from Mustatunturi Ridge to Hill 109.0 (south of Kutovaya): timber-reinforced firing positions—11; firing positions (for 2–3 men each)—40; communications trenches—800 m; barbed wire obstacles—4.3 km; mortars—10; guns—six; heavy machine guns—seven; light machine guns—20; automatic rifles—43; rifles—420; and infantry soldiers—520 men.

In combination with the rocky, non-trafficable terrain, the system of defense was durable, and the enemy could count on its hardness. The most vulnerable defense was along the coastline of Maattivuono Bay. In the depth of his defenses (figure 1.1), the enemy had individual centers of resistance along the roads and on the most threatened axes.

Units of the Northern Defensive Region occupied defensive positions on the isthmus of Sredniy Peninsula, by the beginning of the operation having 347th and 348th Separate Naval Infantry Machine Gun Battalions there, combined with the units of 12th Red Banner Naval Infantry Brigade that were there previously. In reserve, the commander of the Northern Defensive Region had 349th Separate Naval Infantry Machine Gun Battalion and one tank company; for operations as an amphibious landing force, he also had 63rd Naval Infantry Brigade with the attached 716th Chemical Platoon (Heavy Mortar), one sapper company of 388th Separate Engineer Battalion, a platoon of the dock-amphibious company, and the reconnaissance detachments of the Northern Defensive Region and Headquarters, Northern Fleet.

The artillery group, along with the artillery of two naval infantry brigades and three naval infantry machine gun battalions, consisted of the batteries of the 113rd Separate Red Banner Coast Artillery Battalion and 104th Cannon Artillery Regiment.

The total strength of the artillery group reached 209 barrels. For support of the ground forces and for suppression of the enemy's artillery batteries, an operational aviation group numbering 30 aircraft was sent from Northern Fleet Air Forces to Pummanki [a primitive airstrip on the northeast quadrant of Rybachyy Peninsula] and was increased by a factor of almost two during the operation. The disposition of the units of the Northern Defensive Region on Sredniy Peninsula before the start of the operation is shown in figure 1.2.

The enemy's combat actions on the isthmus of Sredniy Peninsula were limited to artillery and mortar shelling of combat formations of the Northern Defensive Region and rifle and machine-gun fire.

In over two years the enemy had never undertaken any active measures with its manpower, but unceasingly improved its defenses regarding fortifications and obstacles to prevent penetrations of the defended sectors by the reconnaissance groups of the Northern Defensive Region. After Finland's departure from the war, the German command along the northern flank of the Soviet-German front anticipated that the Red Army would go over to the offensive. In connection with this, the enemy conducted a full registration of their artillery and mortar batteries on the isthmus of the Sredniy Peninsula to cover the approaches to the forward edge of their defensive line and to individual strongpoints.

Infantry and artillery units of the Northern Defensive Region carefully studied the enemy's disposition along the isthmus of Sredniy Peninsula by persistent reconnaissance patrols, the interrogation of prisoners of war, and daily observation of the enemy; they were fully prepared for the breakthrough of the enemy's defenses.

Thus, the situation on land had unfolded in such a manner that by the beginning of October 1944, the enemy in front of the forces of the Northern Defensive Region was holding their occupied defensive line firmly, had improved it with engineer fortifications, and had sufficient forces to defend it. At the same time, along the line of the Western Litsa River, the Germans in front of the forces of the Karelian *Front* were also holding an occupied position, with the goal, it seems, of maintaining it, despite Finland's departure from the war, since it connected with northern Norway and the Barents Sea. Holding this area, the Germans could export nickel ore and other strategic minerals from northern Finland.

The enemy was delivering reinforcements and supplies by sea to its forces operating in northern Finland through Varangerfjord ports, and therefore the sea lines of communication held great significance.

For the defense of their Tromso–Varangerfjord sea corridor against the pressure of the Northern Fleet submarine and air assets, the enemy positioned antisubmarine minefields at a great distance from the coastline, mined Varangerfjord in several areas, developed a complex of shore and antiaircraft defenses on the coastline, increased the number of escort vessels based in ports in northern Norway, and increased the number of airfields on the coast so that its aviation could get nearer to the areas of convoy movement. Enemy measures for the defense of its sea lines of communication grew, particularly after Northern Fleet's torpedo cutters began to operate successfully.

Along with the defense of sea lines of communication and defense of the coastline, the enemy strove to operate actively against Allied Sea lines of communication in the Norwegian and Barents Seas, and as well on Northern Fleet's internal sea lines of communication between Murmansk and Arkhangelsk, and in the arctic. For this effort, the enemy concentrated a great quantity of submarines, large surface vessels, and aviation in and near northern Norwegian fjords.

Existing data on the enemy showed that by 1 October the enemy fleet in northern Norway and Varangerfjord consisted of the following: one battleship (*LK*) (*Tirpitz*); 12–14 destroyers (*EM*) and destroyer escorts (*M*); about 30 submarines (*PL*); about 50 patrol ships (*SKR*) and minesweepers (*TShch*); two minelayers (*ZM*); two antiaircraft ships (*PVO*); about 50 patrol craft (*SKA*), small submarine chasers (*MO*), and minesweeping cutters (*KATShch*); 30–35 fast amphibious assault barges (*BDB*); 12 special craft (*VSON*); and about 40 transports (*TR*) and tankers. The known disposition of these enemy vessels on 1 October is shown in table 1.1.

Of the enemy ships located in northern Norwegian ports, it was believed that the following were most likely to be employed against the ships of the Northern Fleet: 2–4 destroyers; 20–25 patrol ships, minesweepers, and cutters; and 10 fast amphibious barges.

In October 1944, Northern Fleet was employing the following assets for operations in Varangerfjord: 6–8 submarines, 20 torpedo cutters, 10 or 11 large submarine chasers, and 8–12 small submarine chasers.

Enemy ships did not undertake active operations at sea, but a significant number of them were called upon to guard transports in connection with the increase of cargo shipping between the ports of Narvik, Tromso, and Hammerfest, and particularly in Varangerfjord. Although the enemy moved convoys mainly at night and during nonflying weather, 15–25 escort vessels were frequently assigned for a convoy of two or three transports.

The enemy constantly had three or four submarines in the Barents Sea, one of which was located near the Kola Peninsula coastline, and three in the center and western sectors of the Barents Sea. In addition to these submarines, the enemy had an additional 20 submarines in northern Norwegian ports for action against Allied convoys.

Northern Fleet submarines and torpedo cutters systematically operated against enemy convoys on the Hammerfest–Varangerfjord route.

Thus, the situation on the sea prior to the beginning of the operation was characterized principally by activities against sea lines of communication. The enemy was conducting intensified naval resupply and supporting it with surface ships it was maintaining in northern Norwegian ports. Northern Fleet ships were systematically conducting strikes against enemy transport and combat vessels during their transits between ports.

The situation in the air by the beginning of the operation was characterized by the following. German aviation assets on the Murmansk sector were based on airfields at Luostari, Hoybuktmoen (Kirkenes), Nautsi, Salmiyarvi, and at other locations. By 1 October 1944, a total of 109 aircraft were operating from these fields. Their disposition by airfield is shown in the following table.

In addition, the enemy had up to 20 *Ju-52*-type transports in northern Finland and Norway, and replenishment of its bomber aviation was anticipated, the aircraft arriving from airfields in southern Finland.

Enemy air operations were limited to cover of the airfields, convoys during their sea passage, and ground forces. But from the second half of September, air reconnaissance was strengthened along the forward edge of the defense on the Murmansk sector and along frontline roads, in order to uncover the concentration

TABLE 1.1. German vessels in area of operation

Station	Class of Ship	Quantity
Varangerfjord	Destroyer	2
	Patrol ship and minesweeper	6–9
	Patrol cutter, small subchaser, small minesweeper	17
	Fast amphibious barge	12
Honningsvag	Patrol ship and minesweeper	2–3
	Patrol cutter	3
Lillefjord	Special hydroplane tender	1
Hammerfest	Submarine tender and repair facility	1
	Patrol ship and minesweeper	6–7
	Patrol cutter	5–7
	Fast amphibious barge	3–5
Altafjord	Battleship	1
	(Tirpitz) destroyer escort	2–3
	Antiaircraft ship	1–2
	Patrol ship	3
	Patrol cutter	7
	Fast amphibious barge	3
	Submarine tender	1
	Submarine	1
Tromso	Destroyer	2
	Antiaircraft ship	2
	Special hydroplane tender	2
	Patrol ship and minesweeper	8
	Patrol cutter (flotilla)	12
	Fast amphibious barge	9
Harshtadt	Destroyer	2
	Patrol ship	5
Narvik–Trondheim	Destroyer	5
	Submarines	2 flotillas
	Patrol ship and minesweeper	15–17
	Patrol cutter	7

TABLE 1.2. German aircraft and their airfields

Airfield	Aircraft Type[a]									
	Bf-109	FW-190	Ju-88	Ju-87	FW-189	He-111	Fi-156	Hydro	Misc.	Total
Luostari	18	12	1	–	2	–	2	–	–	35
Hoybuktmoen	–	–	5	–	–	–	–	–	–	5
Nautsi	2	2	8	–	8	–	–	–	1	21
Salmiyarvi	5	–	–	20	–	–	–	–	–	25
Banak	–	–	6	–	–	3	–	–	–	9
Kirkenes	–	–	–	–	–	–	–	7	–	7
Lillefjord	–	–	–	–	–	–	–	7	–	7
Total	25	14	20	20	10	3	2	14	1	109

a. In the interest of preserving the integrity of the two tables on these pages, I have moved all the German aircraft descriptions to the note after table 1.3.—Translator

TABLE 1.3. German reconnaissance flights against Soviet forces[a]

Area of Activity	Aircraft Type						
	Bf-109	FW-190	Ju-88	FW-189	He-126	Ju-87	Total
N. fleet main base	–	–	2	–	–	–	2
N. defensive region	3	–	2	–	–	–	5
Varangerfjord	–	–	1	–	–	–	1
Ground front	31	1	4	3	1	2	42
Total	34	1	9	3	1	2	50

a. The *Messerschmitt Bf-109* was a multipurpose fighter, most often employed as a high-speed interceptor. It was powered by an inverted, liquid-cooled V-12, with a top speed of 320 mph at sea level and 400 mph at 21,000 feet. It was armed with two 13mm machine guns and a single nose-mounted 20 mm cannon and could carry up to 250 kg of bombs or rockets.

The *Focke-Wulf FW-190* was a single-seat fighter, powered by a 14-cylinder, 2-row air-cooled radial engine. Its maximum speed was 405 mph at 19,500 feet, with a range of 250–310 miles. It was armed with two 13mm machine guns, four 20 mm cannon, and the capability of hanging one bomb under the fuselage or four under the wings.

The *Junkers Ju-88* was a twin-engine (liquid-cooled V-12) multirole combat aircraft, crew of four, capable of carrying an approximately 3,000 lb. bomb load, armed with four 7.92 mm machine guns in flexible mounts front, rear, and upper and lower fuselage. Its maximum speed was 290 mph, cruise speed 230, with a range of approximately 1,100 miles.

The *Focke-Wulf FW-189* was a three-seat, short-range reconnaissance aircraft, easily recognized by its large glass-enclosed crew gondola and twin-boom tail assembly. It was powered by two air-cooled, inverted V-12 engines, with a top speed of 214 mph and range of 580 miles. Its armaments included two fixed 7.92 mm machine guns firing forward, a single 7.92 mm machine gun at the rear gunner position in the gondola, and optionally another 7.92 mm machine gun in the rear cone.

The *Heinkel He-111* was a twin-engine (liquid-cooled V-12) bomber, crew of five, capable of carrying 4,400 lb. bomb load, armed with up to seven 7.92 mm machine guns in various configurations. Its maximum speed was 270 mph, with a range of approximately 1,400 miles.

The *Fiesler Fi-156 Storch* (stork) was a small German liaison aircraft, a high-wing monoplane with a crew of two and long, fixed landing gear. It was powered by a liquid-cooled, inverted V-8, which gave it a top speed of 109 mph and a range of 240 miles. It was armed with a flexible 7.92 mm machine gun at the rear of the cockpit.

The *Hydro* named in the table was most likely the *Blohm & Voss-138*, a trimotor (diesel 2-stroke, opposed 6-cylinder) boom-tailed flying boat used for long-range maritime patrol and naval reconnaissance. It had a crew of six men, maximum speed of 177 mph, and range of 760 miles. It was armed with two 20 mm cannons, one 13mm cannon, with a payload of six 50 kg bombs or seven 150 kg depth charges.

[Second table] The *Henschel He-126* was a two-seat, high wing monoplane reconnaissance and observation aircraft, powered by a 9-cylinder, air-cooled radial engine to a top speed of 221 mph and a range of 620 miles. It was armed with a fixed, forward-firing 7.92 mm machine gun and a flexible 7.92 machine gun mounted in the rear turret. It could carry up to 150 kg of bombs.

The *Junkers Ju-87 Stuka* was a single-engine (liquid-cooled, inverted V-12) dive bomber and ground attack aircraft, easily recognized by its inverted gull wing and fixed undercarriage. It had a crew of two (pilot and rear gunner), was capable of a top speed of 211 mph and a range of 370 miles. Its armament consisted of two wing-mounted 7.92 mm machine guns and a flexible 7.92 mm machine gun for the rear gunner. Its payload was a single 250 kg bomb hung on the centerline and four under-wing 50 kg bombs.—Translator and regrouping of Karelian *Front* forces. The number of transport aviation flights between airfields also increased significantly.

Enemy reconnaissance flights in connection with the operation conducted in October are shown in the following table. As shown in this table, air reconnaissance was carried out primarily by fighter aircraft that reconnoitered the forward edge of our defenses and the road system leading to it with 10–12 sorties per day.

For participation in the operation, Northern Fleet Air Forces set aside from its resources 55 bombers, 35 ground attack aircraft, 160 fighters, and 25 reconnaissance aircraft that were positioned at their airfields: Vaenga, Gryaznaya, Ura-guba, and Pummanki. The aircraft operated systematically against enemy convoys on the Varangerfjord–Tanafjord route, conducting strikes independently and in cooperation with submarines and torpedo cutters. Fleet aviation also attacked the ports of Petsamo, Liinakhamari, Kirkenes, Vardo, Vadso, and others from the air.

Northern Fleet Air Forces' ground targets included shore batteries on the coastline of Petsamovuono Inlet and enemy batteries and firing positions on the isthmus of Sredniy Peninsula. Air reconnaissance was conducted to detect enemy convoys in Varangerfjord ports and in transit. Air reconnaissance was significantly increased before the operation.

Thus, the situation in the air favored the conduct of the planned offensive operation, particularly the actions of the forces of the Northern Fleet on the coast and in the waters of Varangerfjord, because the correlation of forces and tempo of air activity of the Northern Fleet air forces were superior to that of the enemy's aviation.

CHAPTER II

Commander's Concept and Operational Plan

1. Concept of the Operation and Plan of Actions of the Forces of the Karelian *Front*

The Karelian *Front* command group planned to conduct an offensive operation on the Murmansk axis even before Finland withdrew from the war. Based on considerations submitted to *STAVKA*, permission was received to regroup the forces of the Karelian *Front* and reconcentrate them. The original date to complete the regrouping of forces and begin the offensive was originally 27 September, but that date slipped to 7 October 1944.

According to the operational plan, Karelian *Front* forces would conduct an offensive in cooperation with Northern Fleet units. Their goal was to encircle the main enemy forces that were defending positions along the Western Litsa River by offensively striking the enemy's right flank at Lake Chapr and breaking through the defensive positions on the isthmus of Sredniy Peninsula. Subsequently, the offensive would develop in the direction of Pechenga (Petsamo) and Kirkenes, liberating all Pechenga oblast and the Soviet far north from the German invaders.

In accordance with this operational concept, the following steps were proposed:

- Two rifle corps (99th and 131st) with 14th Army reinforcing units would attack on the axis Malaya Karikvayvish–Bolshaya Karikvayvish–Luostari–Petsamo.
- Northern Fleet forces would conduct a breakthrough of the defenses on the isthmus of Sredniy Peninsula.
- Units of Second Chudovskiy Fortified Region (three battalions), 45th Rifle Division, and the Third Naval Infantry Brigade would remain in the sector from Great Western Litsa Bay to Hill 334.2, to defend the right flank of 14th Army's attacking forces and then pursue the enemy during his retreat to Pechenga.
- Two light rifle corps (126th and 127th) would bypass the enemy defenses on their right [our left] flank and, moving toward Luostari, cut the Rovaniemi–Pechenga Road, preventing enemy reserves from approaching the Luostari–Pechenga area.

2. Missions of the Northern Fleet

The commander of 14th Army informed the Northern Fleet command group of the Karelian *Front*'s planned offensive operation on 3 September 1944. His briefing pointed out the axis of the main attack and discussed the fleet mission for cooperation with the troops of the Karelian *Front* and breakthrough of the enemy defenses on the isthmus of Sredniy Peninsula. The *Front* commander personally confirmed the fleet mission on 8 September and additionally directed that, once ashore, the naval infantry brigade link up with 14th Army units and jointly continue the attack toward Pechenga.

After meeting with the Karelian *Front* commander, on 29 September the Northern Fleet commander definitively stated the fleet's mission: "The naval infantry brigades, in coordinated action with fleet aviation and surface ships, will break through the enemy defenses in front of the Northern Defensive Region. After breakthrough of the defenses on the isthmus of Sredniy Peninsula is accomplished, the naval infantry brigades will capture the Titovka–Porovaara road, cut off the retreat of German forces from Western Litsa River positions, and upon linkup with 14th Army units, jointly develop the attack on Petsamo. The fleet will support movement of 14th Army troops and supplies from Murmansk to the western shore of Kola Bay."

CHAPTER III

Decision of the Commander, Northern Fleet, and Plan of Joint Operations with the Karelian *Front* for the Liberation of the Soviet Far North

The commander of the Northern Fleet developed his plan for the actions of the forces subordinated to him in the operation for the liberation of the Soviet far north based on information received from the commander of 14th Army on 3 September. At 1100 on 8 September, the Military Council of the Northern Fleet signed combat directive No. 0049/*ob*,[1] which set forth the missions for the commander of the Northern Defensive Region, commander of Torpedo Cutter Brigade, commander of Submarine Brigade, commander of Surface Squadron, commander of the Main Base Approaches Defense Command, commander of Shore Defense Command, and commander of the Northern Fleet Air Forces.

Order No. 0048/*op* (appendix 1), concerning the organization and composition of forces for the operation in cooperation with 14th Army for the defeat of the Germans' Western Litsa grouping of forces, was issued on this same day. The operation received the code name "West."

The operational plan was published on 1 October, and combat directive No. 0052/*op* (appendix 2), which replaced the earlier published combat directive, was issued. The decision of the commander, Northern Fleet, for the operation and grouping of forces is shown in figure 1.2.

1. The Decision and Operational Plan on Land

To accomplish a joint offensive with 14th Army, the fleet commander ordered a breakthrough of enemy defenses on the isthmus of Sredniy Peninsula and the capture of the Titovka–Porovaara Road in the area of Rasvatunturi mountain, thus cutting the enemy's path of retreat to Pechenga. He designated two naval infantry brigades with attached units for this effort. One brigade, with the support and cover of surface vessels and aviation, would break through the enemy defenses on the isthmus. The other was to land on the southern coast of Maattivuono Bay into the rear of the defending enemy force. The amphibious landing was to occur prior to the breakthrough attack against the defensive positions.

---

1 The Military Council was comprised of the commander, his chief of staff, and the senior political officer of the command. This political officer institution existed throughout the Soviet armed forces at all levels of command down to at least brigade and is visibly manifested in the signature blocks on all significant combat documents.—Translator

TABLE 3.1. Composition of forces, embarkation, and landing times

Wave	Composition of Forces	No. of Men	No. of Cargo	Embarkation Time	Landing Time
1st	Eight small subchasers, one torpedo cutter. Recon detachments of HQ Fleet and NDR. Recon company of 63rd NIB, platoon 508 Sep Eng. Assault Co., 1st and 2nd Rifle Co., Submachine gun Co., recon platoon of 2nd Rifle Bn. Forward observer section and Pathfinder Company.	606	10 t.	2130	2300
2nd	Eleven large subchasers, one torpedo cutter. 1st Rifle Bn., 3rd Co of 2nd Rifle Bn., machine-gun Co, 2nd Mortar Co, Anti-tank Rifle Co, chem platoon, signal co, AAA plat. NCO Academy, medical co, brigade support and command post, 716th Chem Plat, NDR Forward Observer Section.	1,628	21 t.	2200	2330
3rd	Eight torpedo cutters. 3rd Rifle Bn., Engineer Plat and Forward Observer Section.	517	4 t.	2230	2400

The following sub-missions were contained within this plan of action:

IMMEDIATE MISSION: The 63rd Naval Infantry Brigade was to capture the coastline of Maattivuono Bay in the sector of Cape Punaynenniemi and Cape Akhkioniemi and then attack into the rear of the enemy defenses in the western sector of the isthmus between the mainland and Sredniy Peninsula.

SUBSEQUENT MISSION: Supported by artillery of the Northern Defensive Region and fleet ships and aviation, the amphibious landing force, with 12th Naval Infantry Brigade, which was attacking from the front, was to break through enemy defenses in the western sector of the isthmus.

FOLLOW-ON MISSION: 12th and 63rd Naval Infantry Brigades will move to the Titovka–Porovaara road, hold it firmly, and prevent the retreat of enemy forces along it toward Pechenga.

Keep in mind the combined attack with 14th Army units on Pechenga and the capture of the port and town. The plan of action on land envisaged the following components:

1. The amphibious assault on the coastline of Maattivuono Bay was to be executed in three waves. The composition of forces by wave, time of embarkation, and time of landing is shown in table 3.1.

   - Actions of the assault force after landing were planned so that after its first 24-hour period ashore, its units would reach the southern shore of Lake Selyarvi, and reference points 203 and 64 on the western shore of the lake.
   - After the second 24-hour period, the assault units would reach Rasvatunturi mountain and Lake Ustoyarvi.
   - After the third 24-hour period, the assault force would reach the Titovka–Porovaara Road and occupy positions from Larasyarvi to Hill 388.9.

2. Breakthrough of enemy defenses on the isthmus of Sredniy Peninsula by the forces of 12th Red Banner Naval Infantry Brigade [NIB]:

   The 12th NIB's breakthrough in the sector from Kazarma to Lake Raseyarvi was planned so that units would reach the western edge of the enemy defenses by dawn, after 63rd NIB's night amphibious landing. The attack was to be developed in the direction of the Titovka–Porovaara road, culminating in its capture by combined action with 63rd NIB in the sector of Lake Larasyarvi and Hill 388.9 on the third day.

3. The amphibious assault and breakthrough of the enemy's defenses on the isthmus of Sredniy Peninsula was to be supported by preliminary (three days prior to the operation) suppression of enemy batteries on the coastline of Petsamovuono Bay and on the isthmus of Sredniy Peninsula by Northern Defensive Region artillery and fleet air forces, by shelling 63rd NIB's beachhead in the event of enemy resistance, and a massed 30-minute artillery barrage by the Northern Defensive Region on enemy command posts, firing positions, and troops just prior to the breakthrough. During the development of the attack, the brigades were to be accompanied by artillery and airstrikes on enemy command posts, batteries, defensive fortifications, and troops.

4. To distract the enemy's attention during the time of the amphibious assault on the coastline of Maattivuono Bay, the operational plan provided for a demonstration landing on the coastline of Motovskiy Bay between Cape Pikshuev and Cape Mogilnyy.

5. Defense of the isthmus of Sredniy Peninsula was to be accomplished by units of 347th and 348th Separate Machine-Gun Battalions. The 349th Separate Machine-Gun Battalion was left in reserve on Sredniy Peninsula, and 125th Naval Infantry Regiment around the fleet main base at Polyarnoye.

2. Decision for Actions at Sea

The commander of the Northern Fleet planned to protect 14th Army offensive and the amphibious landing against enemy ships moving toward the Varangerfjord coastline by actions at sea and, at the same time, prevent the introduction of German reserves into the Pechenga area or the evacuation of the area by sea.

He planned to cover the amphibious landing by a mobile screen of three torpedo cutters in Varangerfjord. A support detachment of two destroyers was to be positioned in Motovskiy Bay to support the breakthrough of German defenses on the isthmus of Sredniy Peninsula. The following assets were to attack enemy convoys and unaccompanied ships: 6–8 submarines deployed in the sector between Vardo Island and the meridian 20°00' east, a strike group of 10 torpedo cutters positioned at Pummanki, and four destroyers based in Kola Inlet.

3. Decision for Actions from the Air

Up to 275 of the fleet's available aircraft were to support the offensive, protect the fleet against enemy air attacks, conduct air reconnaissance, and attack enemy forces at sea and on land. This number included an operational group, consisting of 10 *Il-2*,[2] 10 *Yaks*, and 10 *Kittyhawks*,[3] based on Pummanki airfield. At the time of the operation, the group was subordinated for operational purposes to the commander, Northern Defensive Region. The number of aircraft stationed at Pummanki was more than doubled during the operation.

Northern Fleet Air Forces were to execute the following tasks:

- Conduct systematic reconnaissance of enemy defensive dispositions on the isthmus of Sredniy Peninsula and along the coastline of Varangerfjord.
- Provide cover to troop concentrations and the assembled amphibious assault force.
- Eliminate and destroy enemy defensive fortifications prior to and during the operation.
- Suppress enemy shore batteries on the coastline of Petsamovuono Inlet and on the isthmus of Sredniy Peninsula.
- Support the attacking naval infantry units with strikes against enemy command posts, troops, and firing positions, and protect friendly forces against enemy air attack.
- Conduct attacks on enemy convoys and unaccompanied ships at sea.
- Conduct attacks on enemy airfields at Luostari, Hoybuktmoen, and Salmiyarvi in coordination with Karelian *Front* air forces.

---

2 The *Ilyushin Il-2 Shturmovik* (low-level attack aircraft) was a heavily armed and armored ground-attack aircraft, of which 36,183 units were produced during the war. It featured a 1,500 lb. tub that protected the two-man crew, engine, radiator, and fuel cell. Powered by a liquid-cooled V-12, it was capable of 250 mph with a range of 475 miles. It was armed with two fixed forward-firing 23 mm cannons, two fixed forward-firing 7.62 mm machine guns, and a flexible 7.62 mm machine gun at the rear cockpit gunner position and could carry a wide array of up to 600 kg of bombs or 82 mm or 132 mm rockets, in wing bomb bays or on wing hangers.—Translator

3 The Curtiss P-40 *Kittyhawk* was a single-seat fighter, delivered to the Soviet Union initially in the *Tomahawk* version early in the war in limited numbers and later as the improved *Kittyhawk* (P-40E and beyond) in extremely large numbers (2,200 units). It was powered by a liquid-cooled V-12 engine, it had a top speed of 334 mph, it had a range of 716 miles, and it was armed with six .50-caliber machine guns in the wings. It could carry 910 kg of bombs on one fuselage and two wing hard points.—Translator

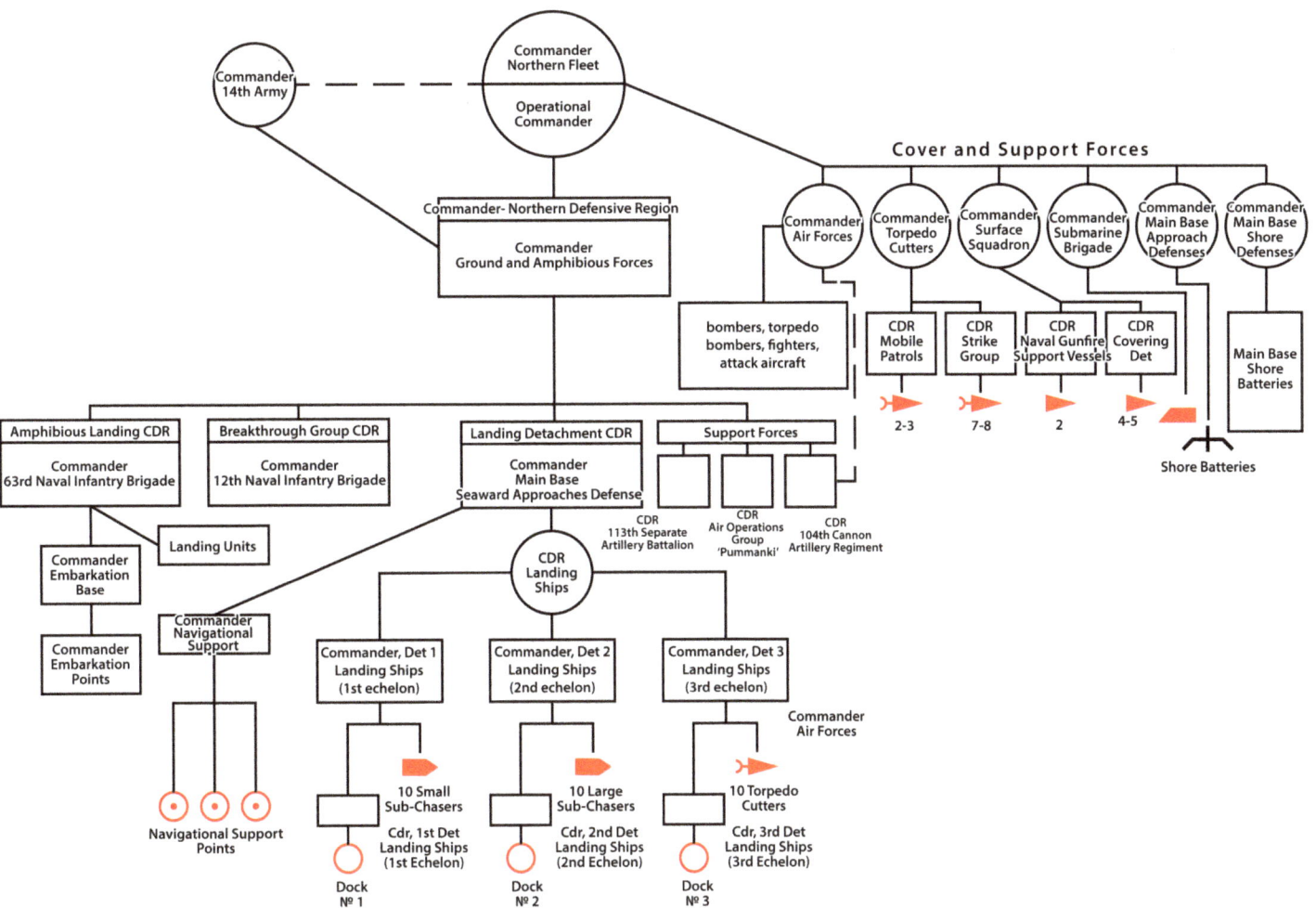

FIGURE 3.1. Organization of command and composition of forces

4. Organization of Command and Composition of Forces

The fleet commander's order No. 0048/*op* of 8 September 1944 specified the composition of the forces for the operation. In accordance with this order, the following assets were subordinated directly to the fleet commander, Admiral Golovko:

- the commander of the group of ground and amphibious assault forces, commander Northern Defensive Region Major General (now Lieutenant General) Dubovtsev;
- acting commander of Fleet Air Forces, Major General Preobrazhenskiy;
- commander of Surface Squadron, Captain First Rank (now Rear Admiral) Fokin;
- commander of Torpedo Cutter Brigade, Captain First Rank Kuzmin;
- commander of Submarine Brigade, Captain First Rank (now Rear Admiral) Kolyshkin;
- commandant of Main Base Shore Defense Force, Major General Kustov.

The organization of command and composition of forces are shown in the schematic (figure 3.1).

On 9 October, the fleet commander and a group of fleet staff officers (mobile staff) positioned themselves at Hill 342.0 on Sredniy Peninsula to control the operation, collocated with the forward command post of commander, Northern Defensive Region. Northern Fleet's main staff and its chief remained at the fleet main command post on shore at Polyarnoye.

When the fleet commander arrived on Sredniy Peninsula, the commanders of the principal formations that were participating in the operation, along with their mobile staffs, were already in place. The command posts of commander, Northern Defensive Region, and Commander, 12th Naval Infantry Brigade, were located in the area of Hill 342.0, and the command posts of Commander, Northern Fleet Air Forces and Commander, Torpedo Cutter Brigade, were located in the vicinity of Hill 200 (Pummanki area).

The positioning of command posts of the formation commanders proximate to each other and the area of combat activities permitted them to have direct observation of the [area of combat activities], facilitating rapid and reliable communications. It also favored timely and precise information concerning the situation and permitted the conduct of coordination between them.

Liaison officers were sent from the Northern Fleet staff to the Karelian *Front* and 14th Army staffs and from the staff of the Northern Defensive Region to the staff of 14th Army to facilitate coordination with the forces of the Karelian *Front*.

CHAPTER IV

Preparation for Execution of the Assigned Missions

Preparation for the operation began in the Northern Fleet long before the operation itself. It included not only direct preparation of the forces participating in the operation but also combat activities intended to weaken the enemy in advance of the operation, to create favorable operational conditions in the battle area.

In this regard, air, submarine, and torpedo boat attacks were systematically conducted against enemy sea lines of communication. Airstrikes were launched against Varangerfjord ports and enemy airfields, and air and artillery attacks methodically destroyed firing positions in the German defenses.

Beginning on 29 September, with the receipt from commander, Karelian *Front* of missions for Northern Fleet and the designated be-prepared time for the operation, preparation was intensified and was focused on the execution of the assigned missions. The be-prepared time for Northern Fleet for the conduct of the operation was initially set at 4 October, and later slipped to 9 October. The forces of the Karelian *Front* would begin the offensive for the breakthrough of enemy defenses on 7 October.

An examination of the amphibious landing area and enemy defenses on the isthmus was conducted during the preparatory period, using available intelligence documents and on-the-ground reconnaissance of officer staffs of the units and formations designated for participation in the operation. Units and ships were simultaneously preparing for the fulfillment of their assigned tasks and were working out the measures for comprehensive support of upcoming combat activities (navigational, engineer, logistic, and medical).

All preparation was conducted under strict observance of security measures, and a limited number of staff officers were involved in preparation of the necessary documents.

1. Staff Work During the Preparation for the Operation

During the preparation of this offensive operation involving the participation of significant and diverse forces, designated for actions on land, on and under sea, and in the air, a large and complex set of activities had to be undertaken by staffs of fleet units and formations.

Work of the staffs of formations was conducted with the following goals:

- the collection of all necessary data for the success of the amphibious landing and breakthrough of the defenses, and the transmission of this data to the users;
- the preparation of all materials for the evaluation of the situation and the making of the commander's decision;
- the preparation of the forces and assets that would participate in the operation;
- the working out of coordination[4] between the various forces participating in the operation;
- the organization of communications;
- and the working out of measures for support of the operation.

The end result of the work of the staffs was the preparation of appropriate documents. The following documents were developed and transmitted to users by the fleet staff during the preparatory period:

- combat directive,
- organizational order,
- planning schedule,
- planning table [synchronization matrix],
- scheme of the organization of command,
- scheme of radio and teletype communications,
- communications instructions,
- scheme of navigational support equipment,
- instructions to the demonstration landing support ship detachment.

The organizational order was issued to formation commanders over the course of several days after the fleet commander's receipt of information from commander, 14th Army, on 3 September, that is, almost a month prior to the start of the operation. Combat Directive No. 0052/*op* was delivered to formation commanders a week before the operation.

The documents developed by the fleet staff pertained only to the first phase of the operation—the amphibious landing on the coastline of Maattivuono Bay and the breakthrough of the defenses on the isthmus of Sredniy Peninsula.

---

4 The Russian term used here is *vzaimodeystviya*, the actions of forces coordinated relative to aims, missions, place, time, and methods of mission accomplishment to achieve the goal of a battle (operation). This term is most frequently translated into English as "coordination" or "cooperation," but in the current operational and tactical lexicon of the US Armed Forces can sometimes be understood as "synchronization." For consistency, it is translated in this document as "coordination."—Translator

Formation staffs developed the documents necessary to their activities based on the documents from fleet staff. Northern Defensive Region staff prepared the following documents:

- combat order (appendix 3);
- scheme of the organization of command;
- communications instructions;
- planning table [coordination matrix];
- order from the chief of artillery;
- order to rear services;
- schematic for the organization of radio communications for the operation;
- schematic for wire communications for Northern Defensive Region units, ships, and aviation;
- call-sign table for the officer component;
- schematic of the combat formations of NDR's artillery concentrated for the operation;
- table showing the composition of the artillery supporting the breakthrough on the ground sector of the front [firing in support of 14th Army];
- schedule of embarkations and landings by 63rd NIB amphibious force; and
- schematic of reference points placed on a 1:50,000 map of the Titovka River area [the area of main effort by 14th Army units].

Fleet Air Force staff developed the following documents:

- combat order,
- planning table [synchronization matrix] of combat actions,
- reconnaissance plan,
- communications instructions,
- organizational order,
- navigational instructions with tables of bombing calculations,
- signals for cooperation with ground forces.

The staff of the Northern Fleet Surface Squadron developed the following documents:

- combat directive,
- communications instructions,
- naval gunfire support instructions,
- planned table of fires.

The amphibious landing force staff (Main Base Seaward Approaches Defense Force staff) developed the following documents:

- combat directive,
- planning table [synchronization matrix],

- schematic of the amphibious landing force commander's plan,
- communications instructions,
- table of coded signals,
- instructions for the return of the landing force to its ships,
- organizational order with a schematic of the organization of command.

The staff of Torpedo Cutter Brigade developed the following documents:

- combat order,
- organizational order.

The Submarine Brigade staff developed the following documents:

- combat order,
- communications instructions,
- supplemental combat instructions,
- table of coded signals.

A particularly important issue in the work of all the staffs during the preparation for the operation was the provision of appropriate reconnaissance data to all the affected units and formations. Accordingly, the fleet staff intelligence department developed and distributed all the materials it had on hand concerning the enemy's defensive system in the landing area and on the isthmus of Sredniy Peninsula. Reconnaissance of all types was planned and conducted during the preparatory phase of the operation to support these efforts.

Air reconnaissance accomplished the following:

- aerial photography of the ports at Liinakhamari and Kirkenes, and of the engineer aspects of the enemy artillery and mortar battery positions;
- systematic observation of the enemy's road network along and behind the front line, in order to determine locations of their main groupings and traffic along roads;
- systematic observation of enemy airfields, with the mission to determine the positioning of their air assets, and of Varangerfjord ports and sea lanes, with the mission of detecting the shipment of forces and combat equipment and transit of convoys.

Fleet Air Forces staff worked up all this data and sent 164 aerial composites and 2,890 photographs of individual objects to its own units, units of the Northern Defensive Region, and the fleet's ships. Intensive aerial reconnaissance was conducted during the preparatory period.

Troop reconnaissance assets of the Northern Defensive Region accomplished the following tasks:

- pinpointing and reconnoitering individual targets;
- confirmation of enemy composition of forces and groupings in front of the Northern Defensive Region, determination of the system of fire of the defenses and the quantity and calibers of artillery and mortar batteries in the breakthrough sector;
- detailed reconnoitering of engineer fortifications, approaches to the forward edge of the defenses in the breakthrough sector and at amphibious landing sites.

Reconnaissance subunits of 12th and 63rd NIBs and 347th and 348th Separate Machine-Gun Battalions conducted 10 ambushes and 36 reconnaissance patrols between 1 and 10 October to obtain the necessary information. As a result of the patrols, the approaches to the forward edge of the enemy's defenses and firing positions were studied, along with the system of fire, and the nature and quantity of man-made obstacles in front of the defensive system. Up to 700 linear meters of barbed wire obstacles were destroyed, 846 mines were removed, and five pressure-activated high explosive devices were neutralized in 37 penetrations of the barrier system.

At the same time, troop artillery reconnaissance by Northern Defensive Region units, with the support of 225th Separate Artillery Reconnaissance Battalion, determined the locations of six artillery and 15 mortar batteries and the area of activity of individual roving guns in the breakthrough sector.

As a result of troop reconnaissance and the photographing of various objects, the Northern Fleet staff intelligence department put together schematics of the engineer fortifications of the defensive system, showing the locations of artillery and mortar batteries. These schematics were distributed to the entire officer component of units participating in the breakthrough of these enemy defenses on the isthmus of Sredniy Peninsula.

Fleet submarines and torpedo cutters also conducted reconnaissance. Submarines conducted nine combat sorties against enemy sea lines of communication during the preparatory period for the operation. During these patrols, supplemental reconnaissance was carried out of enemy convoy movements, their defenses, changes in the sailing regime, and so on. During this period, torpedo cutters carried out 19 group patrols, during which six combat actions occurred with enemy convoys or separate ships.

Heightened communications intelligence collection was also conducted during the preparatory period for this operation. Its purpose was to achieve complete control over enemy radio traffic in the Varangerfjord region. For this purpose, in addition to its daily activities, communications intelligence undertook the following:

- monitoring the main transmitter/receivers of the enemy ground forces in the Murmansk sector;
- interception of transmissions of enemy chiefs of air services [airfield operations];
- monitoring of radio traffic of base stations in Varangerfjord, Kirkenes, Vardo, Vadso, Petsamo, and shore defense transmitter/receivers;
- special monitoring of radio traffic of air units operating from airfields at Luostari, Kirkenes, Banak, Salmiyarvi, and Nautsi;
- monitoring of ship radio traffic in Varangerfjord.

It is important to note that communications intelligence collection was conducted to facilitate a more complete analysis of the grouping and activities of enemy forces, and to establish that the German command did not know the time of the launching of the offensive in northern Finland by the forces of the Karelian *Front*. This was confirmed by the fact that by the beginning of the operation, the enemy had not made any substantive changes in the composition or disposition of his forces and had not prepared their radio net or portable radio transmitters on the coastline of Varangerfjord. This net was in total chaos.

An intensification of the training of staff officers for the upcoming activities associated with the operation was noted in the work of Northern Defensive Region staff during the preparatory period. Staff officers conducted exercises aimed at deliberating and resolving issues; they assembled various instructions and planning tables; they planned for the rapid transmission and oversight of these instructions; and they checked the functioning of communications assets with subordinate and superior staffs.

In addition, a war game was conducted in the headquarters of the Northern Defensive Region, with the participation of staff officers of the naval infantry brigades. The theme of the game was "Breakthrough of an enemy defense on a land sector with a simultaneous amphibious landing on the enemy's seaward flank." The naval infantry brigade headquarters in turn conducted four exercises with their battalion headquarters.

In this manner, the staff work during the preparatory period, conducted for the purposes of comprehensive support of the upcoming combat, to a large degree enabled the units execution of their combat missions.

2. Preparation of Units and Ships for the Amphibious Landing

PREPARATION OF THE LANDING FORCES. Units of 63rd Naval Infantry Brigade were prepared to be the amphibious landing force. The brigade's Second and Fourth Battalions were concentrated in Pummanki for this purpose, and First and Third Battalions in the area of Eyna Bay. They conducted training for actions in amphibious operations from the second half of August. Three exercises were conducted to train the troops in rapid embarkation on cutters with weapons and ammunition, and landing on an unprepared shore that was similar in terrain to the enemy-occupied coastline.

Units also practiced firing their heavy and light machine guns from the decks of torpedo cutters during their approach to shore and worked on their skills in utilizing signal devices within their formations during the landing and in battle once ashore. Altogether, one brigade-, 16 battalion-, and 28 company-level tactical exercises were conducted for the purpose of training the units in their actions ashore after the landing.

The following issues were worked out in exercises for the officer component:

- arrival of assault force units at the embarkation point, procedure for loading on the cutters and offloading;
- development of sound habits in organizing cooperation within units and subunits, and also with attached and supporting units;
- organization of continuous command and control of subunits and units in combat;
- means of conducting battle ashore;
- on-the-ground reconnaissance [*rekognostsirovka*[5]] of the terrain.

---

5 *Rekognostsirovka* is reconnaissance conducted by commanders at any level, whenever possible conducted at a site from which the battlefield is visible. It permits the higher commander to point out to his subordinates, on the terrain, the important elements of the upcoming operation, such as approach routes, main axis and supporting axes, known and suspected enemy locations, and other features that influenced his decision (the plan for conducting the battle). At sea, this activity was sometimes conducted using an air platform, or even through a submarine periscope in the case of an amphibious landing operation. The practice was employed by both ground and naval forces throughout the war.—Translator

TABLE 4.1. Tactical-technical data on Northern Fleet vessels that participated in the amphibious assaults on the south coast of Varangerfjord (9–31 October 1944)

Type of Craft	Displacement (tons)	Length Width Draft (meters)	Max and Econ Speed (knots)	Range (nautical miles)	Horsepower	Armament	Mines	Landing Force (men)	Cargo (tons)
Large Sub chaser	108.0	33.6 / 5.5 / 2.3	12/15 5	2,800	2 × 1,200	I 40 mm Bofors III 20 mm Oerlikon	8-rail depth charge M-20 B-1–18	150	4.5
Small Sub chaser	56.5	26.9 / 4.9 / 1.3	15/27 4	610	3 × 850	II 45 mm II 12.7 mm machine guns	Torpedo launcher BS-45 B-1–2 M-1–30	60	1.0
Torpedo cutter A-2 "Higgins"	59.0	26.0 / 5.1 / 2.0	12/41 6	715	3 × 1,200	II 20 mm Oerlikon IV 12.7 mm "Colt" machine guns	Torpedo launcher 53cm ABS	45–70	1.2
Torpedo cutter A-1 "Vosper"	43.9	22.1 / 5.2 / 2.0	12/39 6	825	3 × 1,200	I 12.7 mm "Colt" machine guns		35–60	1.0
Torpedo cutter D-3	37.2	22.3 / 4.3 / 1.8	12/37 6	550	3 × 850	II 12.7 mm DSHK machine guns	Torpedo Launcher 53cm "B-1" 4 "M-1" 8	20–30	0.5

The basic method of officer exercises was group activities on the terrain, involving the solution of brief tactical problems on maps.

PREPARATION OF SHIPS AND THEIR CREWS. All the cutters designated for the amphibious landing received a technical inspection; then were provided with the necessary spare parts, safety equipment, and materials; and finally took aboard the special assault gangplanks. Torpedoes were removed from torpedo cutters, and depth charge launchers, acoustical ranging equipment, and other extraneous equipment were removed from the small and large subchasers.

Additional radio communications gear was placed aboard the cutters designated for the amphibious force commander and the landing force commanders. Tactical and technical data on the vessels that participated in the operation are contained in table 4.1. A rescue group was prepared and sent to Pummanki, consisting in part of a single patrol cutter, for use in rendering timely assistance to damaged cutters.

Training exercises were conducted to prepare the cutter crews. They practiced rapid approaches to undeveloped shorelines, placement of the special gangplanks on the shore by a gangplank team, and landing of the assault force and unloading of weapons. Special attention was given during the conduct of these exercises to mastering the task of holding the bow of the cutter to the shore during the ebb and flow of the surf by manipulating the throttles, to firing from the cutters, to laying down smoke screens and maneuvering in smoke during the approach to or withdrawal from shore, and to removal of the cutter from rocks and the struggle for survival.

A portion of the exercises was conducted with the participation of 63rd NIB subunits, main base shore defense units, and training teams of the Patrol Cutter Brigade.

Unfamiliar with the operational area, the Second Large Subchaser Division conducted training sorties in pairs to Pummanki, where it studied the moorage layout and undertook training in the uploading of soldiers on the vessels and landing them on an undeveloped shore.

During the preparation of ships for the operation, crews developed plans for communication between vessels and for radio communications on call from fleet staff, especially in the event of jamming by the enemy. Four such exercises were conducted using short wave, which was the basic means of radio communication used by the Northern Fleet staff.

The officer component studied intelligence data about the enemy, the region of operations, the character of the coastline, the relief of the sea bottom, and the hydrometeorological conditions of the passage to the landing site in special sessions.

3. Hydrometeorological Support

Hydrometeorological support of the amphibious landing had extremely great significance, in connection with the fact that Northern Fleet lacked special amphibious landing craft and was forced to a large degree to employ vessels inappropriate for the task. At the same time, the meteorological condition in the Barents Sea in the autumn period was characterized by changing weather with storms on many days.

As a consequence of this, at the insistence of the command, the fleet hydrometeorological service published a long-range weather forecast for the month on 3 October. In addition to this, a weather forecast was developed for each week for the main base and for the Norwegian and Murmansk coastlines. Daily forecasts were provided for the coastlines at Murmansk, Kola Inlet, Motovskiy Bay, Varangerfjord, the Norwegian coastline, and White Sea for the period[s] of three days, 24 hours, and each 15 hours. Special weather forecasts were developed for Kola Inlet, and Rybachyy and Sredniy Peninsulas for the period[s] of seven days, three days, 24 hours, and each 12–15 hours.

The forecast for Maattivuono Bay from 1900 9 October to 1900 10 October was as follows: unstable wind, primarily out of the northwest and west, force 2–4,[6] gusting to force 5. The sea at night—force 2, and up to force 3 in the daytime. Dying swells from the north, weakening. Cloudiness 5–9/10ths, at night lessening to 3 to 7/10ths, during snow squalls 7–10/10ths, ceiling 600–1000 meters. Weak snow squalls. Haze. Visibility 5–10 miles, 1–3 miles in precipitation. Temperature −4 to +2°C.

During preparation for the operation, it was considered as well that on 10 October there would be 11 hours 40 minutes of darkness (beginning at 1848), and with the addition of twilight, 14 hours (beginning at 1737). Moon from 2130 to 1900. Low tide at 0709, high tide at 0042 and 1321.

4. Navigational-Hydrographic Support

Navigational-hydrographic support had the following missions:

- support of the passage of the amphibious forces by sea from Pummanki to the deployment point;
- support of the deployment and movement of the amphibious forces to the landing zones in Maattivuono Bay;
- identification and marking of landing sites on the shore before the approach of the main landing force;
- support of the actions of the demonstration landing and naval gunfire support vessels in Motovskiy Bay;
- support of safe passage of vessels to the docks in Pummanki in the period of uploading the amphibious force on the cutters.

There were six pathfinder sections with two or three men in each in both groups.

Marking lights *FS-12* and *SP-95* were selected for equipping of the light posts.[7] *SP-95* marking lights, as the most transportable, were utilized for marking the landing sites, along with marking lights *F-300* and *F-140*, which could be seen from a great distance. Three pairs of alignment lights and two navigational lights

---

6 The Soviet Navy used the Beaufort Wind Force Scale, a somewhat subjective measure of wind velocity and wave conditions. "Force 2–4" equates to a 4–16 knot wind, shown by small wavelets to small waves.—Translator

7 The Russian here is *stvor*. These were lights of various colors or fires placed on land to assist vessels at sea in navigating from or to a fixed point, using the lights as a point of reference.—Translator

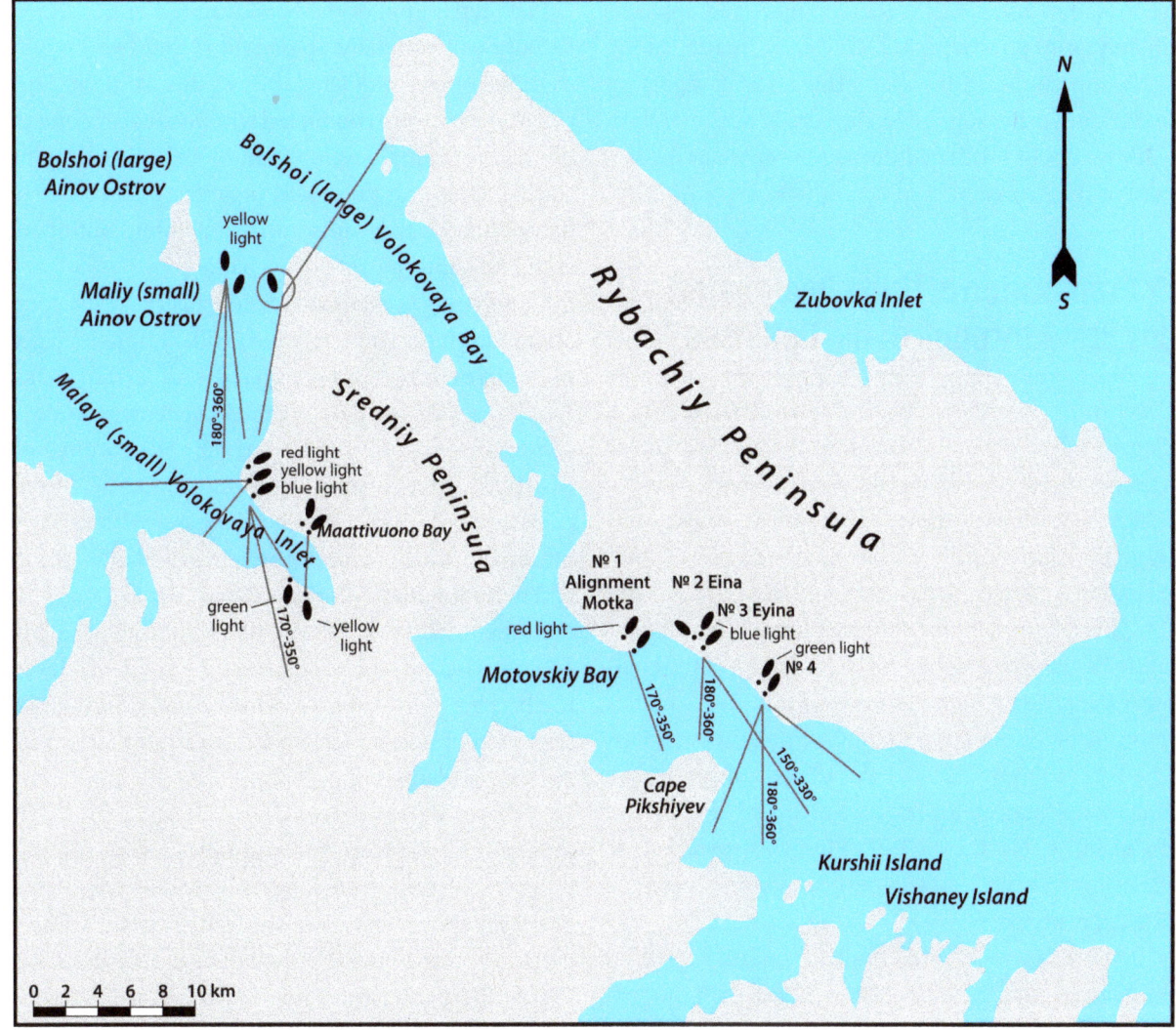

FIGURE 4.1. Placement of navigational support lights

were established to assist the ships in crossing from Pummanki to Maattivuono Bay.

Four pairs of light posts were set up on the southern shore of Rybachyy Peninsula for support of the actions of the demonstration landing and the naval gunfire vessels in Motovskiy Bay (figure 4.1).

All the navigational equipment was designed for continuous operation, but provision was made for its employment on demand. Turning the lights on was done on order from the fleet command post through the commanders of the pathfinder groups, who received their instructions by a specially assembled table of code words. The marker control posts were to turn on the lights in sequence in conjunction with the movement of the assault force ships.

In addition to the specified measures of navigational support for the ships, units and formations were equipped with all the necessary aids and military-geographic descriptions of the area of operations. For example, the amphibious landing force commander was issued 12 copies of overlays of Maattivuono Bay, scale 1:100,000; the amphibious force commander was given local maps of the landing area in scales 1:100,000 and 1:25,000, 50 copies of each. The naval gunfire support vessel commanders received artillery firing tables with goniometric coordinates specially prepared for this operation.

Three photographic montages of Petsamovuono Inlet were assembled, altogether 15 military-geographic descriptions of the Pechenga and Kirkenes areas were made, and 14 plans bearing the coordinates of up to 500 military objects in the forward edge of the enemy's defenses were prepared. As many as 1,500 military objects in the forward edge of the enemy's defenses and in Petsamovuono Inlet were identified, and approximately 100 photographic sets were made, along with 200 copies of the plan. This all-encompassing navigational-hydrographic support of the operation without doubt facilitated the actions at sea and guaranteed their success.

5. Preparation of Units Designated for Breakthrough of the Defenses

Twelfth Red Banner Naval Infantry Brigade, 614th Separate Punishment Company,[8] the entire artillery component of the Northern Defensive Region (104th Cannon Artillery Regiment and 113th Separate Coast Artillery Battalion), and fleet engineer units (338th Separate Engineer Battalion, 508th Separate Assault Engineer Company, the sapper platoon of 180th Separate Engineer Battalion, 4th NCO School of the engineer department of the Northern Fleet, the road platoon of 357th Separate Road Company) comprised the forces designated for the breakthrough of the enemy defenses on the isthmus of Sredniy Peninsula. In addition, Northern Fleet's First Destroyer Escort Division (two vessels) was designated for naval gunfire support.

Twelfth Naval Infantry Brigade conducted special exercises during the preparatory period, with the goal of developing among the troops the skills of fighting in close battle, of rapidly combining light infantry subunits for actions in mountainous terrain, and [of] practice in land navigation and terrain orientation at night.

Each squad was equipped with assault ladders and ropes for surmounting steep slopes and descents in the mountains. Each battalion assembled two or three assault groups for blocking and destroying enemy firing positions during the breakthrough of the fortified zone. Each of these groups rehearsed on specially prepared terrain that was similar in nature to that on which the actual combat would occur during the breakthrough.

---

8 *Shtrafbats* (*штрафбат* or *штрафной батальон*) were disciplinary frontline-combat punishment battalions where soldiers who deserted, who retreated, or who were sentenced to death were assigned for up to three months. They had a chance to redeem themselves through frontline combat at the most hazardous points. Battalions were normally some 800 men and companies up to 150. Release from a *shtrafbat* or *shtrafrot* (company) was by death, wound, or decoration for valor. Preceding an attack by clearing minefields by running through them was a common punishment battalion or company mission.—Editor

For preparation of the breakthrough of the enemy defenses, 14 company, 10 battalion, and two brigade exercises were conducted, principally at night. Special exercises were conducted with the officer component, concerning development of skill in occupying start positions for the attack, organizing coordination between and within units, and maintaining continuous command and control during battle.

Concerning preparation of the artillery for the operation, the officer component of artillery units engaged in group exercises and command-staff terrain walks. Emphasis was placed on organizing offensive battle in conditions of heavily broken terrain, and coordination of artillery units with infantry units. Joint field exercises were held with the same emphases with infantry officers, in which common terrain orientation points and mutual signals were established. During this process, the infantry officers pointed out to the artillery officers where it would be necessary to blow lanes in the barbed wire obstacles, which enemy firing positions to suppress, and in what order to shift fires from one line to another.

Forward observer teams were formed to enable infantry commanders to communicate with artillery units. Three teams from long-range artillery, two from direct support artillery, and one from the coast artillery battalion were sent to the battalion in the first echelon. Artillery unit commanders personally coordinated with infantry units on common numerical designators for targets, order of priority for forward observers, and call signs and frequencies for maintaining communication. In addition, exercises were conducted with forward air controllers.

Four group exercises were conducted with the officer component during the preparatory period, along with two command post field communications exercises, and two command and control exercises.

At the same time, the enlisted and non-commissioned officer personnel conducted systematic training in the rapid deployment of their guns at night. Much attention was given to the study of targets on the terrain.

The artillery section of the Northern Defensive Region corrected all observed deficiencies during the preparation of artillery unit support sections for combat.

Regarding the preparation of destroyer escorts for naval gunfire support to the breakthrough units, vessel commanders, their navigators, and gunnery officers studied target lists. Forward observer teams were prepositioned on the coastline of Rybachyy Peninsula and in the area of Ozerko and Eyna, and their communications with headquarters and artillery units of the Northern Defensive Region and their vessels were confirmed.

Preparation of engineer units for the operation was conducted with the goals of accomplishing the following missions for engineer support:

- conduct of engineer reconnaissance for the confirmation of data on the enemy defenses;
- construction of passages through the obstacle system and clearing paths through minefields for the attacking units;
- engineer preparation of assembly areas and departure positions;
- complete clearing of mines in liberated territory, populated areas, and roads;
- setting up of field troop shelters in newly occupied areas.

In preparation for the accomplishment of these missions, engineer reconnaissance units conducted a careful examination of minefields and fortifications in the forward edge of the enemy defenses in September. Exercises were conducted with naval infantry units, using actual engineer equipment on terrain quite similar to the terrain in the breakthrough sector.

Immediately prior to the start of the offensive, from 6 to 10 October, six reconnaissance parties totaling 236 personnel prepared 37 passage lanes in the barbed wire obstacles, varying in width from 4 to 70 meters, and removed 846 Soviet mines from five Soviet minefields in the attack sector. At 0320 on the morning of 10 October, during the period of concentration of troops at their attack positions for launching the breakthrough, engineer troops and attached naval infantry groups detonated demolitions and line charges in the enemy barbed wire obstacles, resulting in the creation of a one-kilometer-long passage lane.

6. Preparation of Aviation

Northern Fleet Air Forces accomplished their assigned missions in the preparatory period for the operation: reconnaissance, suppression of the shore batteries at the entrance to Petsamovuono Inlet and of the artillery batteries on the isthmus of Sredniy Peninsula, and the destruction of enemy transports and combatants detected at sea.

Fleet Air Forces conducted nine war games, 135 group exercises, eight command and control exercises, [and] four tactical flying exercises, and resolved over 500 tactical problems with flight crews during the preparation. In preparing the officer component, special attention was given to resolving issues of coordination with the ground troops and surface vessels. With this in mind, liaison officers were placed in the headquarters of the Northern Defensive Region, [in] the naval infantry brigades, on the naval gunfire support vessels, and at Seventh Air Army [Karelian *Front*] prior to the start of the operation.

With the participation of these liaison officers, several exercises were conducted before the operation for the development of cooperation between air and ground forces during the offensive. In these sessions, the liaison officers explained the tactical and technical capabilities of their aircraft and how they could best be used in combat.

Also during the course of the preparation of aviation units, the entire area of operations was photographed from the air and then studied by aviation personnel. The results of this effort were of great value during the presentation of missions to air crews and specifying their targets for destruction from the air.

7. Logistic and Medical Support

Preparation for the operation regarding logistic support was directed toward one fundamental mission—the accumulation of reserves of all types of supplies at assembly points of units and ships participating in the operation and the uninterrupted resupply of the forces from these points during the operation. Prior to the operation's start, formations designated for participation in it were logistically supplied at the following locations:

- Units of the Northern Defensive Region were supplied from rear area dumps on Rybachyy and Sredniy Peninsulas, because main bases (Eastern and Western Ozerko) and docks there were under intense enemy observation, and the dock at Western Ozerko and the entrance to Motka Bay were subject to systematic enemy artillery fire.
- Ships of the seaward approaches' security force were supplied through their own shore base at Kuvshinsk and through their logistic section in Polyarnoye.

- Surface Squadron ships were supplied through their logistic section in Vaenga.
- Torpedo cutters were supplied through the shore base in Dolgaya Bay and at the forward base in Pummanki on Sredniy Peninsula, where a shore base section was set up.
- Aviation based on airfields at Vaenga, Gryaznaya, Ura-guba, and Pummanki were supplied through the organizations that maintained these airfields.

Fleet logistic units took all possible measures in the preparatory period to stockpile all necessary reserves at Northern Defensive Region supply dumps for complete satisfaction of all supply demands that might arise.

One month's supply of various types of goods was unloaded for the Northern Defensive Region from 5 to 13 September. This included 970 tons of food and forage, 211 tons of troop issue and ships stores, 667 tons of fuel, and 660 tons of ammunition. Along with this, measures were taken to accelerate the movement of supplies from central Soviet Navy supply dumps, and requests were submitted for an increase in ammunition drops for artillery and mortars, for aviation fuels *B-70*, *B-78*, and *B-100*, and automotive fuel.

Northern Defensive Region logistics command issued and delivered the following items to units preparing for the operation from 11 September to 10 October: 1,970 tons of ammunition, 426 tons of food and forage, 130 tons of troop issue and ships stores, and 497 tons of petroleum products.

In 63rd Naval Infantry Brigade, designated for the amphibious landing, logistic units were relocated to the area of "North-2" dock (Pummanki), and the following supplies were stocked at brigade dumps: a six-day supply of provisions; three units of fire of ammunition;[9] 37 tons of engineer, chemical, medical, and other supplies; and 100 percent of the brigade's requirement for winter-issue clothing.

In addition, a staging base of 21 men was formed in the brigade, the mission of which was to land with the amphibious assault on a cleared shore and organize a forward unit supply point capable of receipt and distribution of required materials and enemy property.

By the beginning of the operation, Northern Defensive Region units had been provided with the following: six units of fire of artillery ammunition, up to 13 days' issue of food and forage, up to 14 days' supply of fuel, and all the troop issue items requested.

By 1 October, the following quantities of ammunition were on the ground at coast and field artillery firing positions:

45 mm gun	16,164
76 mm gun	20,411
100 mm gun	1,773
107 mm gun	772
122 mm gun	3,971
122 mm howitzer	4,210
130 mm gun	3,909
152 mm gun	4,143
82 mm mortar	22,870
107 mm mortar	1,078
120 mm mortar	5,555
Total	84,856

In addition, the Northern Defensive Region had the following items in its rear area supply dumps on 10 October: 2–3 units of fire of artillery ammunition, 12 units of fire of small arms ammunition, seven days' supply of rations and forage, 118 tons of fuel, and a complete issue of winter clothing items.

The following comprised the equipment items for the troops of the amphibious landing and breakthrough forces: a quilted padded jacket (for women) or double-breasted jacket (for men), quilted trousers, boots or overshoes, pile caps, foot bindings [worn by Soviet military personnel in lieu of socks], one pair of warm and two pairs of standard underwear (one in an equipment bag), gloves or mittens, and a camouflage cape.

On-hand tentage was prepared for troop warming sites, and where tentage was not available, warming sites were fabricated from waterproof capes.

A significant shortcoming in the preparation of fleet units was in transportation.

They had only 26 percent of authorized wheeled transport, 66 percent of authorized pack animals, and 50 percent of tracked transport.

Logistic support to the Fleet Air Forces was accomplished by the creation of necessary stocks of fuel, ordnance, food, and aircraft spare parts at operational airfields (Pummanki and Ura-guba). By the beginning of the operation, 400 tons of aviation gas and 750 tons of ammunition were on the airfield at Pummanki, and 181

---

9 In Russian, *boyevoy komplekt* (combat load), which in essence is a "basic load" for a weapon system based on estimated expenditure for a given type of tactical employment of the weapon system.—Translator

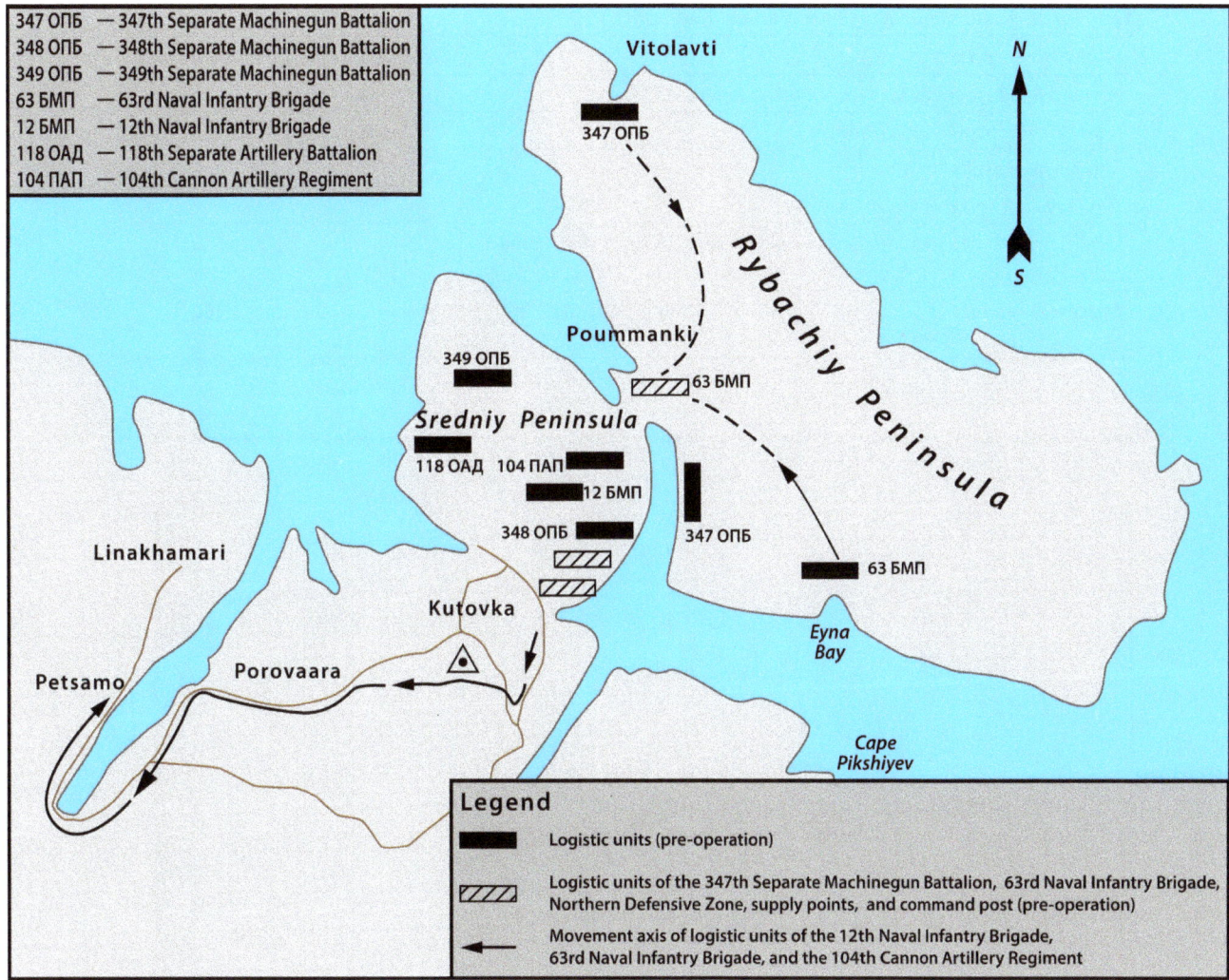

FIGURE 4.2. Location and movement of Northern Defensive Region logistic facilities

tons of ordnance, 427 tons of aviation gas, 36 tons of oil, and 50 tons of aircraft spare parts were delivered to the airfield at Ura-guba.

Three hundred tons of *B-70* aviation fuel, artillery ordnance, spare parts, and other items were issued for logistic support of vessels at Pummanki. The remaining classes of supply for vessels were to be issued from Northern Defensive Region supply depots. The location of Northern Defensive Region logistic facilities is shown in the schematic (figure 4.2).

Preparation for the medical evacuation and treatment aspects of the operation included the following actions:

- primary hospitals were emptied out as much as possible and patients moved to the rear;
- an 86 percent increase in bed space in existing hospitals was created by consolidation of existing facilities, utilization of auxiliary rooms, setting up of bunk beds, and utilization of tents in Forward Field Hospital 2215;
- field hospitals were prepared for reception of sick and wounded on Kildin Island (100–120 beds), Set-Navolok (100–120 beds), 30th Air Brigade at Vaenga (78 beds), the Submarine Brigade in Polyarnoye (30 beds), in the former space of 72nd Naval Hospital and rest home in Tyuba-guba (up to 120 beds), in the rest home at Kildinstroye (up to 60 beds), and in the Naval Air Forces rest home at Gryaznaya Bay (80 beds), altogether an additional 670 spaces. This number of beds could be increased on demand in an extreme emergency by placing hospitals in the building of the former 72nd Naval Hospital in Vladimir Port (300 beds), and at School No. 6 in Murmansk (1,000 beds).

TABLE 4.2. Available and reserve medical bed space

Name of Hospital	Deployed Beds	Reserve Beds
Forward Field Hospital 2215 on Rybachyy Peninsula	500	
Naval Field Hospital in Polyarnoye	648	
74th Naval Hospital in Murmansk	397	
71st Naval Hospital in Gryaznaya Bay	150	
Treatment facilities in Kildin, Set-Navolok, Vaenga, Gryaznaya, Tyuba-guba, Polyarnoye, and Vladimir (first reserve)		970
Treatment facilities in White Sea Flotilla and school for hospitals in Murmansk (second reserve)		1,300

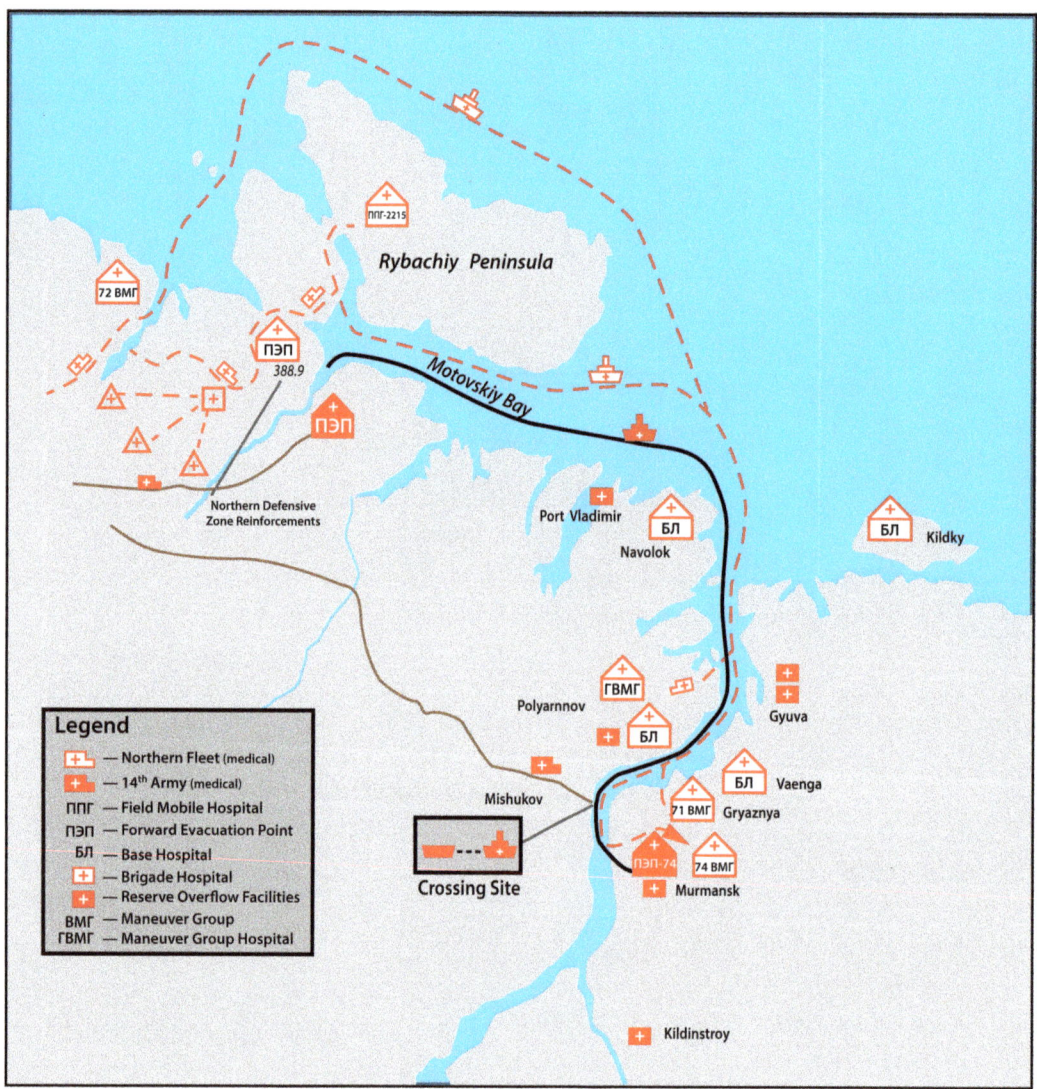

FIGURE 4.3. Location of medical treatment facilities

28 CHAPTER IV: PREPARATION FOR EXECUTION OF THE ASSIGNED MISSION

In addition, bed space in treatment facilities of White Sea Flotilla was increased by 300 beds. The total amount of bed space, deployed and in reserve, is shown in table 4.2.

A special schedule and work plan for caring for sick and wounded were established in each hospital in the event of mass casualties.

For bolstering medical assistance in the combat zone, Northern Defensive Region medical service units, which administered Forward Field Hospital 2215 and a medical company in each naval infantry brigade, were reinforced by a special group of 27 personnel, who became the intermediate link between the medical companies and the forward field hospital. This group was in effect a mobile surgical detachment, designated to follow behind the naval infantry brigades.

The medical companies were responsible for evacuation of wounded from the battlefield to forward evacuation points. For the support of wounded evacuated by boat, an aid station was set up at dock "North-2" in Pummanki. Two hospital barges (*PMB-87* and *PMB-88*) were designated for the evacuation of the Northern Defensive Region's sick and wounded by sea [see figure 4.3 for destination facilities]. The passenger ship *Sosnovets* was designated for the evacuation of 14th Army's [Karelian *Front*] sick and wounded from Titovka. Two vessels were designated for transport of wounded across Kola Bay (Cape Mishukov to Murmansk).

Evacuation of wounded to the rear was to be accomplished through 14th Army's forward evacuation point (*PEP-24*), which had at its disposal the passenger terminal at Kabotazh Pier, Murmansk Port, which adjoined the rail line.

8. Preparation of Military Transportation Units for the Operation

In fulfillment of their assigned missions, during the preparatory period Northern Fleet military transportation units transported Karelian *Front* units across Kola Inlet and carried supplies and concentrating Northern Defensive Region units. At the same time, they completed all preparatory actions for the support of the upcoming sea transport effort to service the coastal flank of the forces and evacuate wounded.

All computations were made in consonance with forecasting memorandums of 14th Army chief of military transportation, who established the daily transport requirement at 1,500 tons. The transport of concentrating Karelian *Front* units began on 6 September and was completed on 1 October (see figure 4.4).

From 3 to 5 October, a war game was conducted in the military transport department of fleet staff with the theme "Providing troop and cargo transport to Northern Fleet and 14th Army from Kola Inlet to points in Motovskiy Bay and to the Petsamo area." The conduct of this game significantly helped to confirm the established organization of command and control of sea transport, the existing calculations of transport capability, and the organization and conduct of various scenarios of uploading and offloading.

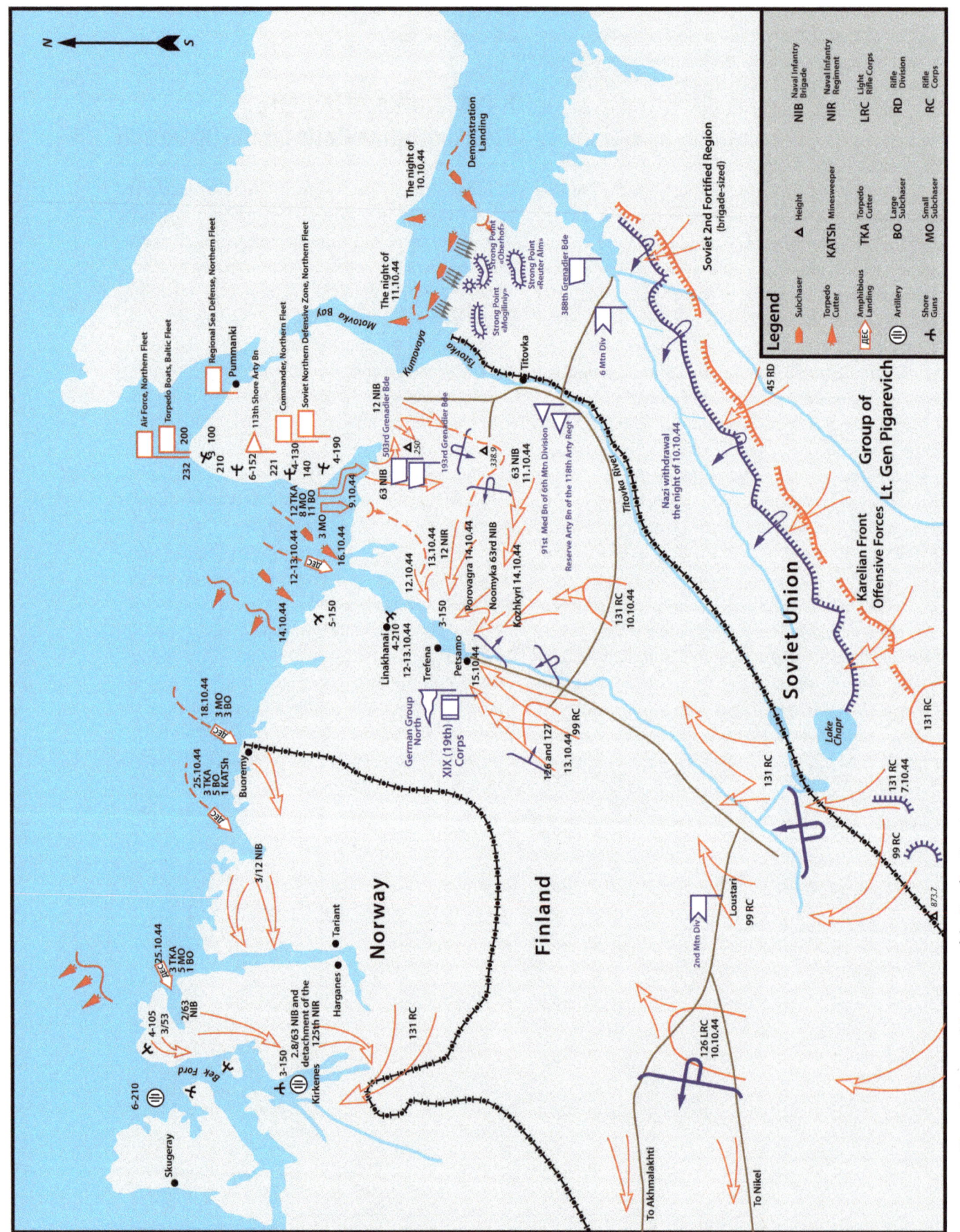

FIGURE 4.4. Plan of advance of the Forces of the Karelian Front

CHAPTER V

Execution of the Assigned Missions

1. Actions of the Forces of the Karelian *Front*

In early October, troops of the attacking the Karelian *Front* formations concentrated on 14th Army's left flank south of Lake Chapr (24 km southeast of Pechenga[10]). On 7 October, after an artillery and mortar barrage on enemy defensive positions along the Western Litsa River, these forces attacked the German positions in the sector Lake Chapr to Lake Bolshoy Karik-yavr. Overcoming fierce resistance, the attacking units advanced 4–10 kilometers by the close of the day.

The attacking units had to overcome extremely untrafficable terrain, interlaced with lakes and streams, under enemy fire. The stiffest resistance was in the area of Hill Bolshoy Karikvayvish (elevation 873.7). Earlier indications that the enemy was strengthening its forces on the Murmansk axis with units taken from the Kestenga axis (6th *SS* Division *Nord*), and units arriving from northern Norway (Bicycle Regiment *Norway*), were confirmed by statements of prisoners captured in these battles and documents recovered from enemy dead.

Preliminary data on enemy losses for the first two days of battle were cited in the operations summary of the Red Army General Staff for 9 October. The number of captured personnel was shown as 210, along with 34 guns, 19 machine guns, eight mortars, 12 radios, 90 horses, 20 wagons, and nine assorted supply caches. The enemy lost more than 2,000 soldiers and officers through death alone.

Offering stubborn resistance in the contested sector, the enemy retreated toward the northwest, but continued to hold firm in the center and on the left flank of its defensive line on Western Litsa River.

Pursuing 14th Army units developed the offensive toward Pechenga. As a part of this effort, two light rifle corps (126th and 127th) executed a deep bypass of the enemy's right flank in the tundra. Units of 99th Rifle Corps crossed Titovka River near Lake Layya and consolidated on the west bank.[11]

Units of Lieutenant General Pigarevich's operational group continued to hold their defensive areas in the

---

[10] Pechenga is the Russian name for the former Finnish city of Petsamo.—Editor

[11] Titovka River was then part of the official border of the Soviet Union in this region.—Editor

center and on the right flank [German left flank] of the Western Litsa line. But on the morning of 10 October, the enemy began to withdraw their troops in these sectors of his defenses. The following was contained in Order No. 18 of Sixth Mountain Division on 9 October:

1. Sixth Mountain Division, abandoning positions in the main line of defense, is to withdraw to the Titovka River at night on 9.10.44.
2. 388th Grenadier Brigade (minus 3rd Battalion), with its attached First and Second Artillery Battalions of 118th Mountain Artillery Regiment, is to occupy a temporary defense on dominating terrain as follows: in grid square 0264-1, Hill 281.4 (grid square 0262), Hill 288.0 (grid square 0260).
3. The mission of those units that remain in the main defensive positions is to delay the enemy as long as possible, to support the withdrawal of the main force.

This order continued with instructions concerning the sequence of withdrawal of units in the Western Litsa grouping. Lieutenant General Pigarevich's forces pursued the retreating enemy units, and on the first day reached the Western Litsa River.

On the following day, the enemy offered serious resistance on his right flank, and counterattacked more than once. During the night of 11 October, he even drove units of 131st Rifle Corps from the Titovka-Pechenga Road, positions they had reached as a result of three days of attacks. However, on the morning of 12 October, corps units once again seized the road, and enemy units withdrawing from the Western Litsa River line were forced to retreat cross-country.

Fierce battles occurred on 11 October on the approaches to Luostari. Forces of 99th and 131st Rifle Corps drove the enemy from the settlement by 1145. The enemy continued to retreat, under threat of being cut off from Petsamo by Northern Defensive Region units attacking westward from the isthmus of Sredniy Peninsula. Prisoners captured west of Luostari on 11 October indicated that fresh forces arriving from Rovaniemi had been immediately thrown into battle. According to prisoners, more new units were anticipated.

Thanks to these arriving reinforcements, on 12 October two battalions from 143rd Mountain Regiment and units of Bicycle Regiment *Norway* attacked 14th Rifle Division,[12] which was occupying a defile between Lakes Santo-yarvi and Kaakkuri-yarvi, and managed to push the division to the south.

---

12 14th Rifle Division and 10th Guards Rifle Division were part of the 131st Rifle Corps.—Editor

Nevertheless, despite local counterattacks, the situation of 14th Army units that had occupied Luostari was stable. They continued the advance toward Petsamo. By 14 October, after the occupation of Liinakhamari Port by Northern Fleet's naval infantry amphibious landing, the arrival of 63rd NIB units at Porovaara and Isamukka on the eastern shore of Petsamovuono, and linkup with 14th Rifle Division, the enemy's Petsamo force was in immediate danger of encirclement.

Despite this, on this same day (14 October), units of this enemy force conducted 16 strong, yet unsuccessful, counterattacks against 131st Rifle Corps units. These enemy counterattacks attest to the stubbornness of their defense on the approach to Pechenga. German resistance was broken after 14th Rifle Division of 131st Rifle Corps forced the Petsamo-ioki River near Kaakkuri and reached the immediate approaches to Petsamo (Pechenga). At 0215 on 15 October, 131st Rifle Corps units drove the enemy from Pechenga. Developing this success in a northward direction, these troops captured the settlements of Parkkino and Hyasyukka. More than 2,000 bodies of dead enemy soldiers and officers were counted after the battle in the Pechenga area, principally from units of XIX Mountain Corps, which had been defending in this area.

With the occupation of Pechenga, forces of the Karelian *Front* pursued the enemy in two directions: to the north, into northern Norway, and to the west, into Finland along the road to Salmiyarvi.

Pursued by our forces, despite the support of units arriving from the Kandalaksha axis that acted as rear guards, the enemy continued to retreat. Units of 14th Army, having overcome the strongest resistance in the Tarnet [Norway] area, occupied this village on 22 October. On the same day, after stubborn battles, the Germans were driven out of the settlements of Sturbukt, Akhmalakhti, and Kosioki. Our forces occupied the nickel mine area. With their advance to this line, 14th Army units had divided the enemy into two groups: those withdrawing to the north toward Kirkenes [Norway], and those retreating to the south into Finland toward Nautsi.

The enemy was defending the approaches to Kirkenes along the coast with coastal defense artillery and naval gunfire, which on 23 and 24 October alone fired up to 45,000 artillery rounds at advancing 131st Rifle Corps formations. Stubborn German resistance was broken, and corps units reached the immediate approaches to Kirkenes. At 1045 on 25 October, 14th and 45th Rifle Divisions of 131st Rifle Corps forced Bekfjord [to surrender] and,[13] in cooperation with 99th Rifle Corps units [attacking from the south] and Northern Fleet ships, aviation, and naval infantry operating on the coastal flank, captured the port and town of Kirkenes.

Enemy troops retreating to the south destroyed the roads and bridges, but pursued by 14th Army were driven from the Mayatola settlement and airfield on 26 October, and from Nautsi on 27 October. On 29 and 30 October, our forces occupied Virtoniemi and Nollim, and by 1 November 1944 the entire Pechenga (Petsamo) oblast was cleared of German forces.

2. The Landing of Amphibious Assault Forces by Northern Fleet Vessels (maps: naval 2531 and ground 1:100,000)

During the conduct of the operation for the liberation of the Soviet far north from the German invaders, Northern Fleet forces carried out naval infantry amphibious landings in conjunction with the offensive. In accordance with the plan of the commander of the Northern Fleet, the first landing was conducted on the night of 9–10 October on the southern shore of Maattivuono Bay, and simultaneous with it a demonstration landing occurred in Motovskiy Bay.

The second amphibious landing was conducted for the capture of Liinakhamari Port on the night of 12–13 October. At this time, Karelian *Front* forces were reaching the approaches to Pechenga from the south and southeast and 63rd and 12th Naval Infantry Brigades were moving toward the eastern shore of Petsamovuono Inlet. Under threat of encirclement in the Pechenga area, the enemy had begun to destroy the port facilities at Liinakhamari.

Subsequent amphibious landings were conducted with the purpose of operating in conjunction with the Karelian *Front* forces advancing toward the Norwegian border. These landings were organized and conducted in the coastal bays of Suolavuono and Aresvuono on 18 October, in Kobbholmfjord on 23 October, and in a coastal bay of Holmengerfjord on 25 October.

---

13 Actually, the 45th Rifle Division belonged to Group Pigarevich, another Corps-sized Soviet formation. The 14th Rifle Division was part of the 131st Corps.—Editor

A. AMPHIBIOUS LANDING ON THE SOUTHERN COAST OF MAATTIVUONO BAY

According to existing intelligence data, there were no anti-landing defenses on the southern coast of Maattivuono Bay, and therefore it was the most favorable place for an amphibious landing coordinated with the breakthrough of enemy defenses on the isthmus of Sredniy Peninsula. The landing in Motovskiy Bay to bypass the Germans' [coastal] right flank did not promise great success, because our forces had conducted landings here more than once before, and each time met stiff resistance in the enemy's well-organized coastal defensive network.

CONCENTRATION OF FORCES. It was necessary to concentrate landing craft and landing forces at Pummanki in advance for the amphibious landing on Maattivuono coast. For this purpose, on 9 October, nine torpedo boats made a transit from Dolgaya Bay to Pummanki by 0050, eight small subchasers arrived at Pummanki from Pala Bay by 0250, and one torpedo boat arrived from Kola Bay by 0450.

In this manner, counting the four large subchasers and two torpedo boats that had arrived earlier, by 9 October, 11 *BO-I* large subchasers, eight *MO-IV* small subchasers, [and] eight *A-2* (Higgins) and four *A-1* (Vosper) torpedo boats had arrived at Pummanki. In addition, patrol cutter *SKA-619* from the crash-rescue division and three torpedo boats of the mobile screen arrived at Pummanki.

The amphibious landing forces of 63rd Naval Infantry Brigade and attached units were concentrated in Pummanki at embarkation points by 1800 on 9 October. By this time, aviation assets had been positioned at forward airfields at Pummanki and Ura-guba. Through the course of the entire day of 9 October, the air forces maintained a strengthened air curtain over Pummanki and blockaded enemy airfields to protect the concentration of troops and equipment.

The destroyers *Gremyashchiy* and *Gromkiy* were at Vaenga in readiness to sortie for naval gunfire support of the landing and 12th Naval Infantry Brigade's attack on the isthmus of Sredniy Peninsula.

MISSION OF THE AMPHIBIOUS LANDING FORCE. Northern Fleet Directive No. 0052/*op*, dated 1 October 1944, assigned to the commander of the amphibious landing force the mission to land 63rd Naval Infantry

Brigade and attached units covertly on the southern coast of Maattivuono Bay in the area of Cape Punaynenniemi and Cape Akhioniemi.

After the landing, the amphibious force was to move to the flank and rear of the enemy's defenses on Mustatunturi Ridge for coordinated actions with 12th Naval Infantry Brigade, which was executing the breakthrough of the enemy's prepared defenses on the isthmus of Sredniy Peninsula.

ORGANIZATION OF COMMAND AND COMPOSITION OF FORCES. Overall command of both the amphibious landing and breakthrough of enemy defenses on the isthmus was placed on the commander of the Northern Defensive Region, Major (now Lieutenant) General Dubovtsev. Rear Admiral Mikhaylov, commander, Northern Fleet Main Base Seaward Approaches Defenses, was named commander of the landing force. He also was the Northern Defensive Region's deputy commander for naval units. The commanders of the landing ship detachment and mobile screen were subordinated to him.

Captain First Rank Klevenskiy, commander of Patrol Cutter Brigade, was named commander of the landing ship detachment. The three assault detachment commanders were subordinated to him.

Commander of the first assault detachment was Guards Captain Zyuzin. The following vessels comprised his detachment: small subchasers *MO-423, MO-424, MO-428, MO-429, MO-430, MO-431, MO-433,* and *MO-434,* and torpedo boats *TKA-214, TKA-215,* and *TKA-211.*

Captain Third Rank Gritsuk was named commander of the second assault detachment, consisting of the following vessels: large subchasers *BO-213, BO-214, BO-215, BO-216, BO-217, BO-218, BO-219, BO-220, BO-221, BO-222,* and *BO-224.*

Commander of the third assault detachment was Captain Second Rank Alekseev.[14] The following vessels comprised his detachment: torpedo boats *TKA-204, TKA-206, TKA-207, TKA-208, TKA-210, TKA-213, TKA-222,* and *TKA-240.*

Captain-Lieutenant Antonov was named commander of the mobile screen force, consisting of the following vessels: torpedo boats *TKA-234, TKA-238,*[15] and *TKA-246.*

The following units were subordinated to the defensive region commander for support: 113rd Separate Artillery Battalion, 104th Cannon Artillery Regiment, and the air assets at Pummanki.

In accordance with the plan for organization of command, the locations of commanders during the operation were as follows: commander, Northern Defensive Region—at his forward command post on Hill 342.0. Collocated with him were the commander of the amphibious landing and the commander of the pathfinder detachment. The entire landing area was clearly visible from this point. The landing ship detachment commander was located on the specially equipped torpedo boat *TKA-241,* which carried no assault troops. The first assault detachment commander was on *MO-423,* the second assault detachment commander was on *BO-221,* and the third assault detachment commander was on *TKA-240.*

Radio communications between the amphibious landing commander and the landing ship detachment commander were arranged so that the landing force commander could listen to radio traffic between the landing ship commander and the commanders of the three assault detachments.

UPLOADING THE AMPHIBIOUS FORCE. Three moorages were used at Pummanki for uploading the amphibious force: Moorage No. 1 (North-1 near the airfield), moorage No. 2 (North-2), and moorage No. 3 (North-3, floating) (see figure 5.1). Uploading began with the onset of darkness in the following weather conditions: southerly wind at force 3 to 4, sea at force 2, visibility 0.2 nautical miles, and temperature +2°C. The distribution of the landing forces and cargo on the vessels of the landing detachment is shown in table 5.1.

On the average, small subchasers took on board approximately 60 men and 0.9 ton of cargo each; large

---

14 Vladimir Nikolaevich Alekseev (1912–unknown) entered maritime ("merchant marine") service at age 15 in 1927, completed Leningrad Naval Academy in 1932, and served in the Pacific Fleet until 1942. After completing Naval Academy in 1944, he was reassigned to Northern Fleet, where he commanded the 3rd Torpedo Cutter Division in the Petsamo Operation. The forces under his command sunk 17 enemy vessels. He was awarded Hero of the Soviet Union on 5.11.44 [5 November, 1944]. *Geroi Sovetskogo Soyuza: Kratkiy Biograficheskiy Slovar* (Heroes of the Soviet Union: Brief biographical dictionary, hereinafter cited as *GSS*) (Moscow: Voyenizdat, 1987), vol. 1, p. 42.—Translator

15 This *TKA* is shown in Berezhnoy, *Flot SSSR*, p. 27, to have been moved by rail and inland water means from the Northern Fleet to the Black Sea Fleet on 21.04.44 [date format day.month.year], arriving in Yeisk on 27.06.44.—Translator

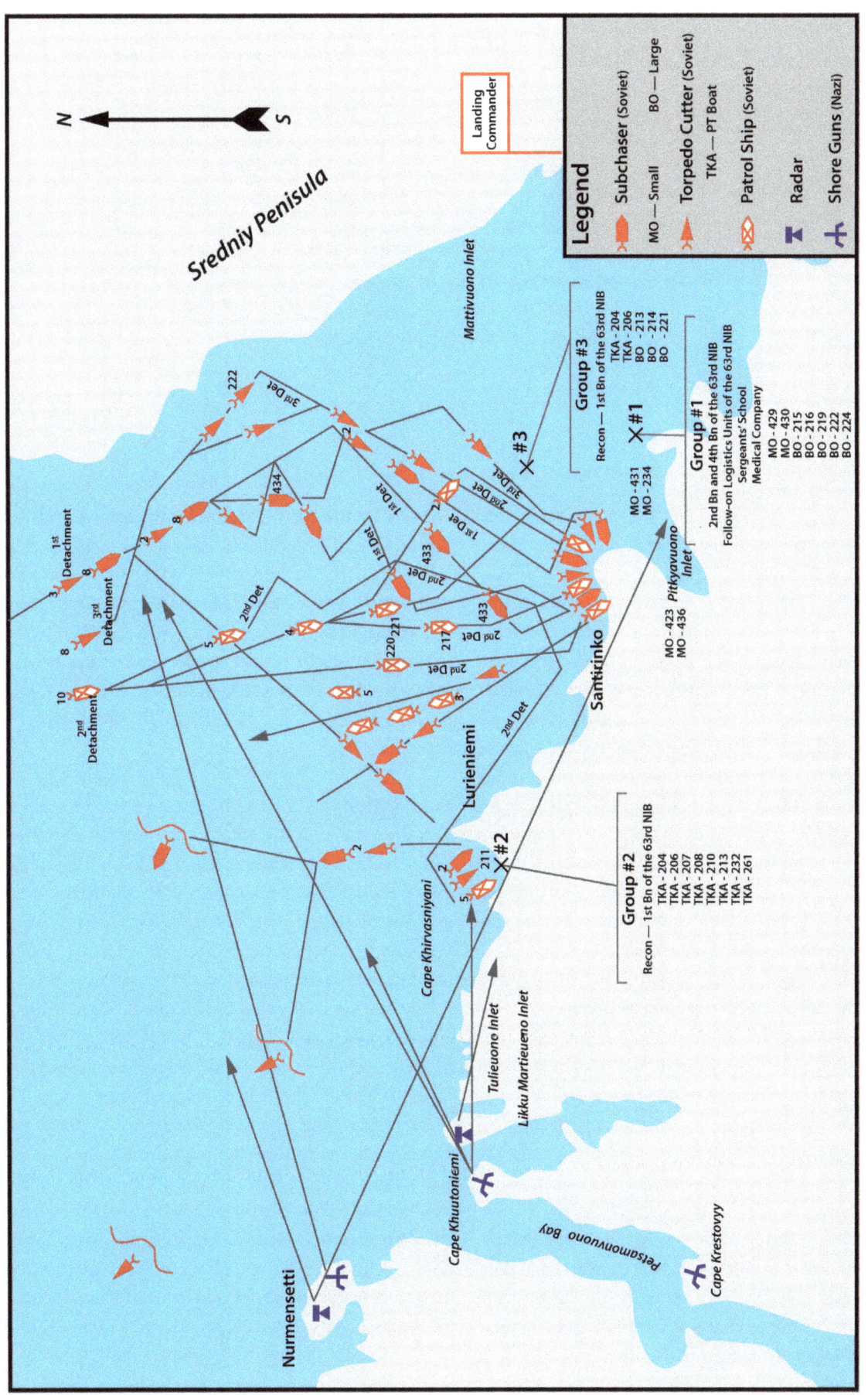

FIGURE 5.1. Transit of naval infantry and their assault landing by moorage group on the Maattivuono coast

TABLE 5.1. Uploading the amphibious force

Upload Site	Upload Times Start	Upload Times Finish	Vessels to Be Uploaded	Units to Be Uploaded, Troops	Quantity of Cargo (kg)
Moorage No. 1	1830	2220	MO-428, MO-431, MO-434, MO-433, MO-423, MO-424, TKA-214, TKA-215	2nd, 4th Rifle Battalions, 63rd NIB; scout and submachine-gun companies, 471 men total	5,580
			BO-213, BO-214	757 men total	22,758
Moorage No. 2	1845	2154	MO-429, MO-430, TKA-211	Recon detachments of NDR and HQ Fleet, 190 men total	
			BO-219, BO-220, BO-221, BO-222, BO-224, TKA-241	1st Rifle Battalion, 63rd NIB Headquarters, 958 men total	22,000
Moorage No. 3	1900	2031	TKA-204, TKA-206, TKA-207, TKA-208, TKA-210, TKA-213, TKA-222, TKA-240	3rd Rifle Battalion	9,119

subchasers, up to 150 men and 4.5 tons of cargo; and A-2 torpedo cutters (Higgins), from 60 to 65 men and 1.2–1.3 tons of cargo.

Difficulties occurred during the upload of the assault force on the cutters, stemming from the fact that there were no navigational aids for the cutters' approach to moorages 1 and 2. The shallow depth of the waters near the docks demanded a relatively complicated approach to them, and required appropriate navigational markers. As a result of the absence of navigational lights near moorage No. 2, large subchaser *BO-218* damaged its propellers and was removed from the landing ship detachment. This led to the necessity to redistribute the personnel and cargo designated for loading on this ship to other vessels, because there were no ships available in reserve to replace damaged vessels. As a result, there was a delay of almost one hour in completion of the uploading of the second assault detachment.

The uploading of the first assault detachment was also finished 1 hour and 10 minutes late. The cause of delay was the commander of the first assault detachment, who was passing out instructions to the cutter commanders concerning changes of place in the landing and navigational support. The dissemination of instructions at a time when troops were to be received on board the cutters led to the absence of cutter commanders from their vessels during the upload and caused violations of the loading plan. The on-time completion of the upload was particularly important because the departure time of the amphibious landing detachments to the landing site depended on this.

The nighttime conditions of the upload and the assembling of a significant quantity of landing ship resources in the harbor demanded the utmost in precision of all participants. The most important aspect was to meet the time requirements of the plan. Delay in the uploading of the first and second landing detachments on their ships attests to the fact that this phase of the operation was not organized as precisely as it could have been.

THE TRANSIT BY SEA AND AMPHIBIOUS LANDING. The first wave of the amphibious assault departed Pummanki to the landing site at 2140 on 9 October. At sailing time, the meteorological conditions were as follows: southerly wind at force 4–5; sea at force 3; visibility 1–2 nautical miles; overcast at force 3–4 with ceiling at 2,000 meters; moon in the first quarter.

The first wave, moving in column at 12 knots, held close to the shore. To maintain the security of the movement, all torpedo boat engine exhausts were diverted beneath the surface of the sea.

Upon reaching Malyy Aynov Island at 2209, the detachment fell under searchlight beams from Cape Ristiniemi, which periodically illuminated Maattivuono Bay. Soon after the illumination of the bay, the enemy began to conduct shore battery fire with illumination rounds from Cape Numeroniemi, and turned on a second searchlight, located on Cape Khuutoniemi. The entire reach of Maattivuono Bay was so powerfully illuminated that cutters falling in the light beam had to decrease speed to seven knots to lessen their bow waves and their visibility against the background of the shore. The detachment continued movement, and at 2300 was detected by German observation posts during their approach to Cape Volokovaya. The shore batteries on Capes Ristiniemi and Numeroniemi immediately increased their firing of illumination rounds out over the bay.

The cutters then increased their speed to 16 knots and, under cover of a smoke screen laid with onboard dischargers and from the water, began to dash into their landing sites with the support of shore batteries of 113th Artillery Battalion.

The group under the command of Guards Senior Lieutenant Lyakh[16] (*MO-429*, *MO-430*, and *TKA-211*) moved out of column toward their landing site on the western shore of Cape Punaynenniemi. Small subchasers *MO-429* and *MO-430* immediately began to offload Captain Barchenko's reconnaissance detachment. *TKA-211* attempted to approach the shore three times but was unable to extend its gangplank and land its small force. Only after landing his troops from *MO-429* did Guards Senior Lieutenant Lyakh, learning of the problem with *TKA-211*, order the torpedo boat by megaphone to come alongside his *MO-429*. *TKA-211* returned to shore and, coming alongside *MO-429*, landed its troops across the other boat.

The vessels of this group completed their landings by 2316 and, moving away from shore north–northwest at full speed, laid down a smoke screen to cover the other landings occurring at that moment in the area of Cape Akhioniemi. After accomplishing this task, *MO-429*, *MO-430*, and *TKA-211* took up patrol positions between Cape Volokovaya and Cape Punaynenniemi to screen the amphibious landing from light enemy surface craft.

Approaching the shore at 2315, small subchasers *MO-423*, *MO-424*, *MO-428*, *MO-431*, *MO-433*, [and] *MO-434*, and torpedo cutters *TKA-214* and *TKA-215*, landed their troops in the area of Cape Akhioniemi. The landings were completed in 15 minutes, and the commander of the landing vessel detachment was informed by radio at 2347 that the landing of the first detachment had been executed under insignificant enemy artillery and mortar fire.

Upon completion of the landing, the cutters withdrew north of Cape Akhioniemi to cover the approach and landing of the second and third waves of the amphibious force. During their withdrawal, the cutters laid down a smoke screen with their onboard dischargers.

The second landing detachment began to approach this same landing site near Cape Akhkioniemi at 2330, even before the first wave completed its landings. It had departed Pummanki at 2235 and was detected by enemy searchlights and taken under fire by their shore batteries in the area of Cape Volokovaya at 2315. Maneuvering at full speed in an anti-artillery zigzag, the detachment reached the set of green navigational marker lights in Maattivuono Bay and turned toward the landing zone. But because the large subchasers had a draft of seven feet, they had to come into shore several times, looking for the deepest waters. In some cases, they were even forced to lay just offshore, and disembark their troops across a smaller vessel between themselves and the shore. This occurred, for example, with *BO-213*.

During the landing of the second wave, only enemy shore batteries from Capes Ristiniemi and Numeroniemi laid down a barrage. By the fall of the rounds, it was observed that the enemy seemingly was simply targeting the areas around the capes on the Maattivuono shoreline. There were places in which the landings were not fired upon. Batteries of 113rd Separate Artillery Battalion conducted counterbattery fire against enemy artillery and searchlights, which assisted the assault waves in reaching shore and executing their landings.

An insufficient knowledge of the region on the part of the commanders of some of the vessels allowed five large subchasers (*BO-219*, *BO-215*, *BO-216*, *BO-222*, and *BO-224*) to approach the coastline west of the designated landing site and deposit their troops (NCO Academy, 3rd Company of 2nd Rifle Battalion, 2nd Company of 4th Rifle Battalion, and the brigade medical company) near Cape Punaynenniemi, and not near Cape Akhkioniemi.

The pathfinder teams turned on their markers one after the other as the cutters proceeded past them, and

---

16 Boris Mitrofanovich Lyakh (1918–unknown) entered naval service in 1937, and completed Ordzhonikidze Naval Communications Academy in 1938 and Frunze Naval Academy in 1941. As commander of *MO-429*, Second Guards Division of small subchasers, Patrol Vessel Guard of Offshore Area of the Northern Fleet Main Base, executed more than 130 sorties in searching and destroying enemy submarines, escorting our own vessels, and in landing amphibious assault forces and reconnaissance groups. During the Petsamo–Kirkenes Operation, commanding a group of cutters, landed an assault force without losses in the Liinakhamari harbor. Awarded Hero of the Soviet Union on 5.11.44 [5 November 1944]. *GSS*, vol. 2, 1988, p. 8.—Translator

this should have fully supported en route orientation of the landing ship detachments. A pathfinder team went ashore with the first wave, and after seven minutes determined its location and turned on its marking lights. By 0050 on 10 October, the second wave had landed, and its landing vessels began the withdrawal to base at Pummanki.

The third wave cast off their moorings in Pummanki at 2212 and proceeded to the landing site at 12 knots. In the transit, the cutters of this wave were illuminated by enemy searchlights and illumination rounds and, just like the first two waves, were fired upon by artillery. By 2316, the third wave had overtaken the second and had to stop for seven minutes. During the resumption of movement, the cutters moved toward shore under cover of a smoke screen. By this time, several smoke screens hung over Maattivuono Bay, placed there by vessels of the first and second waves (figure 5.2).

The laying of smoke screens was accomplished both from onboard cutters and from devices placed in the water. Practice had shown that the latter gave excellent results. The rapid withdrawal of the cutters away from the drop site of the smoke discharger precluded aimed fire against them because the enemy normally laid concentrated fire into the smoke. It is important to note that most of the smoke screens were laid not for concealment alone, but to facilitate mutual support of all three assault waves. Massive utilization of smoke was a reliable means of defense against aimed enemy fire (figure 5.2).

The following smoke-producing equipment was employed: smoke apparatus *DA-TK-42*, smoke mixture *S-4*, and smoke charges *MDSh* and *NS-M4*. The following quantities were expended: 1,100 kg of smoke mixture *S-4*, 263 rounds of smoke charges *MDSh*, and 181 rounds of *NS-M4*. Six *DA-TK-42* smoke dischargers were employed. The best smoke device in this operation turned out to be smoke charge *MDSh*. During employment of the American smoke charge *NS-M4*, it was discovered that a cone of flame erupted above the device during its burning, which exposed the ship to detection and created a serious fire hazard.

The smoke screens laid down in Maattivuono Bay during the assault by the first and second waves considerably hindered the maneuverability of the third wave. *TKA-222* went aground about 5–10 meters from shore during its approach. The order to the commander of *TKA-210* to tow the torpedo boat from the rocks was executed at 0025, while other torpedo boats (*204*, *206*, *207*, *208*, *213*, and *240*) were landing their troops on the shore from 0015 to 0040. Torpedo cutters *210* and *222* landed their troops about one-half hour later.

The cutters returned to their base upon completion of the landings. Thus, 63rd Naval Infantry Brigade's landing was complete by 0110 on 10 October. It had gone quickly. However, some of the men were not put ashore where they were supposed to be. Brigade units suffered one dead and five wounded during the landing. There were no casualties among the ships' crews. Several cutters suffered minor damage from shell fragments or rock strikes during the landings.

The landed units left one battalion for defense of the landing site and immediately began moving inland from the shore. Not meeting any enemy resistance, they occupied a sector of the southern coastline of Maattivuono Bay from Cape Punaynenniemi to Cape Akhkioniemi. A single small group of enemy soldiers illuminated the landing site with flares, fired several rifle and mortar rounds, and withdrew from the shore.

The Third and Fourth Battalions, along with the brigade headquarters, moved inland, and by 0500 on 10 October had reached the area northwest of the lake marked 15 and Hill 124. Brigade staff did not have communications with First Battalion and other brigade subunits that had landed in Punaynenniemi Bay. It was subsequently learned that the battalion commander, unable to determine his exact location, had taken command of all units that had landed with him and had begun to move inland to the south. First Battalion reached the southwest slope of Hill 141 by 0400 on 10 October.

Meanwhile, Third and Fourth Battalions, moving inland to act in concert with units of 12th Naval Infantry Brigade, which was breaking through enemy defenses on Sredniy Peninsula, attacked a German mortar battery on the southern slopes of Mustatunturi Ridge, capturing 17 prisoners. The Third Battalion linked up with 12th Naval Infantry Brigade units in the area of Lake Tie-yarvi by 1200 on 10 October.

At the same time, the composite detachment made up of the reconnaissance detachments of the Northern Defensive Region and Headquarters, Northern Fleet, under the overall command of Captain Barchenko, began its cross-country movement over extremely untrafficable terrain in the direction of Cape Krestovyy.

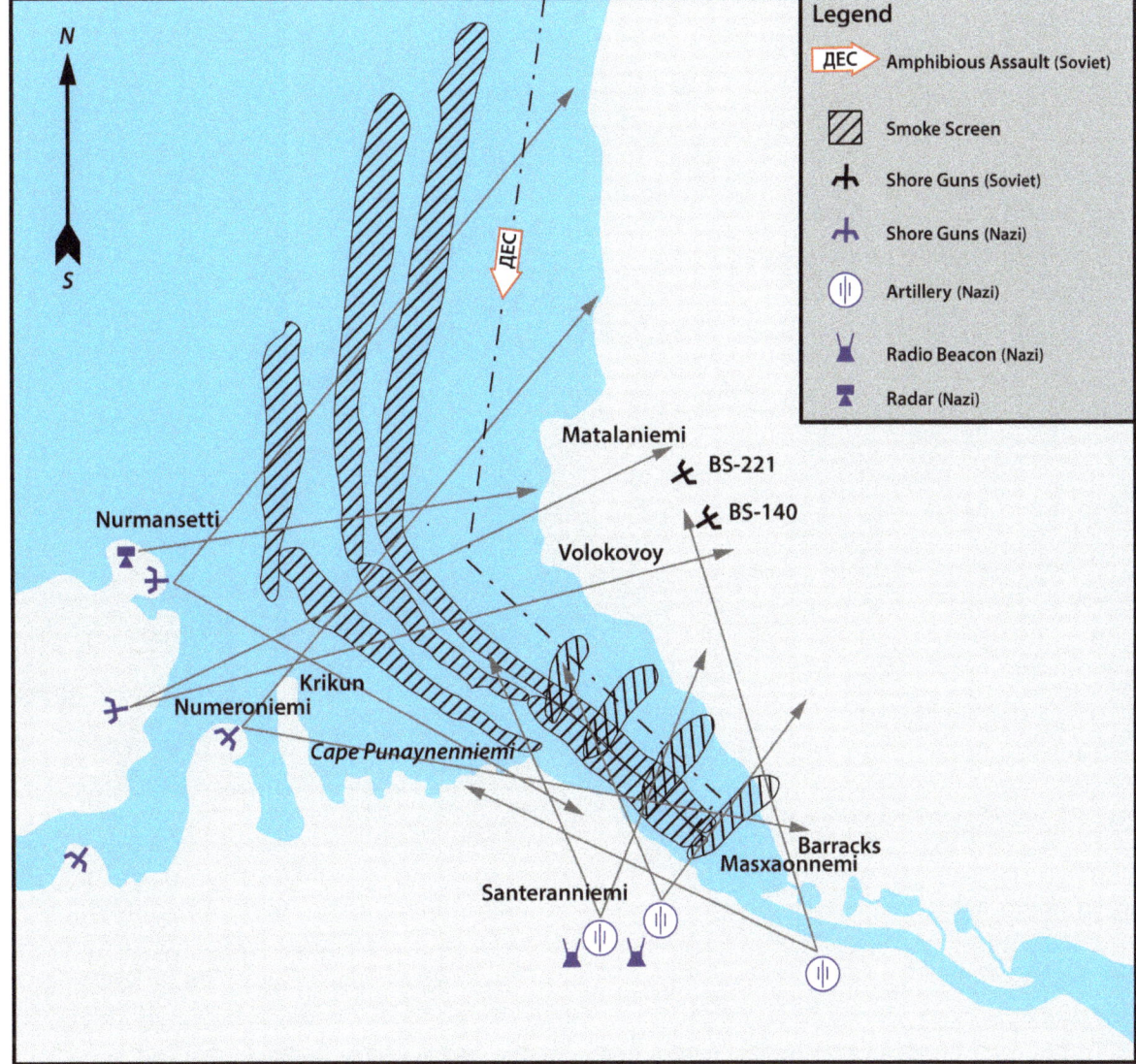

FIGURE 5.2. Smoke screens laid down by cutters during the amphibious landing on Maattivuono coastline

Their mission was to liquidate the batteries located on this cape.[17]

---

17 The actions of the composite detachment are described in detail by both of the detachment commanders. See Hero of the Soviet Union I. P. Barchenko-Emelianov, *Frontovyye bydni Rybachevo* (Frontline life on the Rybachyy Peninsula) (Murmansk: Knizhnoye Izdatelstvo, 1984); and Twice Hero of the Soviet Union Viktor Leonov, in *Blood on the Shores: Soviet Naval Commandos in World War II* (Annapolis: Naval Institute Press, 1993), chap. 8. These accounts are excerpted and appended to this study at translator's appendix 2. Another briefer version, based on accounts of both Leonov and Barchenko, is contained in James F. Gebhardt, *The Petsamo-Kirkenes Operation: Soviet Breakthrough and Pursuit in the Arctic, October 1944*, Leavenworth Papers No. 17 (Fort Leavenworth, KS: US Army Command and General Staff College, 1990), chap. 6.—Translator

B. ACTIONS OF THE COMPOSITE RECONNAISSANCE DETACHMENT

The composite reconnaissance detachment (reconnaissance detachments of the Northern Defensive Region and Headquarters Northern Fleet), totaling 195 personnel, did not meet any enemy resistance during its movement to Cape Krestovyy. The detachment had to penetrate deep into the enemy's rear, overcoming the difficulties of moving across heavily broken terrain over the course of two days (10–11 October). By 0200 on 12 October, the detachment reached the isthmus of Cape Krestovyy (see figure 5.3) undetected by the enemy, and at dawn on 12 October attacked the four-

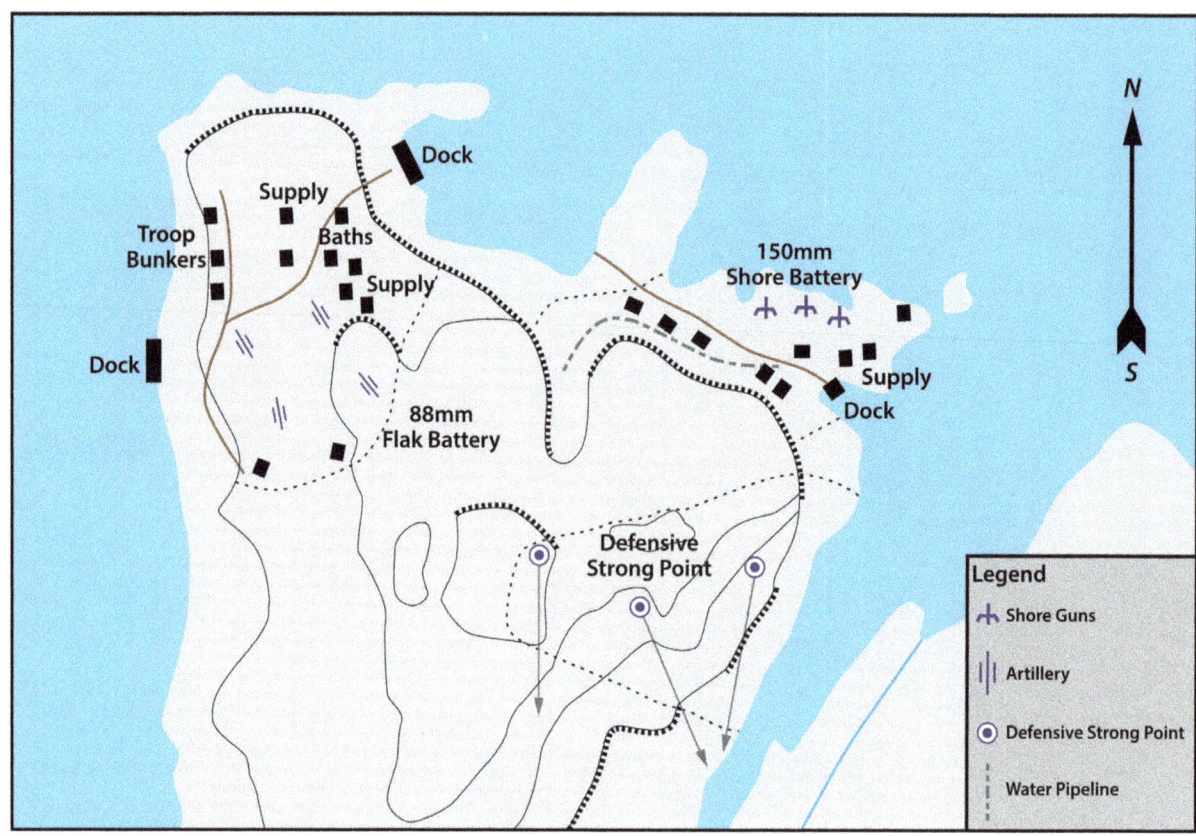

FIGURE 5.3. Disposition of the batteries on Cape Krestovyy

weapon 88 mm antiaircraft battery, capturing it after a brief fight. Three working guns and three prisoners were captured.

The remaining battery personnel took flight.

With the capture of the antiaircraft battery, the detachment began the battle for capture of the 150 mm shore battery, which covered the entrance to Petsamovuono Inlet and the immediate approaches to Liinakhamari Port with its fires. On 12 October, the enemy twice sent 50 men across Petsamovuono Inlet to reinforce the shore battery garrison. These troops attacked the reconnaissance detachments with fire support from shore batteries on Cape Numeroniemi and the Liinakhamari Port area. Four enemy attacks were defeated with the assistance of fire support from shore batteries of 113th Separate Artillery Battalion. But the reconnaissance detachment's ammunition supply was running low, and this caused the composite detachment commander to request by radio: "I need air support. We can live for three days without food, but we can't hold on for even several hours without ammunition."

A group of *Il-2* and *Kittyhawk* aircraft with *Yak* fighter cover was dispatched from Pummanki airfield for support of the detachment. The actions of the air support were made difficult by the proximity of our men and the enemy on the limited space of Cape Krestovyy. But on the approach of the aircraft, the reconnaissance detachment marked the location of their perimeter with flares, and designated enemy positions with tracer rounds. This facilitated the accuracy of the air strikes. As a result of the air attacks, a significant number of enemy soldiers were destroyed, two wooden barracks and one dock were set afire, and one launch was sunk and two others damaged.

At the same time as these air strikes were being conducted against the enemy, multiple *A-20 Boston* aircraft,[18] also launched from Pummanki, were dropping

---

[18] The Soviet Union received altogether 3,414 *A-20* medium bombers from the USA through Lend-Lease, many of which were the G-model. Although its standard crew was three (pilot, bombardier-navigator, and dorsal turret gunner), the Soviets modified many aircraft with the installation of a ventral flexible machine gun (to fire downward in departure from low-level attacks) with a designated gunner. It was powered by two air-cooled 14-cylinder, two-row Wright Cyclone engines, and had a top speed of approximately 320 mph and a range of 945 miles. The G model was armed with a combination of nose-mounted 20 mm cannons and .50 caliber machine guns, which made it a lethal attack aircraft against enemy vessels. This aircraft was also widely reconfigured for use as a torpedo bomber

food and ammunition parcels into the reconnaissance detachment's position. Five supply canisters were dropped altogether on 12 October, receipt of which was acknowledged by radio.

Meanwhile, the actions of the detachment against the enemy on Cape Krestovyy forced the Germans fully to concentrate on defense of their batteries from the landward side, and to begin destruction of their equipment. The enemy continued to resist fiercely.

At 0800 on 13 October, the reconnaissance company of 63rd NIB, reinforced by a platoon of submachine gunners and a platoon of sappers, arrived to assist the composite reconnaissance detachment. At 1500, 50 additional men joined with the detachment. They were from the amphibious landing force that captured Liinakhamari Port during the night of 12–13 October and had mistakenly landed on the eastern shore of Petsamovuono Inlet.

On 13 October, the enemy garrison on Cape Krestovyy was given a surrender ultimatum, with the guarantee that their lives would be preserved. After some time, the battery's 60-man garrison laid down its weapons and surrendered. As a result of the battles on Cape Krestovyy, the enemy lost approximately 100 soldiers and officers killed and wounded and 63 captured. The reconnaissance detachment had seized four 88 mm antiaircraft guns (one disabled), one 150 mm gun (the barrels of the other three had been blown up), 1,200 150 mm shells, a dump of ammunition for the 88 mm guns, six submachine guns, six MG-34 machine guns, 100 rifles and carbines, tens of thousands of rounds of small arms ammunition, and two supply caches of food as trophy property.

The composite reconnaissance detachment lost 19 men killed and 34 wounded during the battle for Cape Krestovyy.[19]

---

and used in that role in all four Soviet Fleets. With extra fuel cells in the bomb bay, it was also an excellent long-range photographic reconnaissance aircraft, with over 2,000 miles of range. Northern Fleet employed the *A-20G* in all these roles.—Translator

19 Six of the [killed in action] KIA were in Leonov's Northern Fleet Reconnaissance Detachment, all named in his memoir; the remaining 13 were in Barchenko-Emelyanov's Northern Defensive Region Reconnaissance Detachment and are not named.

The award Hero of the Soviet Union was given to four participants in this action: Barchenko-Emelyanov, Leonov, and two of Leonov's men—Semyon Agafonov and Andrey Pshenichnykh.

Ivan Pavlovich Barchenko-Emelyanov (4.01.1915–16.01.1984) [dates throughout in form of day.month.year] was born in the village of Okulovskoy, Novgorod rayon, to a peasant family. He completed a forestry technical school and undertook employment as a bookkeeper-inspector. He entered naval service in 1941 and completed a course for junior lieutenants. As commander of the composite

---

The composite reconnaissance detachment was reconnaissance group, he landed with his force on enemy territory on the night of 10.10.44 and on 12 October seized an enemy battery and defensive position on Cape Krestovyy, which enabled the amphibious landing into Liinakhamari port. Awarded Hero of the Soviet Union [HSU] on 5.11.44. After the war, he continued service in the *VMF*, retiring at the rank of colonel in 1951. His decorations, in addition to HSU, include the Order of Lenin, two Orders of the Red Star, and other medals. A school in Murmansk bears his name; he is buried in Leningrad. *GSS*, Vol. 1, p. 123.

Viktor Nikolaevich Leonov (21.11.1916–7.10.2003) was born in Zaraysk of present-day Moscow oblast to a working family. He completed middle school in 1931 and undertook employment as a sheet-metal worker in the "Caliber" concern in Moscow. He entered service in the Soviet Navy in 1937, trained as a "motorman" and was assigned to the Northern Fleet's submarine brigade. Within days of the German invasion of the USSR, he volunteered to serve in the nascent Northern Fleet Reconnaissance Detachment, where he worked his way up through the ranks from seaman to junior lieutenant (September 1942), serving in positions from squad leader to becoming the detachment's political officer in December 1942, and eventually its commander at an unspecified date in 1943. He received his first award of Hero of the Soviet Union on 5.11.1944 for his courage and heroism displayed in battle for the liberation of Petsamo [at Cape Krestovyy] and his second award of HSU on 14.9.1945 for outstanding performance while leading the reconnaissance detachment of the Pacific Fleet in combat in north Korean ports against Japanese forces. Leonov completed the Caspian Higher Naval Academy (one of his classmates was 2HSU Aleksandr Shabalin) in 1950 and was assigned to the central Soviet Navy apparatus in Moscow. He retired as a Captain Second Rank in 1956. In addition to HSU (two awards), his decorations include the Order of Lenin, two Orders of the Red Banner, the Order of Aleksandr Nevskiy, Order of the Patriotic War First Class, the Red Star, and foreign decorations. A Russian Navy Vishnya-class intelligence vessel (*CCB-175*) named after Viktor Leonov has cruised up and down the American East Coast and in the Caribbean since 2015. *GSS*, Vol. 1, 1987, p. 862, with annotation by the translator.

Semyon Mikhailovich Agafonov (13.9.1917–01.01.1955) [was born] in the village Pushlakhta, today Primorsk, in Arkhangelsk rayon and oblast, to a working-class family. He completed ninth grade in 1938, then began his military service that same year. In 1942 he became a member of the Communist Party. He was serving in Northern Fleet when the war began. On the night of 12 October 1944, Senior Sergeant First Class Agafonov, in his role as a squad commander in the Northern Fleet Reconnaissance Detachment, participated in the surprise attack on a German battery. He was one of the first men of his element to burst into the battery, capturing a gun, and commencing fire with it on the enemy. The detachment captured the enemy position in extremely difficult conditions, which enabled the breaching by cutters with an amphibious assault force into Petsamo Inlet and capturing Liinakhamari. The rank of Hero of the Soviet Union was awarded to him on 4.11.44. Agafonov was demobilized in 1948, and lived in Evpatoria, where he worked in a factory. He was awarded the Order of Lenin, three Orders of the Red Banner, and the Order of the Patriotic War Second Class, along with numerous medals. He died at the age of 52. In my September 1990 interview of Leonov in Moscow, he called Agafonov "the most fearless sailor" he had ever known. Leonov credited Agafonov with having personally killed 60 Germans at Cape Krestovyy, with submachine gun, hand grenades, and hand-to-hand combat.

Andrey Petrovich Pshenichnykh (25.5.1914) was born in the village Nizhniy Ikorets, in present-day Liskinskiy rayon of Voronezh oblast to a peasant family. He received an elementary education, then worked as a stoker in a railroad depot. He served in the Soviet Navy 1936–1938 again from 1942 until demobilization at the conclusion of the war. During his second term of service, he held the rank of senior sailor in the Reconnaissance Detachment of the Northern

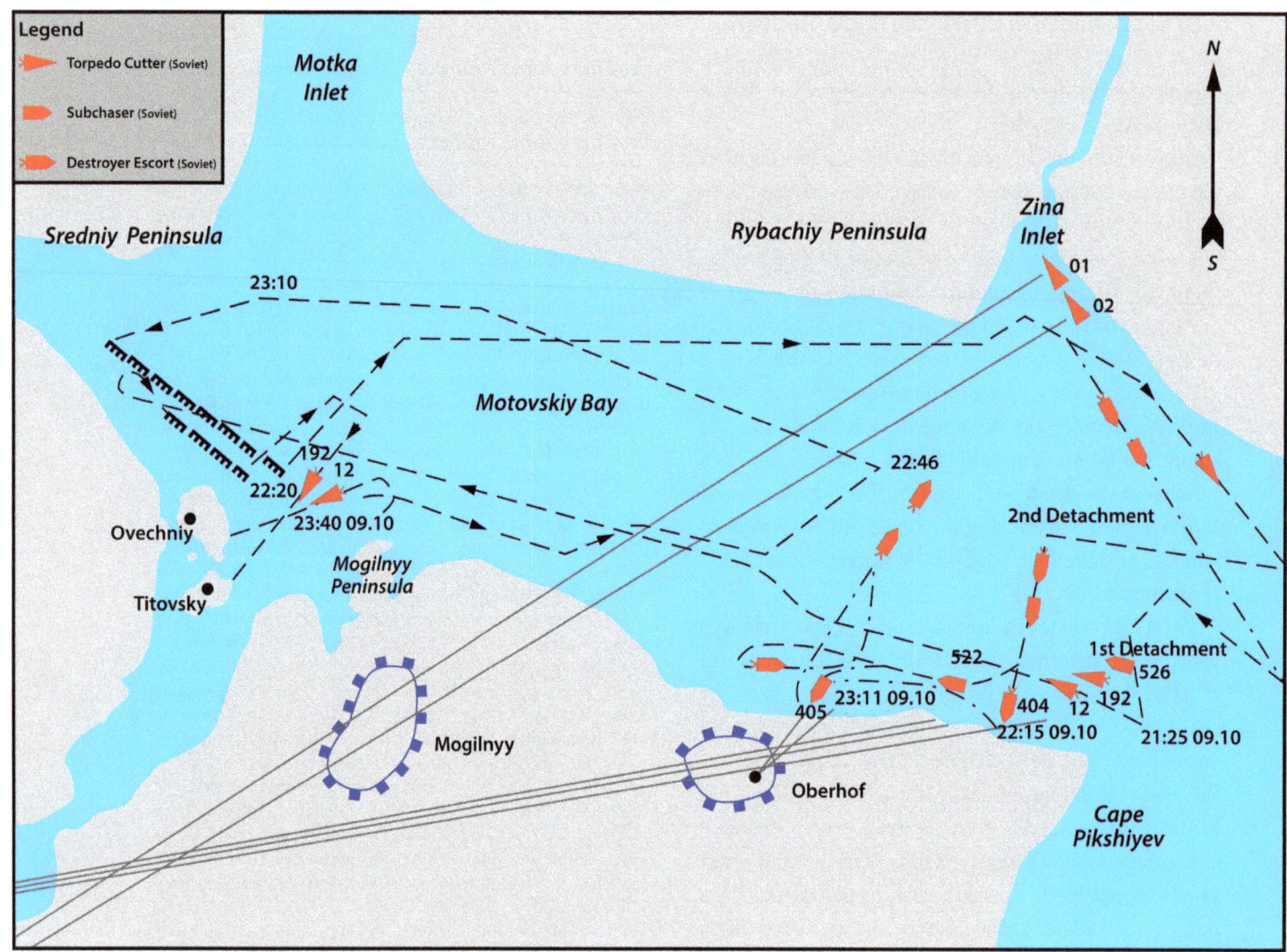

FIGURE 5.4. The demonstration amphibious landing in Motovskiy Bay

transported across Petsamovuono Inlet on torpedo cutters into Liinakhamari Port on the following day.

C. ACTIONS OF THE DEMONSTRATION LANDING

The purpose of the demonstration amphibious landing was to distract the enemy's attention from the main landings on the coast of Maattivuono Bay. The force

> Fleet, participating in several tactical actions behind enemy lines. In October 1944 he performed in an outstanding manner during the combat for the liberation of the Soviet far north during the seizure of two artillery batteries on the eastern shore of Petsamo Inlet, which guarded the entrance to the enemy-held port at Liinakhamari. Destruction of this battery enabled the rushing into the port of our cutters with the amphibious assault force. He was awarded the rank Hero of the Soviet Union on 5.11.1944. After the war, Petty Officer Second Class Pshenichnykh was demobilized, and worked in the mining industry in Kazakhstan. His awards include the Order of Lenin, two Orders of the Red Banner, Order of the Patriotic War First and Second Class, and several medals. *GSS*, Vol. 2, 1988, p. 336.—Translator

was landed in two groups: two torpedo cutters and one patrol cutter in the first, and one patrol cutter and two minesweeping cutters in the second. Both groups departed from Vladimir Port at 1942 hours on 9 October. The first group landed its troops at 2215, the same time as the first wave of 63rd NIB was moving across Maattivuono Bay under the light of enemy searchlights and illumination rounds. The second group was landed at 2311. The landings were conducted on the shoreline of Motovskiy Bay, west of Cape Pikshuev (figure 5.4).

During the landings, the enemy illuminated the shoreline with flares and conducted unorganized light machine-gun fire. This did not interfere with the landing and movement of the groups inland to a depth of one kilometer, in the direction of enemy strongpoint *Oberhof*. After putting their troops ashore, the cutters of the demonstration landing force remained near the shore, conducting intensive cannon and machine-gun fire on the shore and laying smoke screens to create the appearance of large-scale landings.

At the same time, two destroyer escorts from the fleet surface squadron farther out in Motovskiy Bay placed naval gunfire on strongpoint *Oberhof*, batteries, and enemy crossing assets near Titovka. Having fulfilled its mission without losses, the demonstration landing force was withdrawn by the cutters at 0035 on 10 October.

D. THE AMPHIBIOUS LANDING IN LIINAKHAMARI PORT ON THE NIGHT OF 12–13 OCTOBER

The Significance of Liinakhamari Port and Its Defense to the Enemy

Situated on the western shore of Petsamovuono Inlet, Liinakhamari Port was employed by the German command as a supply transloading point for units on the Murmansk axis. Army supply warehouses were located in the Liinakhamari area for this purpose. A good road network connected Liinakhamari Port to Rovaniemi—the hub of northern Finland, to Kirkenes Port—the main army supply base in the north, and to all sectors of the Murmansk axis. The construction of a road with overhead camouflage was completed in 1943. This road ran parallel to the improved Parkkino–Great Litsa River Road.

Movement along the camouflaged road was in both directions.

Naturally, the German command paid attention to the defenses of Liinakhamari Port from both the land and the sea. Four shore batteries covered the approaches to the port from the sea:

- Battery No. 1—four 150 mm guns on Cape Numeroniemi;
- Battery No. 2—four 150 mm guns on Nurmensetti Peninsula (Cape Ristiniemi);
- Battery No. 3—four 150 mm guns on Cape Krestovyy; and
- Battery No. 4—four 210 mm field guns on Cape Neytiniemi (Cape Devkin).

In addition to these batteries, which covered entrances to the bay, antiaircraft batteries in calibers ranging from 20 to 88 mm were positioned on both shores of Petsamovuono Inlet, creating three layers of fires near the entrance to the inlet and five layers of fire in the inlet's inner reaches. The batteries could be used for anti-ship defense.

In addition to the artillery positions on the shore in the area of Liinakhamari Port, there were machine-gun positions in the rocks in cement bunkers, steel-reinforced concrete firing positions, and firing positions made from the armored turrets of obsolete tanks.

The anti-torpedo defense of the port consisted of a two-row, anti-torpedo barrier near moorages Nos. 2, 5, and 6, parallel to the docks and at 80–100 meters from the moorages. The presence of this barrier was confirmed by aerial photographs taken on 16 September.

Strongpoints and pickets located along the coast from Maattivuono Bay to Peuravuono Inlet served as anti-landing defenses and landward defenses for Liinakhamari Port. In addition, barbed wire obstacles and explosive demolitions were placed along the entire coastline near Liinakhamari near the water's edge. A powerful strongpoint was located just north of the port, covering the 210 mm battery position.

Plan for the Capture of Liinakhamari Port

By 12 October, the combat for the liberation of the Soviet far north was characterized by the success of the offensive along the entire front. Karelian *Front* forces had reached the Luostari area and begun their attack toward Petsamo. Naval infantry units were pursuing the retreating enemy along Titovka–Porovaara Road, reaching the units of the composite reconnaissance detachment at the eastern shore of Petsamovuono Inlet in the area of Cape Krestovyy.

Countless fires and explosions were observed in enemy positions in Parkkino, Trifona, and Liinakhamari Port. In order to preserve Liinakhamari Port, which was valuable to the fleet, and to facilitate an increase in the tempo of the operation overall, the Northern Fleet commander decided to seize the port with a dedicated landing force.

In accordance with this decision, he ordered the commander, Torpedo Cutter Brigade, to break through the enemy's defenses at the mouth of Petsamovuono Inlet and land an amphibious assault force directly in Liinakhamari Port. The mission was formulated as follows:

1. Forces were to be landed by small subchasers and torpedo cutters in Liinakhamari Port on the night of 12–13 October. They were to capture the strongpoint of the 210 mm battery in the area of Cape Devkin, seize the port, military garrison, and dominating heights in the port area, and hold them until the arrival of the main force.
2. The force was to create the threat of encirclement of the enemy's Petsamo grouping from the rear by capturing Liinakhamari Port, and by subsequently attacking toward Trifona and Petsamo.

The following forces were designated for the accomplishment of these missions:

   a. **AMPHIBIOUS ASSAULT TROOPS**: 349th Separate Machine-Gun Battalion of the Northern Defensive Region, commanded by Major Timofeev, and a detachment from 125th Naval Infantry Regiment of Main Base Shore Defense under the command of Senior Lieutenant Peterburgskiy, totaling 660 men. Major Timofeev was named overall commander of the assault force.
   b. **LANDING SHIP DETACHMENT**: torpedo cutters and small subchasers, divided into three groups:

   first group: torpedo cutters Nos. *116* and *114*, type *D-3*. Group commander Captain-Lieutenant Aleksandr Shabalin[20] (on *TKA-116*);

   second group: torpedo cutters Nos. *204*, *206*, *207*, *208*, and *213*, type *A-2* [*Higgins*]. Group commander Captain Second Rank Korsunovich[21] (on *TK-204*), also the commander of both groups of cutters that would participate in the breakthrough.

   third group: small subchasers Nos. *423*, *424*, *426*, *430*, and *433*, type *MO-IV*, and *TKA 211*, type *A-2*. Group commander Guards Captain Third Rank Zyuzin[22] (on *MO-423*).

Torpedo cutters Nos. *226* and *172*, commanded by Senior Lieutenant Loshchilin (on *TKA-226* with radar), were designated as the close-in mobile ship screen. Torpedo cutters Nos. *228* and *244*, commanded by Captain Third Rank Fedorov (on *TKA-228* with radar), were designated as the long-range mobile ship screen.

Leadership of the cutters' breakthrough into Petsamovuono Inlet and the assault landing was placed on the commander of the third assault group, Guards Captain Third Rank Zyuzin. The fleet commander planned to be located at Torpedo Cutter Brigade commander's command post on Hill 200 in Pummanki during the conduct of the capture of Liinakhamari Port. The command post of the commander, 113th Separate Artillery Battalion, was selected as the observation point. This position had direct telephone communications with the command post of the Torpedo Cutter Brigade commander.

The Amphibious Assault on Liinakhamari Port

Special air reconnaissance on the eve of the cutters' breakthrough into Petsamovuono Inlet confirmed that there was no anti-ship boom in the bay. Although anti-torpedo nets were noted near moorages 2, 5, and 6 in Liinakhamari Port, they would not create particular difficulties for the cutters' entry into the harbor.

By 1500 on 12 October, all the cutters designated for the conduct of the amphibious assault were concentrated at Pummanki base. The assault troops had also arrived in Pummanki by this time. Prior to setting out to sea, the cutter commanders were instructed to land troops on each dock. Each boat also carried a special assault landing gangplank for use if the troops had to be put directly ashore and not on a dock. The cut-

---

20 Aleksandr Osipovich Shabalin (1914–1982) entered naval service in 1936. After participating in the Soviet-Finnish War, he became the commander of a torpedo cutter in Northern Fleet. By the start of 1944, he had sunk an enemy submarine, four transports, and two patrol vessels. He received his first HSU award on 22.02.44 [dates in format day.month.year]. For his mastery in executing, along with other torpedo boats, the amphibious landing in Liinakhamari harbor on 13.10.44, he was awarded his second HSU on 5.11.44. Throughout the war, he provided a frequent means of insertion of the Northern Fleet reconnaissance detachment elements behind German lines. Shabalin later became the chief of staff of the Northern Fleet. He completed higher-level military schools in 1951 and 1955, and before his retirement served as deputy chief of Frunze Naval Academy. *GSS*, vol. 2, 1988, p. 748.—Translator

21 Sergey Grigoryevich Korsunovich (1912–1964), entered naval service in 1930, completed Frunze Naval Academy in 1934, then commanded torpedo cutters in the Baltic and Northern Fleets. Forces under his command as commander of Second Torpedo Cutter Division, Torpedo Cutter Brigade of the Northern Fleet, executed nine mine-laying sorties that resulted in the sinking of 32 enemy vessels. During the Petsamo Operation, he led the breakthrough of torpedo cutters into an enemy base while executing an amphibious landing of naval infantryman, which ensured the success of the operation. He was awarded Hero of the Soviet Union on 5.11.44 [5 November 1944]. *GSS*, vol. 1, 1987, p. 740.—Translator

22 Sergey Dmitrieich Zyuzin (1911–unknown) entered naval service in 1933 and completed the Black Sea Fleet commander's course in 1935, then served on staffs of Pacific and Northern Fleets. As commander, Second Guards Division of Small Subchasers, Patrol Vessel Guard of Offshore Area of the Northern Fleet Main Base, he successfully landed several assault groups into Liinakhamari Port on the night of 13.10.44 [format day.month.year]; on 18 October, he conducted another amphibious landing at a site on the Norwegian border. He was awarded Hero of the Soviet Union on 5.11.44. (*GSS*, vol. 1, 1987), p. 562.—Translator

ters also took on board 1.5 times the normal supply of smoke charges.

At 2040 on 12 October, the first group of cutters departed Pummanki with their assault troops aboard. The meteorological conditions at that time were as follows: southwest wind at force 3–4, force 2 sea, visibility 1–1.5 miles. To aid in the security of the movement, the cutters' motors were all set to vent their exhaust beneath the surface during the transit. Passing by Aynov Island, the cutters took a course of 185 degrees for transit to Petsamovuono Inlet (see figure 5.5).

A set of navigational lights was positioned on Sredniy Peninsula for hydrographic support of the cutter commanders during transit. In addition, a military harbor pilot who was familiar with the entrance to Petsamovuono Inlet and Liinakhamari Harbor was placed on the lead cutter of each breakthrough group.

During the transit to Petsamovuono Inlet, the first group of cutters was illuminated by a searchlight from Nurmensetti Peninsula, and immediately thereafter fired upon by shore batteries. The cutters fell under artillery and smaller caliber gun fire from Cape Numeroniemi near the entrance to the inlet. The shells fell short of their targets.

Because the enemy was firing both high-explosive and illumination rounds, the cutter commanders easily found the entrance to the inlet. Breaking through the fire curtain, they entered the inlet. The cutters proceeded into the inlet, hugging the western shore and, skirting Cape Devkin, at 2250 found moorage No. 5 (the fueling pier) and Liinakhamari Harbor.

TKA-116 approached the shore east moorage No. 5 at 2302 and landed a 25-man assault force in two minutes. At the same time, the other cutter of this group (*TKA-114*) landed 27 men on the eastern part of moorage No. 4. The cutters came under fire from shore-based artillery, mortars, and machine guns on the approach to the landing site and during the landing. After the landing, *TKA-114* remained near the pier to assist in the landing of men by other cutters. But *TKA-116* withdrew toward Cape Devkin, where it met and led the second and then the third group of cutters toward the docks.

Having completed the upload of their assault troop units, the second group of cutters departed from the dock at Pummanki at 2047. The cutters moved in column toward Petsamovuono Inlet. This group followed the first group of cutters at 2,000–3,000 yards. Just like the leading group, the cutters of the second group fell into the beam of a searchlight, shining from Nurmensetti Peninsula. In addition, they were lit up by illumination rounds. This helped the cutters to determine the location of the entrance to the inlet, which had already been covered by a smoke screen laid down earlier.

It was obvious to the commander of the second group of cutters that the first group in front of them had been illuminated by searchlights and fired upon by shore batteries from Capes Ristiniemi and Numeroniemi. Therefore, he ordered a decrease in speed to slow ahead, and when the searchlight beam fell on cutter *TKA-204* of the second group, he ordered laying a short curtain smoke screen toward Nurmensetti. The remaining torpedo boats, moving out of the searchlight's beam, began to break into Petsamovuono Inlet at full speed. They quickly again fell into the beam of a searchlight from Cape Numeroniemi and were fired upon by an anticutter battery from the same cape. The boats returned suppressive fire at both the battery and the searchlight position and forced their way into the inlet.

The cutters moved into the inlet hugging the western shore. During the approach to Cape Devkin, they were illuminated by flares and received concentrated artillery, mortar, and machine-gun fire. Under the cover of brief smoke screens, which obscured the entire harbor with dense smoke, the cutters almost simultaneously reached their designated landing sites at 2310.

TKA-204 and *TKA-213* landed their troops on the shore just east of the burning pier No. 5. *TKA-206* and *TKA-207* executed their landings on pier No. 4, and *TKA-208* landed its troops 50 meters from pier No. 2. Despite heavy German fire on the five torpedo cutters, only *TKA-208* was struck in the left side, and a second round entered the forward cabin from the right side. As a result, the right motor was disabled, and three men killed. However, the motor was quickly repaired, and the cutter was able to proceed to the exit from Petsamovuono Inlet.

Of the cutters of the second group, *TKA-204* remained in the landing area to meet and guide the cutters of the third group at Cape Devkin. Once having accomplished this, *TKA-204* fell in behind the other cutters of its group and moved toward the exit of the inlet. The smoke screen hanging in the bay was being pushed to the north by the wind, and the cutters were illuminated by a searchlight from Cape Numeroniemi and fired upon by enemy shore batteries during their withdrawal. They had to lay down a new smoke screen,

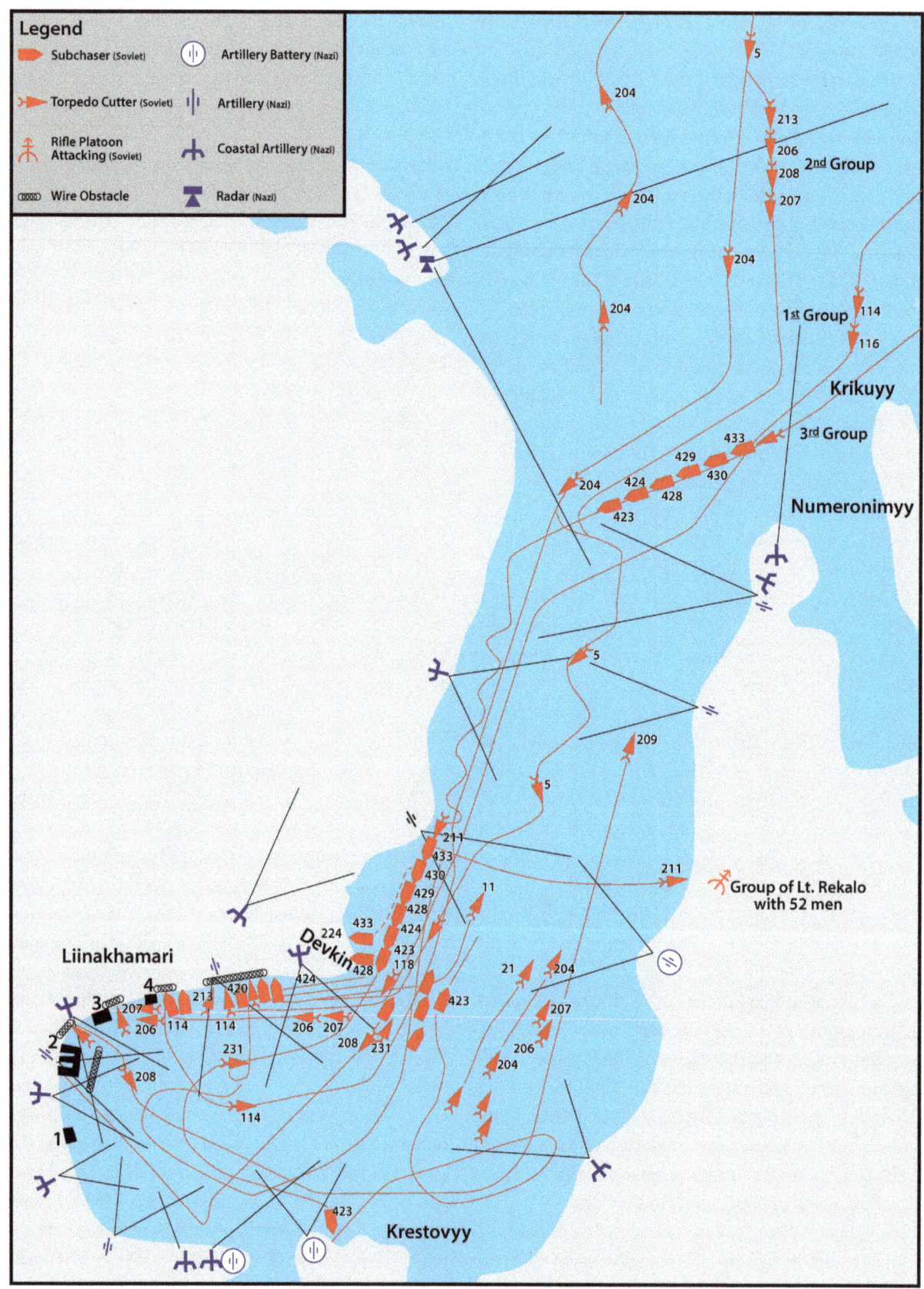

FIGURE 5.5. Breakthrough of cutters with amphibious assault force into Petsamovuono Inlet to capture Liinakhamari Harbor

under the cover of which they exited Petsamovuono Inlet and safely returned to Pummanki.

The cutters of the third group proceeded behind the second group toward their landing sites. The distance between these two groups did not exceed 3,000 yards. Prior to reaching the entrance to Petsamovuono Inlet, the third group set their speed at 8–12 knots. After the second group entered the inlet, the commander of the third group increased speed to 18 knots and at this speed forced his way past the artillery fire from the batteries on Ristiniemi and Numeroniemi.

The smoke from the previously laid screen facilitated the success of this breakthrough, and the cutters entered the inlet without losses. They moved in dense smoke all the way to the landing site, smoke that was particularly thick in the area of Cape Devkin.

TKA-211, moving at the back of the group, veered off from the forward-moving column and lost its orientation in the smoke. This cutter landed its 57 troops under the command of Lieutenant Rekalo not on the western but on the eastern shore of Petsamovuono Inlet, almost opposite Liinakhamari Port.

Under enemy fire, mainly from the area southwest of Liinakhamari Port, the third group reached the landing site between the port's piers. Small subchaser *MO-423* could not land its troops at the designated point between docks 3 and 5, because a mortar round had wounded its navigator and two sailors. The helmsman was also wounded, and the starboard motor damaged. *MO-423* lost orientation and landed its 49 assault troops on the eastern shore of the bay near Cape Krestovyy. Subsequently this group participated in the mopping up of the garrison of the enemy battery on Cape Krestovyy, as part of the composite reconnaissance detachment.

The other small subchaser of this group, *MO-428*, fell under heavy artillery fire after landing its troops. Intending to seek cover in the still-hanging smoke screen near Cape Devkin, *MO-428* increased speed to 20 knots, moved into the smoke screen, and ran aground on rocks near Cape Devkin. Attempts by *MO-429*, which was passing nearby, to pull it off the rocks were unsuccessful. This led the division commander to send small subchasers *MO-430* and *MO-433* to the accident site, and *MO-424* to cover them with a smoke screen. But they were also unsuccessful in their attempts to pull *MO-428* from the rocks. On order of the division commander, the crew and all documents were removed from the vessel. After this incident, all the ships, protected from enemy fires by smoke screens, exited Petsamovuono Inlet.

MO-428 was pulled from the rocks on 15 October at high tide, then towed to Kola Inlet. Thus, there were no ship losses during the capture of Liinakhamari, though almost every ship returned to base with numerous shrapnel and bullet holes in their superstructures and sides. Four men were killed and six wounded among the vessel crews. The three ship detachments had put ashore 658 personnel for the capture of Liinakhamari Port.

Actions of the Mobile Screen

While the ships with the amphibious assault were accomplishing their mission, two groups of torpedo cutters, acting as mobile screens, covered their actions from the sea. One of these groups, *TKA-226* and *TKA-172*, conducted a patrol along the meridian of Peuravuono, with the mission to prevent enemy surface craft from entering the landing area. No enemy vessels appeared in the patrol's sector.

The second group, *TKA-228* and *TKA-224*, patrolling south of Lille-Ekkere Island [in Varangerfjord], was conducting a search for enemy ships exiting from Bekfjord [from Kirkenes Port]. At 2240 on 12 October, *TKA-228* detected on its radar two silhouettes in the area of Cape Korsnes, at a range of 12,000 yards. At 2305, it was determined that the enemy ships were moving on an easterly course. The torpedo cutters immediately set a course to close with the enemy.

In the first minutes of 13 October, the torpedo boats were illuminated by enemy artillery illumination rounds fired from Cape Korsnes. In the glow of the burning flare, the torpedo cutters detected three enemy patrol boats, moving on an intersecting course. It was also observed that at 0013 this group of patrol cutters engaged another group with fire, apparently because of faulty identification, believing they were ours.

Soon one of the groups of enemy cutters veered off to the right from the torpedo boats, and later, covered by a smoke screen, moved off astern. There was no engagement between the German and Soviet vessels, but enemy shore batteries continued to fire at our torpedo cutters until 0042 on 13 October.

Continuing to fulfill their mission, the torpedo cutters remained in this area until they received the order to return to base. Such an order was received at 0436 on 13 October, and both screening forces returned to base at Pummanki by 0655.

Actions of the Amphibious Assault Force Ashore

The composite amphibious assault force for the capture of Liinakhamari Port was landed in two groups. One group, consisting of the officers and men selected from 125th Naval Infantry Regiment, was landed in the immediate area of the port's piers. The other, consisting of units of 349th Separate Machine-Gun Battalion, was landed in the area of Cape Devkin (Neytiniemi).

The first group, commanded by Senior Lieutenant Peterburgskiy, was armed with 18 light machine guns, 193 submachine guns, 80 rifles, and 4–8 hand grenades per naval infantryman, plus 1,500 rounds for each machine gun, 600 rounds for each submachine gun, and 200 rounds for each rifle. The average load per naval infantryman was 12–16 kg [25–35 lbs.], including three days' special rations. This group began rapidly to move into the port, which was swept by heavy machine-gun fire, mainly toward the southwest, toward Lake Puro-yarvi (figure 5.6).

By 0300 on 13 October, this group had driven the enemy from the shore in the port area and had captured a beachhead, a requirement for the development of the attack inland. It was decided to attack toward Lake Puro-yarvi, the sector from which enemy fire was most intense.

The second group of the amphibious force, commanded by Major Timofeev, landed about 20 minutes behind the first. It launched a swift attack on the eastern and southern slopes of the hills of Neytiniemi-tunturi, the location of a strongpoint containing a four-gun 210 mm artillery battery. By 0200–0300 on 13 October, the assault units of this group were moving inland under intense light machine-gun, artillery, and mortar fires. Overcoming barbed wire and stone obstacles, they reached the battery firing positions.

At dawn on 13 October, two companies of enemy infantry, which had made their way to the 210 mm battery firing positions from the isthmus of Lakes Kyante-yarvi and Khinkhno-yarvi, counterattacked and attempted to push the assault force away from the battery position. The enemy was repulsed by the fire of First Machine-Gun Company and several hand-to-hand engagements. By 1200, the entire battery area was in the hands of the assault force and the enemy had withdrawn.

The enemy undertook more deliberate counterattacks in the sector of Senior Lieutenant Peterburgskiy's detachment. At 1200, up to two infantry companies, which came from the direction of Trifona settlement, attacked the detachment north of Lake Puro-yarvi. One of the detachment's platoons was driven to the water's edge, and a unit of 349th Separate Machine-Gun Battalion sent to their aid was insufficient to ward off the ever-fiercer enemy pressure.

New enemy units were arriving on trucks from Trifona, and assembling near Lake Puro-yarvi, with the goal to drive the assault force away from Liinakhamari. Units of Peterburgskiy's detachment came under mortar fire. At this same time, during the afternoon, the enemy again attempted to regain the positions that they had lost in the area of the 210 mm battery, but all their attacks were beaten off with heavy losses.

Soviet aircraft conducting air reconnaissance observed the approach of German units by road from Trifona settlement to Liinakhamari and reported this upon their return to the airfield at Pummanki. At about this same time, the commander of the composite amphibious landing force reported enemy troop concentrations in the area of Lake Puro-yarvi and requested air support.

Despite the approaching darkness (it was nearly 1700), it was decided to dispatch aircraft. Six *Il-8s*,[23] six *Kittyhawks*, and four *Yaks* took off from Pummanki airfield between 1645 and 1800. The pilots made four low-level attacks against the designated targets. The fighter cover also participated in the ground attacks. According to the pilots, the marking of their own positions by the assault force units, as well as designation of enemy targets, was executed in a most helpful manner. Major Timofeev made the following comment to Captain Barchenko on Cape Krestovyy concerning the air support: "Aviation came to our aid quickly, and it struck where I wanted it, leaving smoke and fire everywhere. My heart rejoiced."

The enemy suffered heavy losses as a result of the air strikes on forces in the area of Lake Puro-yarvi and was

---

23 The *Ilyushin Il-8 Shturmovik* (low-level attack aircraft) was an upgraded version of the *Il-2*, with a higher-output engine, which enabled the aircraft to reach a top speed of 294 mph and a range of 611 miles, and a 12.7 mm machine gun in the rear-gunner's position. It retained the same wing-mounted two 23 mm cannons and two 7.62 mm machine guns.—Translator

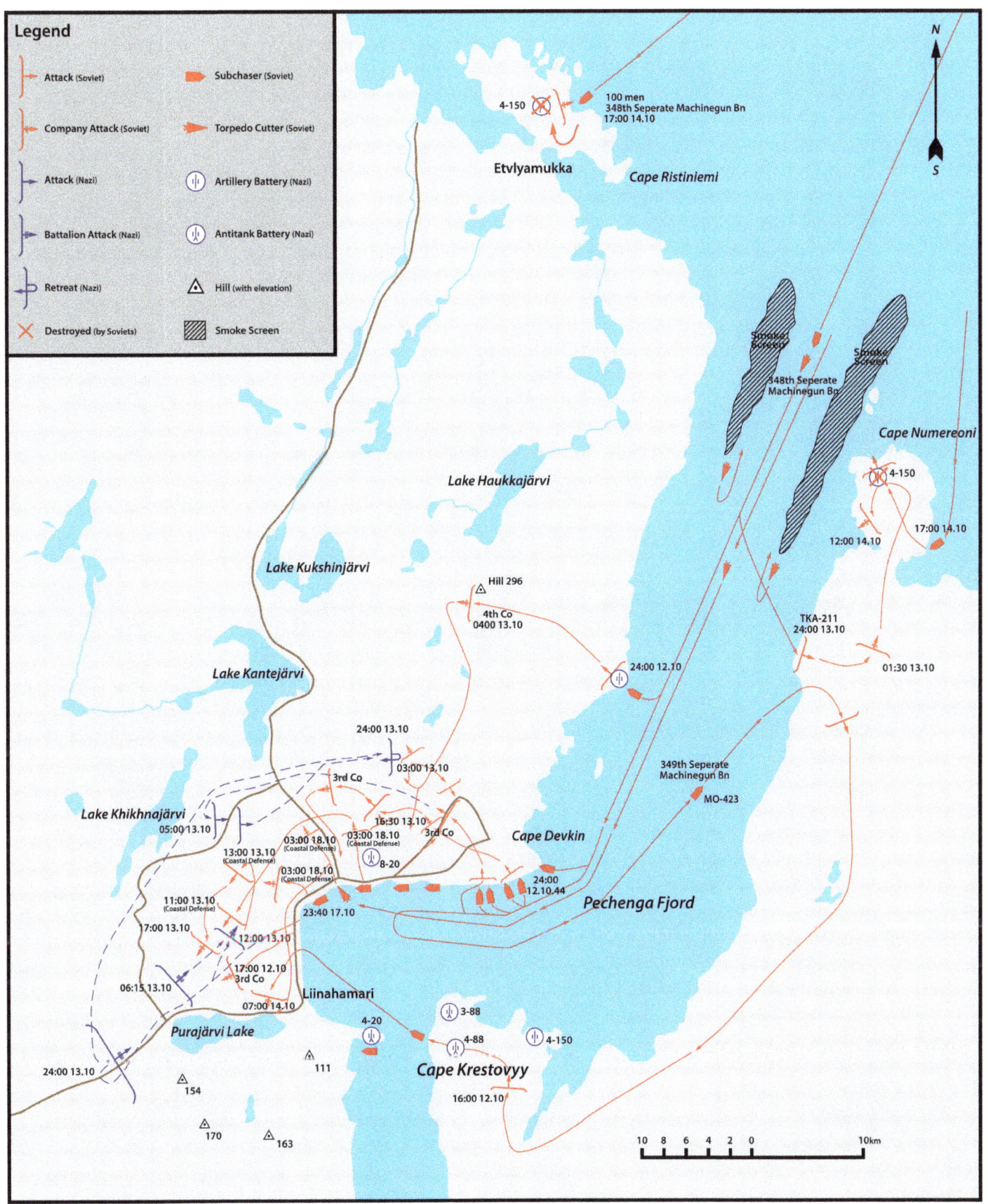

FIGURE 5.6. Actions of the amphibious assault detachment on shore during the capture of the Liinakhamari area

not able to withstand the renewed attack of Major Timofeev's composite detachment, which he had regrouped during the air strikes. The battle lasted until 1800 on 13 October. The enemy could not hold back the forward surge of the naval infantrymen and, suffering heavy losses, began to withdraw toward Lake Trifona-yarvi.

After this, Liinakhamari Port and the entire surrounding area were firmly controlled by the composite detachment, but exchanges of gunfire with and the pursuit of small groups of enemy soldiers continued until 1200 on 14 October. During the night of 13–14 October, the reconnaissance detachment of Captain Barchenko, the reconnaissance company of 63rd NIB, and the NCO Academy of 349th Separate Machine-Gun Battalion were brought over to Liinakhamari from Cape Krestovyy to reinforce the composite amphibious landing force.

E. AMPHIBIOUS ASSAULT FOR THE CAPTURE OF THE BATTERIES COVERING THE ENTRANCE TO PETSAMOVUONO INLET

Enemy shore batteries positioned on Cape Ristiniemi and Cape Numeroniemi, covering the entrance to Petsamovuono Inlet, remained in German hands even after the capture of Liinakhamari Port. These batteries could fire upon our batteries located on Sredniy Peninsula. The fleet commander decided to land an assault force to capture them.

On 14 October, the commander of Torpedo Cutter Brigade selected torpedo boats Nos. *219* and *226* and small subchasers Nos. *423* and *426* for this task. The 348th Separate Machine-Gun Battalion provided 200 men for the assault force, and by 1540 on 14 October they completed uploading on the vessels in Pummanki.

TKA-226 and *MO-423*, with 100 men on board, set out to capture the battery on Cape Ristiniemi (on Nurmensetti Peninsula). *TKA-219* and *MO-426*, also with 100 men on board, set off to capture the battery on Cape Numeroniemi. The weather favored the landing, with the wind from the southwest at force 2, the sea at force 1, and visibility at 12 miles.

Actions by aviation to suppress the batteries with air strikes preceded their capture by the amphibious landing forces. Six *Il-2s*, four *Kittyhawks*, and two *Yaks* carried out low-level strikes against the batteries, dropping fragmentation and phosphorous bombs, and strafing the positions.

By approximately 1800 on 14 October, the assault forces had been landed at their designated landing sites. There had been no enemy resistance during their landing or movement toward their objectives. The enemy had blown up the guns and supply stores, and then abandoned the positions. Apparently, the troops from these batteries had been removed by small boats that arrived before the amphibious assaults, because all landward paths of retreat had been cut off.

On the night of 12–13 October, the mistakenly landed detachment from *TKA-211*, commanded by Lieutenant Rekalo, was already in the rear of the battery on Numeroniemi. This force reached the battery firing position by 1200 on 14 October. It is likely that the enemy had already abandoned the battery by this time. On 15 October, the amphibious forces on Ristiniemi and Numeroniemi were withdrawn by cutters and transported to Liinakhamari.

F. LANDING OF AMPHIBIOUS FORCES ON THE SOUTHERN COAST OF VARANGERFJORD

Naval infantry amphibious forces were landed on the southern coast of Varangerfjord to support the coastal flank of the Karelian *Front*'s 14th Army, attacking along the coast in their advance on Kirkenes. The fulfillment of the missions associated with the preparation of the landing forces became the responsibility of the newly established Pechenga Naval Base on 15 October.

Among the tasks assigned to the commander of this base by the Northern Fleet commander was the mission to be prepared to conduct amphibious landing operations and support the coastal flank of attacking Karelian *Front* units with naval gunfire.

The 18 October Amphibious Landings in Suolavuono and Aresvuono Inlets

The first of these landings was an assault landing with the goal to clear the coastal area from Suolavuono to Vuoremi of small groups of enemy stragglers. The base commander decided to land two groups for this task, the first group at Cape Aresniemi in Aresvuono Inlet, and the second at Cape Munasaari in Suolavuono Inlet. He designated three large subchasers (Nos. *217*, *220*, and *222*), three small subchasers (Nos. *423*, *432*, and *434*), and Fourth Battalion of 12th Naval Infantry Brigade to carry out the assigned mission.

The assault force uploaded in Liinakhamari Port from 0200 to 0240 on 18 October, and the ships departed for the landing site at 0330. The weather currently was as follows: south-southwest wind at force 3, sea at force 2, and visibility of 1–1.5 miles. The assault force was accompanied during the transit by the *Uragon*, which was positioned north of the landing area at 0500, covering it from interference from seaward. A patrol force of two torpedo cutters (Nos. *205* and *215*) was deployed at Sagfjord meridian for the same purpose at 0550.

Arriving at the dispersal point, which was also the rendezvous point after the landing, the assault forces divided into two groups, which then proceeded to their designated sites. The first group conducted their landing from 0650 to 0707 in the area of Cape Aresniemi, and the second landed in the area of Cape Munasaari between 0700 and 0730. Neither group met any enemy resistance during the landing or on shore. After executing the landings, the ships returned without incident to Liinakhamari.

The battalion that had landed on the shore moved along the coastline toward Kobbholmfjord, along the way meeting only small, disorganized groups of Germans who, supported by artillery and mortar fire, offered some resistance. The difficult nature of the terrain slowed the battalion's movement, and it was not able to maintain a sustained pursuit. The enemy was thus able to escape using a self-propelled barge. Later, a battalion of 12th NIB sank the barge with a mortar barrage. The enemy lost 254 men killed as a result of the amphibious landing. Our losses were four killed and 10 wounded.

By 20 October, the battalion was occupying the settlements Afanasev, Turunen, and Vuoremi on the Varangerfjord coastline, and had reached the Norwegian border. The battalion's actions along the coastline contributed to a certain extent to the success of units of 14th Army, which was approaching the outskirts of Tarnet settlement at the time and meeting heavy enemy resistance there.

The Amphibious Landing in Kobbholmfjord on 23 October

By 22 October, the situation was characterized by the farther advance of our forces and enemy destruction of bridges and mining roads on the approaches to Kirkenes. By close of day on 22 October, 131st Rifle Corps of 14th Army had reached the southern shore of Jarfjord, and occupied Sturbukt and Tarnet settlements. By this time, Fourth Battalion of 12th NIB had occupied the settlements Kung-oskar, Nyubygget, and Prestue. At sea, Northern Fleet ships and air forces were operating successfully against enemy sea lines of communication in Varangerfjord and along the northern Norwegian coast.

Given this situation, the Northern Fleet commander decided to support the actions of 131st Rifle Corps and ordered the commander of Pechenga Naval Base to land an amphibious assault in the southern part of Kobbholmfjord. He further ordered the force landed earlier (4th Battalion of 12th Naval Infantry Brigade) to advance and capture Khayokhiation and the hydroelectric station on the river that flowed from Lake Lille-Kobbholmvann. The subsequent mission of the amphibious force was to clear the coastline from Kobbholmfjord to Jarfjord of small enemy groups.

To accomplish these missions, the commander of Pechenga Naval Base ordered Fourth Battalion of 12th Naval Infantry Brigade to continue their attack along the southern coastline of Kobbholmfjord and occupy the hydroelectric station. He decided to land the Third Battalion (432 officers and men) of the same brigade in the northwestern part of Kobbholmfjord, and a detachment (176 officers and men) of 125th Naval Infantry Regiment in the southwestern part of Kobbholmfjord.

The mission of the first landing force was to clear the coastline as far as Lillefjord, and of the second—to capture the settlement of Kroftfeterbukht. The large subchaser *BO-221*; small subchasers *MO-425* and *MO-434*; and minesweeper cutters Nos. *401*, *404*, and *405* were designated for the first landing. Torpedo cutters Nos. *202*, *204*, *205*, and *222* were designated to land 125th Naval Infantry Regiment detachment.

The assault forces loaded up between 0015 and 0100 on 23 October in Liinakhamari Port and set out for the landing area at 0115. The weather was as follows: wind from the southwest at force 5–6, sea at force 3–4, and visibility of 1–1.5 miles. The assault force landings were conducted at designated landing sites beginning at 0608 on 23 October. The torpedo cutters used the undamaged dock in the southwest portion of Kobbholmfjord.

The enemy did not offer any resistance during the landing, which took all of 25 minutes. The assault force immediately set out to accomplish its missions, moving along the coastline in extremely difficult terrain. The Third Battalion reached the eastern shore of Jarfjord on 24 October, and there occupied abandoned shore and antiaircraft battery positions. The 125th Regiment detachment accomplished its mission to capture Kroftfeterbukht settlement on 25 October. Meanwhile, Fourth Battalion 12th NIB, moving along the coast of Kobbholmfjord, reached Khayokhiation settlement and occupied the hydroelectric station, which the Germans had abandoned in working order.

The Amphibious Landing in Holmengerfjord on 25 October

When 14th Army reached the approaches to Kirkenes (the crossing site on Elvenesfjord) by the end of the day on 24 October, and began to contest the crossing area, the enemy offered heavy resistance with the support of tens of batteries, including shore batteries. Attempts by our forces to cross Elvenesfjord were unsuccessful. The naval infantry force landed on 23 October remained in positions at the eastern end of Jarfjord.

Having evaluated the situation, the Northern Fleet commander decided to land an assault force in Holmengerfjord to cooperate with 14th Army in the capture of Kirkenes. He assigned this mission to the commander, Torpedo Cutter Brigade, who was ordered to land two battalions of 63rd Naval Infantry Brigade with attached large and small subchasers.

The landing detachment was divided into two groups. The northern group, landing Third Battalion of 63rd Naval Infantry Brigade, was comprised of large subchaser *BO-221*; small subchaser *MO-434*; and torpedo cutters Nos. *172, 202, 204, 206, 210,* and *222*. The southern group, landing Second Battalion of 63rd NIB, was comprised of small subchasers *MO-423* and *MO-426*, and torpedo cutters Nos. *214, 205, 207, 211, 215,* and *219*. Torpedo cutters Nos. *226, 240,* and *246* were designated to cover the landings from the sea.

The commander of Pechenga Naval Base ordered the landing of a detachment comprised of a submachine-gun company and a scout platoon from Third Battalion, 12th Naval Infantry Brigade on the western shore of Jarfjord to prepare the landing sites.

The upload of the assault forces was conducted in Pummanki from 2240 on 24 October to 0030 on 25 October. Altogether, the ships of the landing detachment took aboard 835 officers and men. Prior to departure of the ships from Pummanki, a message was received from headquarters of Pechenga Naval Base reporting the landing of a group of submachine gunners in the southwest portion of Holmengerfjord. During the approach of the amphibious landing force, these men would mark their positions on the shore with fires and assist the landing units. This information was passed to all the ships and commanders of the assault force.

The last cutter of the assault force had departed the docks at Pummanki by 0050 on 25 October. *BO-222* was leading the detachment. During the passage, the weather was as follows: southwest wind at force 5–6, sea at force 4–5, and visibility at 1–2 miles.

The ships with the assault force began their approach to the landing sites by 0445. At this time, the coastline of Holmengerfjord was lit up by the reflection of the fires in burning Kirkenes. Both assault groups were put ashore at their designated landing sites by 0600 on 25 October, having met no enemy resistance.

The marking of landing sites with fires on the shore did not achieve its goal, because the approaches to the selected sites had not been sufficiently investigated and abounded in underwater hazards. Nonetheless, the landing was accomplished successfully, thanks to the fact that the surrounding area was well illuminated by the reflection of fires in Kirkenes.

After the landing, the assault force proceeded along the coastline of Bekfjord across extremely difficult terrain, and by the morning of 26 October, Third Battalion reached the lighthouse and abandoned 105 mm shore battery on Bekfjord. The enemy had destroyed the battery. Subsequent actions of the landing force were limited to reaching the eastern shore of Jarfjord at Jakobsnes and Ronelven, since by this time 14th Army units had already captured Kirkenes.

3. Breakthrough of Enemy Defenses and Pursuit by Northern Defensive Region Units

Heavy artillery preparation of firing positions, command posts, manmade obstacles, and artillery and mortar battery firing positions preceded the breakthrough of German defenses on Sredniy Peninsula. For this combined artillery effort in support of the breakthrough forces, Northern Defensive Region artillery was divided into long-range artillery, artillery in direct support of 12th Naval Infantry Brigade, artillery in direct support of 63rd Naval Infantry Brigade, shore battery artillery, and direct lay artillery (figure 5.7).

The preliminary destruction of German defensive fortifications was begun 24 hours prior to the beginning of the offensive. It was carried out by batteries of 104th Cannon Artillery Regiment and the howitzer battalion of 12th NIB's direct support group.

Thirty-one firing positions and many enemy observation points were destroyed, which disrupted his system of fires in the breakthrough sector to a significant degree.

Prior to the beginning of the offensive, artillery preparation was conducted in the following phases:

- A five-minute barrage on targets along the forward edge and against command posts and reserves in the area of Hill 388.9 was conducted first. All Northern Defensive Region artillery participated in this barrage (figure 5.8). After the barrage, artillery groups carried out their respective missions for the remainder of the preparatory period.
- The long-range artillery group fired upon batteries and parts of batteries, at fortifications in the forward edge and against observation posts.
- Shore batteries conducted fires on enemy coastal artillery and, in some cases, field artillery.
- Direct-fire artillery groupings engaged enemy bunkers, unimproved positions, and trenches with aimed fire, using vertical and horizontal limits established for their guns during daylight, and illuminated aiming posts.

Batteries designated for blinding and suppressing enemy observation posts fired a combination of smoke and high-explosive rounds and successfully executed their mission. The low intensity, disorganization, and inaccuracy of enemy mortar and artillery fires in response to the Northern Defensive Region's massive artillery preparation attest to this.

Another barrage was fired at the forward edge of the enemy's defenses in the final 10 minutes of the 90-minute artillery preparation. The effectiveness of the artillery preparation was so great that almost all the enemy's fire support was silenced, and only scattered batteries and firing positions were able to conduct unaimed fire. The naval infantrymen, concentrating for the attack, went forward in the offensive almost without losses.

The guns and mortars of the Northern Defensive Region expended 47,000 artillery and mortar rounds during the artillery preparation, which lasted from 0330 to 0500 on 10 October.

The offensive was supported by rolling accompanying fires, fired by 12th and 63rd Naval Infantry Brigade direct support artillery. The shifting of fires from one line to another was accomplished by signals from the infantry. In addition, artillery forward observer teams located with attacking units were able to provide support to the infantry with adjusted artillery fire throughout the depth of the attack.

Northern Defensive Region engineer units prepared an attack position during the preparation for the breakthrough of the German defenses. While the artillery preparation was being fired, engineer troops were clearing passage lanes into the forward edge of the enemy's defenses. Utilizing dead space in the terrain, the breakthrough forces moved unnoticed by the enemy up to the line of attack (figure 5.9).

One or two engineer soldiers accompanied each naval infantry subunit, acting as guides through the minefields and barbed wire obstacles as it began the attack. More than 1,000 anti-personnel mines, four high-explosive, and two flame devices were removed from enemy minefields prior to the attack. An additional 200 anti-personnel mines, 130 high-explosive, and one flame device were removed during the occupation of Hill 146.0.

At 0500 on 10 October, on signal, the artillery shifted fires into the depth of the enemy defenses and the battalions launched the attack on the forward edge of the German positions. The Second Battalion and Third Battalion of 12th Naval Infantry Brigade, along with 614th Separate Punishment Company, advanced slowly under heavy machine-gun fire on their designated axes. The First Battalion was delayed in its sector because on the way to Hill 146.0, it came upon a barbed wire obstacle that the engineers had failed to eliminate. The battalion went to ground at the foot of the hill and managed to reach the top only at 0930. This delayed the tempo of the battle along the entire forward edge, and the breakthrough forces were able to reach the southern slopes of Mustatunturi Ridge only by 1200 on 10 October. There, near Lake Tie-yarvi (Selkyayarvi), they linked up with Third Battalion of 63rd Naval Infantry Brigade, which had landed during the night of 9–10 October on the southern shore of Maattivuono Bay.

					Total
Long-Range Artillery	**281st Artillery Battalion**: 1042nd Battery (4 Guns), 1043rd Battery (3 Guns), 1044th Battery (3 Guns), 1048th Battery (3 Guns), 1050th Battery (2 Guns)		**282nd Artillery Battalion**: 1045th Battery (4-107mm Guns), 1046th Battery (3 Guns)	**283rd Artillery Battalion**: 1049th Battery (3 Guns), 1053rd Battery (4 Guns)	8 — 152mm Guns (M1910/30) 17 — 122mm Guns (M1931/37) 6 — 107mm Guns (M1910/30)
Artillery Support of Infantry (12th Naval Infantry Brigade)	Artillery Battalion: 1st Battery (4 Guns), 2nd Battery (4 Guns), 3rd Battery (4 Guns)	Mortar Battalion: 1st Battery (3 Mortars), 2nd Battery (3 Mortars), 107mm Platoon (2 Mortars)	82mm Mortar Batteries 284/104: 1st Rifle Bn (7 Mortars), 2nd Rifle Bn (7 Mortars), 3rd Rifle Bn (7 Mortars), 4th Rifle Bn (7 Mortars)	1051st Battery (4 Guns), 1052nd Battery (4 Guns)	8 — 120mm Mortar (M1938) 2 — 107mm Mortar (M1938) 4 — 122mm Howitzer (M1938) 4 — 76mm Gun (M1939) 4 — 76mm Gun (M1938) 8 — 76mm Gun (M1927) 4 — 76mm Gun (M1942) 28 — 82mm Mortar
Artillery Support of Infantry (63rd Naval Infantry Brigade)	Artillery Battalion: 1st Battery (4 Guns), 2nd Battery (4 Guns), 3rd Battery (4 Guns)	Mortar Battalion: 1st Battery (4 Mortars), 2nd Battery (4 Mortars)	349th Seperate Machinegun Battalion: Batteries (4 Guns, 4 Guns)	347th Sep Machinegun Bn: Battery (4 Guns)	20 — 76mm Gun (M1927) 4 — 76mm Gun (M1939) 4 — 76mm Gun (M1942) 8 — 120mm Mortar (M1938)
Shore Artillery Group	113th Coastal Artillery Battalion: 140th Battery (4 Guns), 210th Battery (4 Guns), 221st Battery (4 Guns), 232nd Battery (4 Guns)			858th Sep Machinegun Bn: Batteries (4 Guns)	4 — 152mm Coastal Guns (B-4) 7 — 130mm Guns (B-13) 6 — 122mm Guns (M1931/37) 3 — 100mm Guns (B-24)
Direct Fire Group	12th Naval Infantry Brigade: Section of Guns and Section of Antitank Cannon (3 Guns, 10 Guns)	63rd Naval Infantry Brigade: Section of Guns and Section of Antitank Cannon (11 Guns)	347th Sep Machinegun Bn: Artillery Units and Platoons (17 Guns, 1 Gun)	348th Sep Machinegun Bn: Artillery Units (1 Gun, 2 Guns, 7 Guns)	349th Sep Machinegun Bn: Artillery Units (7 Guns, 2 Guns)	1 — 76mm Gun (M1942) 8 — 76mm Gun (M1927) 52 — 45mm Antitank Gun (M1937 and M1937)

FIGURE 5.7. Artillery composition for breakthrough

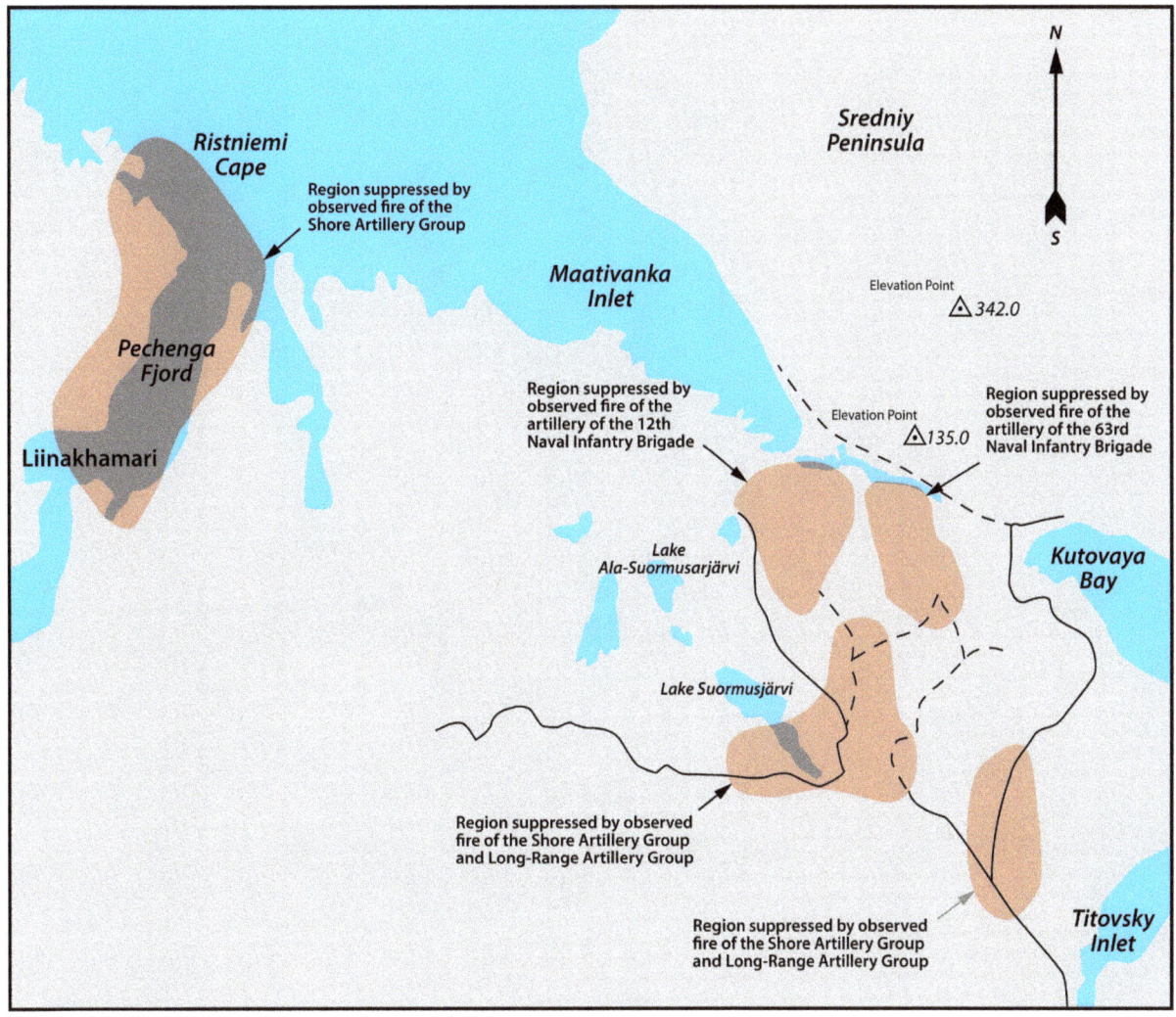

FIGURE 5.8. Distribution of targets for suppression by Northern Defensive Region artillery

Thus, overcoming determined enemy resistance, the breakthrough forces moved only one kilometer in seven hours of action in this sector. The First Battalion lost up to 40 personnel killed and wounded; Second Battalion and 614th Separate Punishment Company lost up to 60 personnel. The 12th Naval Infantry Brigade did not advance farther on this day, but instead consolidated its units and cleared mines in its positions.

During the night of 10–11 October, reconnaissance was conducted of sectors of the German defenses that were not attacked during the day. Several firing positions abandoned by the Germans were occupied. By 0700 on 11 October, reconnaissance had determined that the enemy had abandoned positions in the area of Hill 270. At 0800, it was noted that the enemy had laid down a smoke screen in the areas of Hills 122.0 and 388.9, apparently to cover their withdrawal. The enemy had abandoned all their positions on the isthmus of Sredniy Peninsula during the night.

At 0630 on 11 October, 12th Naval Infantry Brigade commander received the order to continue the offensive and reach the area of Hills 270 and 194.7. The Fourth Battalion, which was in the reserve of the Northern Defensive Region commander, was sent to the area of Lake Ozerko (on Sredniy Peninsula) for employment by the brigade commander.

Brigade units began to move forward to their designated objectives, meeting no enemy resistance. Contact with the enemy was lost. Battalion artillery, which was supposed to stay with the infantry units, moved with extreme difficulty. At first horses pulled the guns, but soon the horses gave out, since the forces were advancing over extremely broken terrain without roads. The guns had to be dragged by hand. This

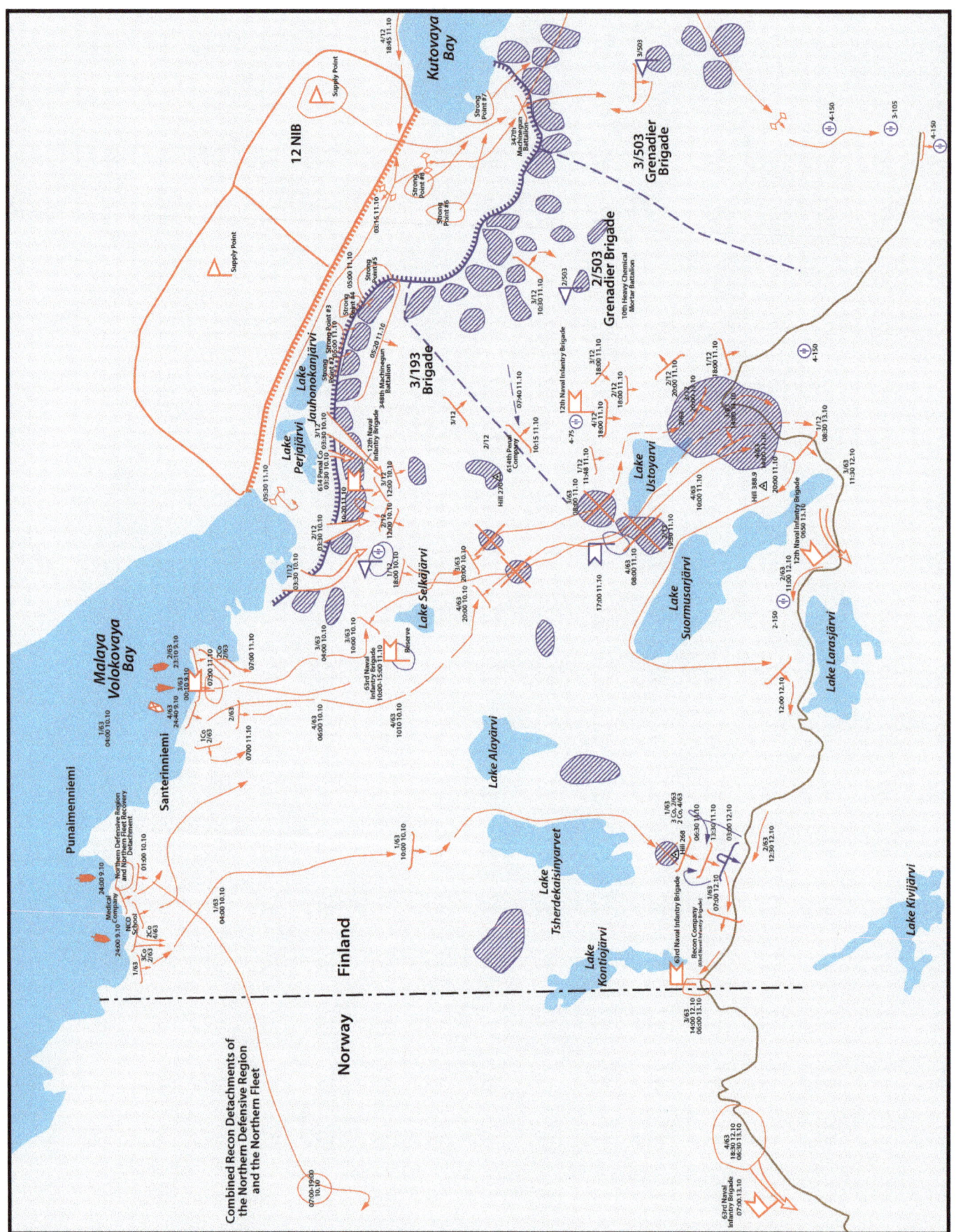

FIGURE 5.9. Start positions of the breakthrough forces at the line of attack and their offensive

demanded a great deal of time and energy. Artillery fell behind and was able to catch up with the infantry only when it reached the road leading from Mustatunturi to Hill 388.9.

The 347th and 348th Separate Machine-Gun Battalions went into the attack at dawn on 11 October, simultaneously with the advance of 12th Naval Infantry Brigade units.

Overcoming barbed wire and mine obstacles in its sector, 348th Battalion reached the southern slopes of Yaukhonokantunturi Hill, and 347th Battalion was occupying the area of Hill 109.0 by 2200.

While units of 12th NIB, attacking on 11 October, were trying to establish contact with enemy forces that had withdrawn during the night, 63rd Naval Infantry Brigade was moving southeastward with its Third and Fourh Battalions. By 1000 on 11 October, they reached the area of Hill 388.9. The battalions attacked the German units on this hill from the march and defeated them.

Pursuing the retreating enemy, 3rd and 4th Battalions of 63rd Naval Infantry Brigade reached the southern slopes of Hills 388.9 and 326.5 by 1400. Here they cut the single road to the west along which the enemy was conducting his withdrawal. The brigade's Second Battalion, comprising the brigade commander's reserve, was moving up to the area of Lake Ustoyarvi currently.

On this day, the 12 NIB brigade's First Battalion fought with enemy forces of up to battalion strength in the area of Hill 268, one kilometer north of Titovka–Porovaara Road. Because of mistaken orientation, however, the battalion commander believed he was located near Hill 299. The enemy counterattacked three times near Hill 368, but each time was driven off by the battalion's submachine-gun and machine-gun fires.

By 1800 on 11 October, up to 35 percent of the men were out of action, and the battalion commander went over to the defense on the southern slopes of Hill 268. At the same time, he requested aid from the brigade commander. The Fourth Battalion, sent by the brigade commander from Hill 388.9 to Hill 299 to support First Battalion, could not find the battalion in that location, because it was not there, but near Hill 268.

The approach of nightfall did not permit the battalions of 63rd Naval Infantry Brigade to continue fighting. By nightfall on 11 October, they occupied the positions shown in figure 5.8:

- 1st Battalion, along with 3rd Company of 2nd Battalion and 2nd Company of 4th Battalion, which had linked up with it during the landing, was in the area of Hill 268;
- 2nd and 3rd Battalions were in the area of Hill 388.9;
- 4th Battalion was in the area of Hill 299.

At this same time, 1st, 2nd, and 3rd Battalions of 12th Naval Infantry Brigade were located east of Lake Ustoyarvi, and 4th Battalion was on the move from Ozerko to the area of Hill 388.9.

The First Obstacle Detachment, which was operating in the second echelon of the breakthrough forces, occupied defensive positions on Mustatunturi Ridge on 11 October.

Thus, by the end of the second day, Northern Defensive Region attacking units had executed their assigned mission, to reach Titovka–Porovaara Road. This was accomplished 24 hours earlier than envisioned by the operational plan, because the enemy offered less resistance than expected. Over two days, the forces advanced only six kilometers (as far as the area of Hill 388.9). This cannot be acknowledged as a sufficiently high rate of advance, given the conditions under which it was conducted. This allowed the enemy to break contact with the naval infantry units that were breaking through their defensive positions and avoid their attacks on the night of 10–11 October.

The necessity to have pursued the enemy more energetically after breaking through their defensive positions is attested to by reports from aerial reconnaissance. An air reconnaissance sortie flown from Pummanki airfield at dawn on 10 October observed, for example, the enemy's southward withdrawal from the isthmus of Sredniy Peninsula. The same pilot observed heavy westward vehicle and cart traffic along Titovka–Porovaara Road on the morning of 10 October. Separate groups of retreating enemy infantry units were also observed.

Fleet Air Forces carried out continuous observation behind the front line and on roads leading out of the battle area to stay informed on the current situation. On 11 October, air reconnaissance observed an accumulation of enemy vehicle transports, carts, and personnel in the road sector near Lakes Suormusyarvi and Mutka-yarvi. Air strikes were called in on these targets, inflicting heavy losses on the enemy (figure 5.10).

With the arrival of naval infantry units in the area of Hill 388.9, air strikes were shifted to German forces retreating along the road to Porovaara. It was clear that the enemy was withdrawing ahead of Northern Defensive Region units, covering their retreat with rearguard units in positions prepared earlier. By this time, the Northern Defensive Region commander was aware of the enemy's retreat along the entire sector of the Western Litsa line, in front of Karelian *Front*'s forces. Liaison officers periodically transmitted operational information about the situation in 14th Army's sector to fleet headquarters.

By dawn on 12 October, it had also become clear that the enemy had abandoned their positions in front of First Battalion, 63rd Naval Infantry Brigade near Hill 268 during the night and was retreating toward Porovaara. The commander of 63rd NIB received the order from the Northern Defensive Region commander to begin pursuit.

With this objective, First Battalion reached the road to Porovaara at 0700. By 1000, the entire brigade was on the march, with the reconnaissance company out in front and Second Battalion acting as rear guard. The enemy did not offer any resistance, and the brigade, clearing the road of mines and explosive demolitions, reached the 1940 international border by 1830.[24] Nightfall forced brigade units to halt and spend the night here.

With the departure of 63rd Naval Infantry Brigade toward the west, 12th Naval Infantry Brigade battalions took up defensive positions southwest and south of Lake Ustoyarvi, with the mission to prevent any enemy withdrawal from Titovka.

Late on 11 October, and again on 12 October, Fleet Air Forces maintained continuous observation on the road to Porovaara and conducted air strikes on retreating German troop and vehicle columns. Air reconnaissance on 12 October observed the retreat of units and movement of German vehicle columns also from Pechenga (Petsamo) toward the west. Air reconnaissance reports indicated that the enemy was apparently not planning to hold in the Pechenga area. This information about the change in the situation should have generated a decision by the Northern Defensive Region commander to employ the forces available to him to move more quickly to the shore of Petsamovuono Inlet. The more so because the arrival of the naval infantry brigade at Titovka–Porovaara Road was the fulfillment of his subsequent mission in his combat order.

Changes in the situation in connection with the fleet commander's decision to capture Liinakhamari Port on the night of 12–13 October, and the rapidly changing situation of the reconnaissance detachments of the Northern Defensive Region and fleet headquarters in the battle on Cape Krestovyy, also should have prompted his thinking.

Nonetheless, until dawn on 13 October, the commander of Northern Defensive Region did not dispatch a single unit from 63rd Naval Infantry Brigade to reestablish contact with the enemy or to reach Cape Krestovyy and support the reconnaissance detachments. Only at 0530 on 13 October, after spending the night at the 1940 international border, did 63rd NIB units set out for Porovaara. Their mission was to assemble on Cape Krestovyy by the end of the day, and to cross over to Liinakhamari for actions to seize Trifona settlement upon the arrival of boats.

The 12th Naval Infantry Brigade units set out from the area of the road intersection between Lakes Ustoyarvi and Suormusyarvi at 0850 on 13 October, for movement to Porovaara behind 63rd NIB.

The insufficiently rapid forward advance of the naval infantry on 11 and 12 October can be explained by delays along the way caused by mine clearing on the road, bridge construction, and obstacle removal, as well as the large gap between the infantry and the supporting artillery. The latter resulted from the fact that artillery units were not able to employ their designated march routes, because the single road across Mustatunturi toward Hill 388.9 was mined. The artillery was forced to bypass through Kutovaya and Titovka. On 11 October, all the artillery and tanks were moving along this road, which was also mined, [was] blocked with rubble, or had bridges destroyed in many places.

Therefore, movement along it was also greatly delayed. Under these conditions, the artillery was able to link up with the forward naval infantry units only by the morning of 14 October.

By 1100 on 13 October, naval infantrymen of the forward elements of 63rd Naval Infantry Brigade were meeting enemy resistance east of Mikulan-tunturi. Having defeated the enemy security forces, the naval

---

24 Recall that Finland ceded territory here to the Soviet Union in March 1940 after being defeated in the brief Winter War (30 November 1939–13 March 1940) between the two nations.—Translator

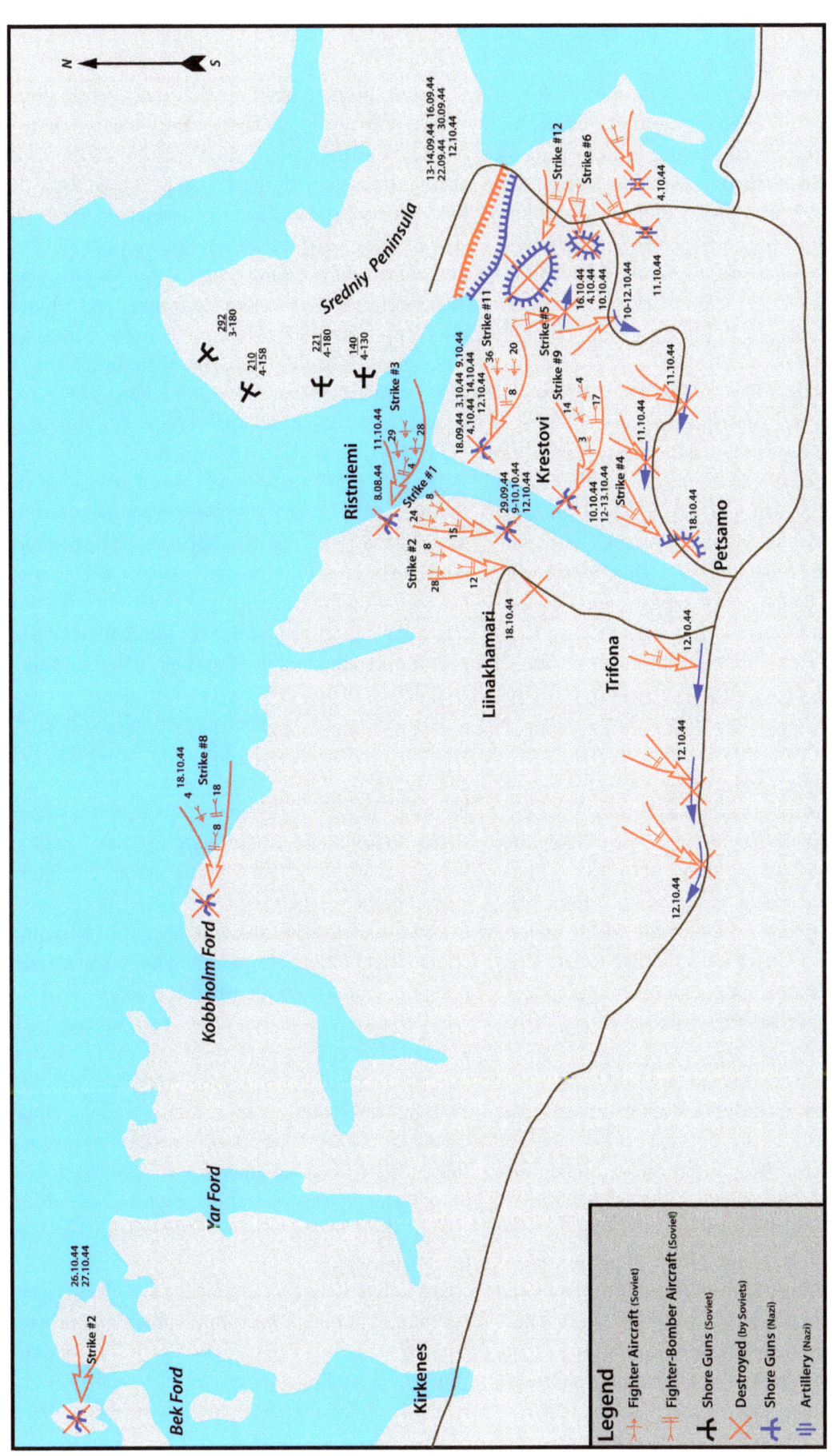

FIGURE 5.10. Northern Fleet Air Forces strikes on ground targets during campaign

infantrymen were engaging in the battle for the approaches to Hill Mikulan-tunturi.

The enemy attempted to delay the attack on Porovaara at this hill with a force of up to a battalion. Brigade units, at this time still lacking artillery support, used their infantry weapons systems and air strikes to defeat the fierce enemy resistance. They occupied the area of Hill Mikulan-tunturi at approximately 1600. While this battle was being fought, Third Battalion of 63rd NIB, operating on the brigade's southern flank, linked up with units of 95th Rifle Regiment, 14th Rifle Division, at 1410.

The capture of the area around Hill Mikulan-tunturi opened the path for subsequent movement of 63rd Naval Infantry Brigade toward Porovaara. But due to the onset of darkness, it was unable to develop a sufficiently energetic pursuit. The brigade had only reached the outskirts of Porovaara by 2000 on 13 October, with Fourth Battalion on the right flank, Third Battalion on the left, Second Battalion in the center, and First Battalion in reserve.

The Northern Defensive Region commander decided that 63rd Naval Infantry Brigade was sufficient by itself to destroy the enemy in this area and reach the shore of Petsamovuono Inlet. He ordered 12th Naval Infantry Brigade to turn off the Porovaara Road on the evening of 13 October and move to Cape Krestovyy. Their mission was to assemble there by 0100 on 14 October for loading on cutters and transit across the bay to Liinakhamari, there to assist in the capture of Trifona.

Carrying out its assigned task, 12th NIB left Porovaara Road at 1800 on 13 October and headed toward Cape Krestovyy. The cross-country movement during darkness was so difficult that brigade units lost contact with each other en route. They had to halt in order to reestablish command and control and reconnoiter the route. As a result of this, the brigade did not arrive at Cape Krestovyy at the designated time but reached it only by 0800 on 14 October. By this time, the reconnaissance detachments had already crossed over to Liinakhamari.

The men of 12th NIB were exhausted by the difficult night march. Their units did not have provisions and ammunition beyond that carried by the troops on their backs. The brigade began to cross the bay to Liinakhamari at noon on 14 October and finished by 1700. Having designated part of its force for extinguishing fires in Liinakhamari, the brigade set off to capture Trifona settlement. The First and Third Battalions of 12th NIB occupied Trifona without a fight by late in the evening of 14 October.

During this time, while 12th NIB units were reaching Cape Krestovyy on 14 October, the battalions of 63rd NIB renewed the attack on Porovaara. Small groups of enemy riflemen, with mortar support fired from the Kakkuri area, showed some resistance by fire to the advancing units. This resistance was broken, and Second and Fourth Battalions captured Porovaara by 1200. The enemy withdrew to Isamukka and, together with the group from Kuobaroaivi, offered yet more resistance to the brigade's Third Battalion. Brigade units approaching Porovaara on the shoreline of Petsamovuono Inlet came under artillery fire. Two guns from the Pechenga area also fired on them.

The 63rd NIB's artillery, which had arrived on the morning of 14 October, deployed from the march to support the attacking battalions. Enemy resistance weakened upon commencement of our artillery fire, and their units began to withdraw to the Pechenga area. The 12th NIB's artillery was unsuccessful in linking up with the brigade and was subordinated to the artillery commander of 63rd NIB.

The Northern Defensive Region's tank company also reached 63rd NIB by 1400. It was immediately employed for the attack on a strongpoint near Isamukka, and drove the enemy from it, fleeing toward Kakkuri. Groups of Germans resisting Third Battalion, which was attacking Hill Kuobaroaivi, also withdrew toward Pechenga (figure 5.11).

Before darkness fell on 14 October, 63rd NIB units cleared the coastline of small groups of Germans, and removed mines from the road. Having received the mission to cross Petsamovuono Inlet, brigade units assembled by 2300 on 14 October in Porovaara and on the cape north of the settlement. Two small subchasers transported brigade units, minus artillery, supply trains, and Second Battalion, across Petsamovuono Inlet to the Trifona settlement area from 0500 to 1000 on 15 October. The Second Battalion was left on the eastern shore of the inlet to secure the artillery and trains left there.

The 14th Army units captured the town Pechenga by storm on 15 October. The enemy withdrew to the west, pursued by 14th Army troops, in coordination with amphibious landings by naval infantry on the Varangerfjord coast and support from the sea of the Northern Fleet ships and Air Forces.

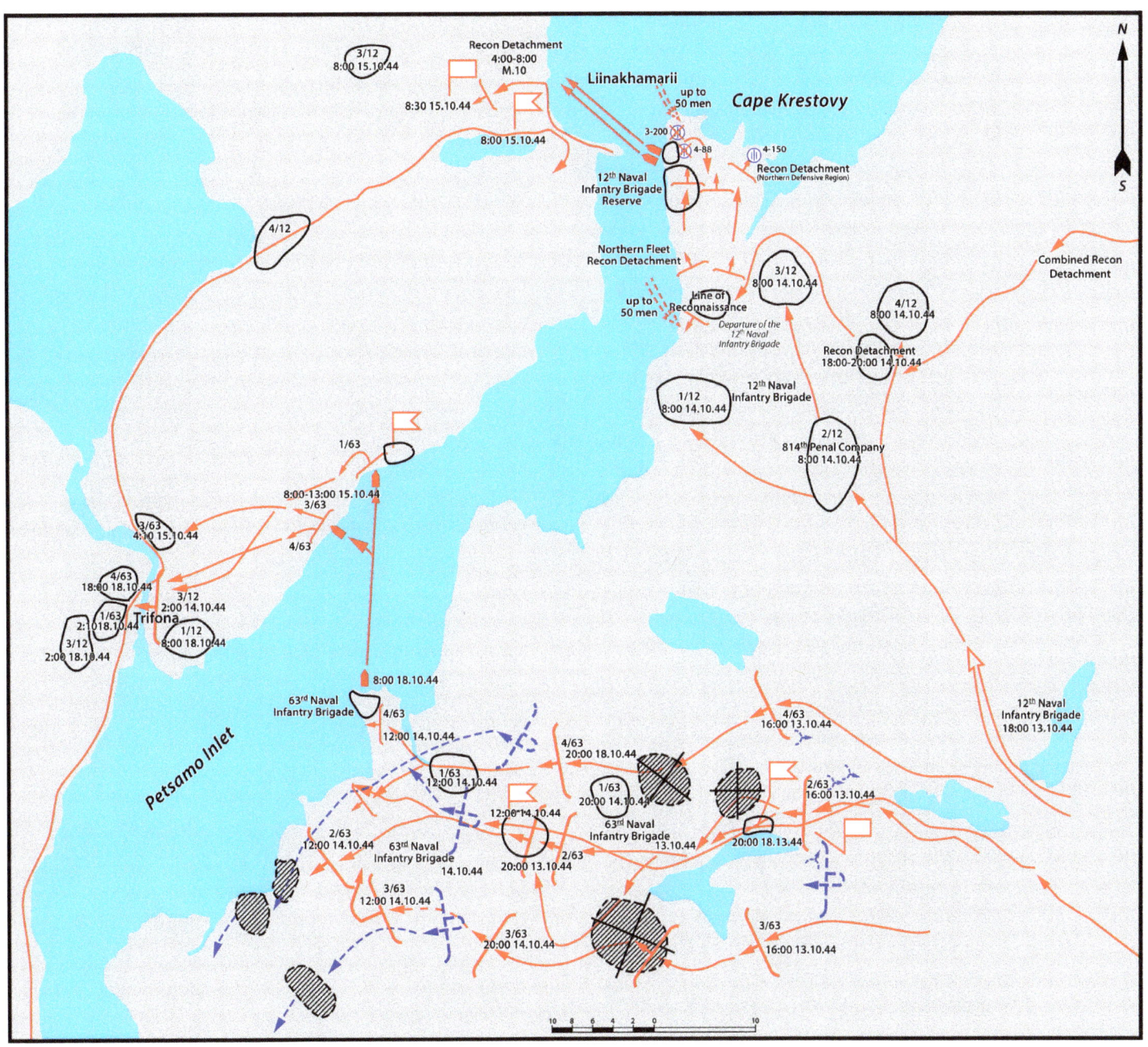

FIGURE 5.11. Pursuit of the enemy by Northern Defensive Region units

4. Actions Against Sea Lines of Communication

During preparations for the conduct of the operation for the liberation of the Soviet far north, Northern Fleet headquarters gave special attention to actions by the fleet for the disruption of the enemy's sea lines of communication. In resolving this issue, it was taken into consideration that because our offensive would develop on the mainland, the enemy would be forced to employ the sea as their main line of communication. Only by sea could the Germans carry out a rapid and massive transfer of reserves toward the front line or, if necessary, conduct the evacuation of retreating forces and valuable supplies from the mainland.

Based on the fleet commander's decision, missions for the disruption of enemy shipping were specified for the Fleet Air Forces, Torpedo Cutter Brigade, and Submarine Brigade. In addition, it was planned to use the Surface Squadron if conditions were favorable.

CHAPTER V: EXECUTION OF THE ASSIGNED MISSIONS   61

Thus, the organization and composition of the designated forces made it possible to maintain control with strikes by the fleet against enemy shipping in the sector from the southern ports of Varangerfjord to Hammerfest meridian.

Taking overall control of this operation upon himself, the fleet commander delegated the necessary operational independence to his principal deputies, restricting them only by their areas of responsibilities. Thus, Fleet Air Forces received approval to operate across the entire length of the sea route from Hammerfest to the southern ports of Varangerfjord. Its targets were specific convoys and lone ships at sea, concentrations of shipping in ports, and harbor installations.

Submarine Brigade was given the area from Hammerfest to Vardo. In this zone, our own forces were forbidden to attack any submarine that they detected, to avoid mistakes.

The area of Varangerfjord up to Vardo was designated as the operational zone for Torpedo Cutter Brigade. Here the torpedo cutters had complete freedom of action, operating independently or with attached Fleet Air Forces in close support (figure 5.12).

The subsequent course of events confirmed the correctness of the decision that was made. Air strikes against enemy shipping gathered in harbors and convoys at sea, the aggressive actions of the torpedo cutters in Varangerfjord, and the submarines to the north and northwest of Vardo all inflicted heavy losses on enemy transport shipping and naval assets.

The combined efforts of all these fleet formations resulted in the sinking of 156 ships with a net tonnage of 139,000 tons during the operation. Of these, 26 were transports and tankers, 3 destroyer escorts, 29 patrol ships and minesweepers, 18 patrol cutters of various types, 12 fast assault barges, and 68 motorized launches and other light craft. Three transports, one destroyer escort, one patrol ship, and two minesweepers were believed sunk. Four destroyer escorts, nine patrol ships and minesweepers, five self-propelled barges, one patrol cutter, 19 transports, and seven motorized launches or other light craft were substantially damaged.[25]

The scale of enemy losses in ships and naval assets gives the basis to conclude that German losses in human and materiel costs were also equally impressive. Thus, the results of the Northern Fleet's actions at sea were a legitimate complement to the successful operations of our forces and amphibious attacks on the land front.

A. ACTIONS OF THE SURFACE SQUADRON

In accordance with the combat directive of the commander of the Northern Fleet No. 0052/*op* of 1 October 1944, the Northern Fleet Surface Squadron had the following mission: conduct strikes on enemy convoys in shipping lanes in the area from Vardo to Nordkin, employing four destroyers acting independently during nonflying weather and with air cover during flying weather.

Because of the situation that developed during the operation, the destroyers went to sea in search of enemy ships only once, on the night of 25–26 October. During the day on 15 October, air reconnaissance confirmed that the enemy was conducting a hurried evacuation of troops from the coastlines of Naydenfjord [and] Bugfjord, and from the areas of Capes Korsnes and Vardo. Our air activity against enemy ship concentrations in Bugfjord and Vardo port were limited due to bad flying weather. Air reconnaissance did not detect any large enemy vessels in Varangerfjord.

On 25 October, fleet commander Admiral Golovko orally passed to Rear Admiral Fokin, Surface Squadron commander, the following missions:

- Conduct a search in the sector from Vardo to Tanafjord on the night of 25–26 October with one destroyer escort division, to destroy enemy combat vessels and transports;
- the ships participating in the search are to shell Vardo port at dawn on 26 October, with the goal to destroy the port and destroy enemy combat vessels, transports, and other vessels.

The destroyer escorts were forbidden to operate south of the line Vardo to Cape Vaytolakhti. Our submarines at sea were informed concerning the destroyer escorts' area of operations. The plan contained a provision for fighter support from Pummanki airfield to fly cover over the destroyer escorts beginning at dawn on 26 October. In addition, eight torpedo cutters were placed on 30-minute standby at Pummanki for additional support.

---

25 These enemy losses are taken from Northern Fleet staff documents, and to date have not been verified from other sources. As a result, there may be discrepancies.—Translator

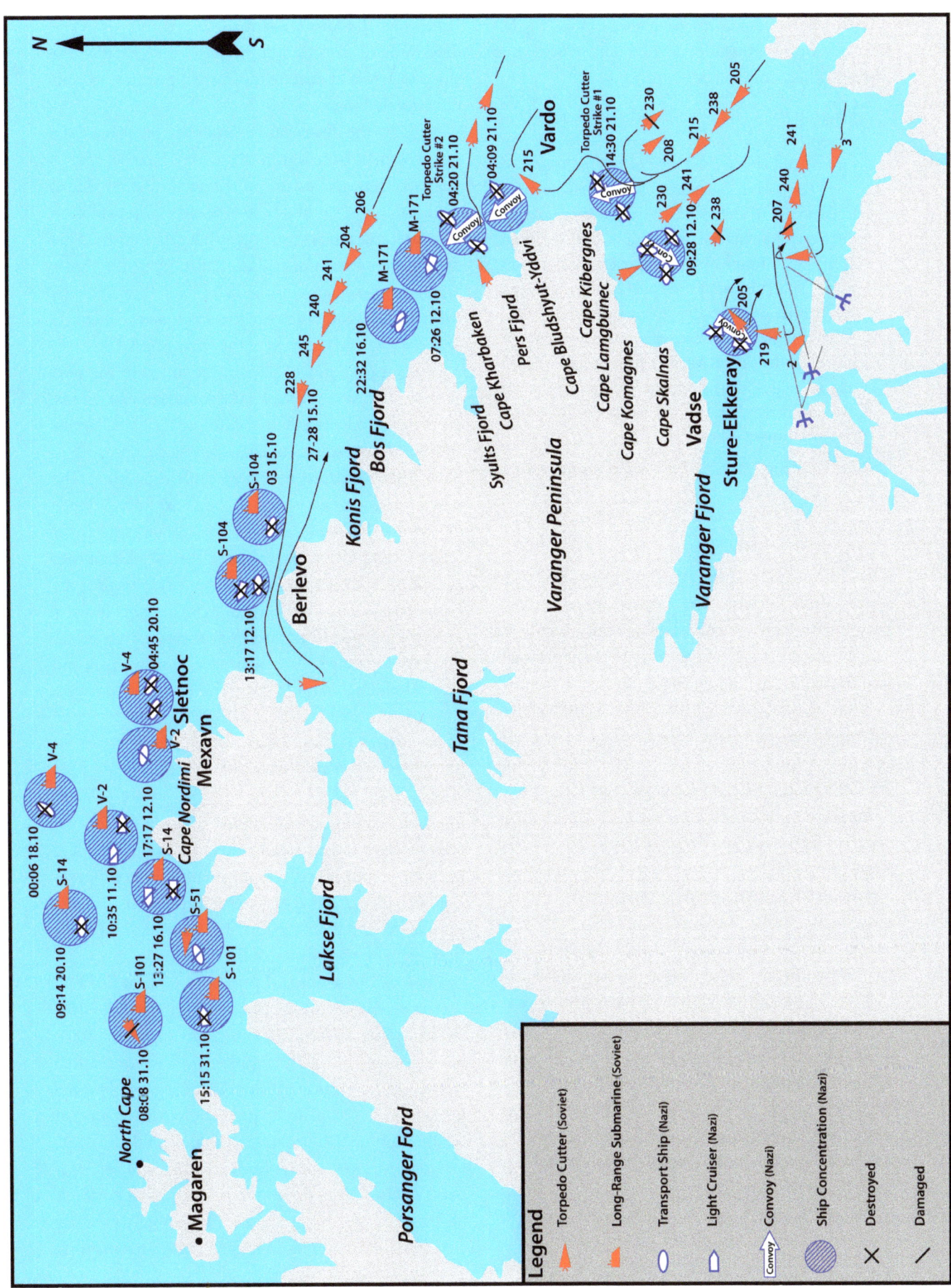

FIGURE 5.12. Submarine and torpedo cutter actions against enemy sea lines of communication

In the refinement of his assigned mission, the Surface Squadron commander devised the following plan, which the fleet commander approved:

1. Flagship *Baku*, destroyer escorts *Razumnyy*, *Gremyashchiy*, and *Razyarennyy* are to deploy at 2000 on 25 October and conduct a search in the area of Cape Harbaken–Tanafjord–Cape Harbaken prior to 0400 on 26 October. The search is to be conducted employing radar apparatus *SF-1*, deployed astern, at a range of 4–4.5 nautical miles from shore. Speed is set at 20 knots in transit to the search area, and 15 knots during the search.
2. After completion of the search, the detachment is to shell the port at Vardo from a range of 6.5–7 nautical miles, also using radar. Shore fires should be concentrated and controlled in the following two groupings:

   first group—flagship *Baku* and destroyer escort *Razumnyy*;
   second group—destroyer escorts *Gremyashchiy* and *Razyarennyy*.

The rate of ammunition expenditure was established at 40 rounds per gun. The Surface Squadron commander conducted a tactical game with his subordinate commanders and officers prior to the deployment, with the theme "Actions on enemy sea lines of communication." Special training exercises were conducted for radar operators and experienced gunners, using radar data to fire upon target panels, on the flagship *Baku*, which was equipped with radars *SF-1* and *284-M4*.

The flagship *Baku* (with the Surface Squadron commander's flag) [and] destroyer escorts *Razumnyy*, *Gremyashchiy* (with the broad pennant of the First Division commander), and *Razyarennyy* departed Kola Inlet at 2000 on 25 October, and took a course initially to the north, later turning westward toward the western sector. The weather favored the mission: west wind at force 5, sea at force 3, and visibility up to 1.5 nautical miles.

At 0019 on 26 October, approaching 70°32' north, 31°08' east, the destroyer escorts lay on course 230 degrees, and began a radar search for enemy ships. They were unable to detect any enemy ships. At 0347, when they had come even with Berlevog, the ships turned in the opposite direction and headed for Vardo, to carry out their shelling of the port.

During the transit they were able to use *Baku*'s *SF-1* and *284-M4* radar equipment for navigational purposes. During the movement from Kongsfjord to Cape Harbaken, the *SF-1* radar made it possible always to determine the position of the ships. This enabled the ships to arrive at exactly the correct position to conduct the shelling.

At 0639, the destroyer escorts were positioned 8.2 nautical miles from Vardo Island, on a bearing of 171.5 degrees. They opened fire on the port while moving at 16 knots. In three minutes, they noted a large explosion on shore, and at 0643 two enemy batteries returned fire on the ships from Cape Bludshyut-udden and Vardo. The destroyer escorts immediately were bracketed by the falling rounds and began to take evasive maneuvers to lessen the effectiveness of the enemy fires.

Four large spouts of flame were noted in the port at 0656, followed in time by the sounds of explosions. The ships conducted their shelling against area targets with the aid of artillery radar, which made it possible to place highly accurate fires even while zigzagging. The destroyer escorts expended 597 high explosive rounds during the shelling.

The ships turned toward base at 0718 and arrived at Kola Inlet at 1045 with no losses or damage. They observed the flames of the fires in Vardo port from 25 miles during their withdrawal. As subsequent reconnaissance data revealed, three moorages, a fishing boat, and several buildings in the town had been heavily damaged.

B. ACTIONS OF RED BANNER TORPEDO CUTTER BRIGADE

The commander of Red Banner Torpedo Cutter Brigade received the mission to interrupt enemy shipping lanes in Varangerfjord, independently and in cooperation with Fleet Air Forces. Twelve torpedo cutters were assembled in the forward base at Pummanki for this mission by the beginning of the operation.

The brigade command post was deployed to Hill 200 on Sredniy Peninsula, along with the mobile staff, on 8 October. Command and control of the cutters' activities against enemy shipping lanes were executed from here. Even during the preparatory period for the operation, the torpedo boats actively participated in the disruption of German shipping. A total of 87 cutters took part in 17 sorties from 3 September to 6 October. Twenty-four of these cutters were laying mines. A destroyer escort, two patrol ships, two minesweepers, a self-propelled amphibious barge, and three transports were sunk because of all these efforts.

The frequency of employment of the torpedo cutters against enemy shipping increased significantly with the beginning of the operation. Ninety boats took part in 23 sorties from 7 to 31 October. Four of these sorties (21 cutters) were carried out in coordination with night air reconnaissance. On most occasions, information gained by air reconnaissance served as the latest intelligence for departing patrols. In three cases, patrols sortied based on data from communications intelligence, and cutters deployed for at-large searches on seven occasions.

The enemy lost 10 transport ships and combat vessels, with a combined tonnage of 28,350 tons, because of these actions by our torpedo cutters. The most instructive mission characteristic of these actions are described below.

Attack on an Enemy Convoy in the Vicinity of Cape Komagnes on the Night of 11–12 October 1944

At 1420 on 11 October, our air reconnaissance detected an enemy convoy of three transports and 10–12 escorts, moving toward Varangerfjord ports. The Torpedo Cutter Brigade received the mission to conduct an attack against this convoy. Four groups of cutters were designated. Coordinating between themselves, they were to conduct a search and then destroy the convoy. The weather favored the mission: southwest wind at force 2, sea at force 1, and visibility up to 2,000 yards.

The first group, consisting of torpedo cutters Nos. *230*, *238*, *241*, and *246*, commanded by Third Division commander Captain Second Rank Alekseev, set out from Pummanki to the area of Lille Ekkere–Stursher at 1910 on 11 October. This group had the mission to conduct a search for the convoy with the aid of radar carried aboard *TKA-230* and attack the convoy in coordination with two *Il-4* illumination aircraft.[26]

At 2100, upon arrival of the group in the search area, *TKA-230* turned on its radar apparatus, and at 2140 the illumination aircraft began the illumination of the search area using *SAB* (parachute flares). Because there had been no prior rehearsal of the use of illumination aircraft in conjunction with torpedo boats, the *SAB* were dropped in a tactically ineffective manner. Sometimes even our own boats were illuminated, which forced them to hide behind their own smoke screens. This abnormal situation led to increased radio traffic between the torpedo boats and aircraft, which was a factor in the violation in the security of the operation.

The brigade commander was forced to impose restrictions on radio transmissions from his command post, and he ordered the aircraft to return to base. The torpedo cutters continued to search on their own. At 2224, *TKA-230* reported the radar detection of the silhouettes of two large and two small ships to the northeast at a range of 6.0 nautical miles. Six minutes later, moving toward the shore, *TKA-230* became convinced that it had mistakenly taken Cape Langbunes, whose terrain relief appeared as several separate silhouettes on the radar screen, for the silhouettes of the ships. The cutter's commander immediately reported, "I do not see the ships." At that moment, *TKA-246*, not even having attempted to identify the target, surged forward and fired a salvo of two torpedoes at rocks, taking them to be enemy ships. The remaining cutters stayed on a course of 60 degrees and continued to search along the shore.

At 2330, *TKA-246* received an order from the shore command post to return to base, and it safely arrived at Pummanki at 0125 on 12 October.

At 0012 on 12 October, when it was near Cape Komagnes, *TKA-230* detected several ship silhouettes by radar at a range of 3.5 nautical miles. Captain Second Rank Alekseev made the decision to attack the enemy from shoreward. At 0021, *TKA-230* reported that the convoy was moving on a course of 240–250 degrees, 1,600 yards from the cutters (the cutters' course currently was 130 degrees). Three minutes later, the cutter visually detected six ship silhouettes, among them one large transport of 6,000–8,000 tons displacement. In addition, there were numerous enemy escort cutters.

At 0028, *TKA-238*, commanded by Lieutenant Nikitin, with his division commander aboard, fired two torpedoes at a large transport at a range of 400 yards and course of 95 degrees off the starboard bow. The torpedo boat then immediately turned to a course parallel to the convoy and laid down a smoke screen. A powerful explosion was observed in the bow section of the transport 30 seconds later.

Enemy escort cutters began a persistent pursuit of *TKA-238*. Finally, after breaking through two picket

---

26 The *Ilyushin Il-4* was a twin-engine bomber and torpedo bomber, developed from the *Ilyushin DB-3*. It was powered by a pair of 14-cylinder, two-row, air-cooled radial engines, which gave it a maximum speed of 250 mph and a range of 1,400 miles with a 1,000 kg bomb load. Armament included two 7.62 mm machine guns, one in the nose and the other in the ventral turret. It also had a 12.7 mm machine gun mounted in the dorsal hatch. Its maximum payload was a single 940 kg torpedo or up to 2,700 kg bombs or mines. Translator.

lines, the cutter managed to elude the pursuit near Cape Skalnes at 0046. *TKA-238* took eight hits from 20 mm and 37 mm shells. The crew lost two men killed and six wounded, including the division navigator, Senior Lieutenant Motrokhov.

Two other cutters, *TKA-230* (commanded by Senior Lieutenant Kosovnin) and *TKA-241* (commanded by Captain-Lieutenant Sherstyuk), attacked the enemy after *TKA-238*. *TKA-230* sunk a transport displacing approximately 5,000 tons, and *TKA-241* another transport displacing 4,000 tons. After their attack, these torpedo boats were subjected to intense pursuit by enemy escort vessels, from which they managed to break off at 0035.

At 0230 on 12 October, torpedo boats Nos. *238* and *241* returned to Pummanki, while the Torpedo Cutter Brigade commander ordered *TKA-230* to remain in the search area to guide the second and third groups of torpedo cutters to the enemy.

The second group of cutters, consisting of *TKA-205* and *TKA-219*, under the command of First Division commander Captain Third Rank Fedorov, was positioned near Bekfjord. Employing intercepts of radio conversations from within the first group, Captain Third Rank Fedorov decided to move northward, closer to the engagement area. At 0020 on 12 October, he observed gunfire, on the basis of which he determined the convoy's location.

His force observed illumination rounds and tracers of two German escort ships on the horizon in the Lille Ekkere area at 0035. At 0037, *TKA-219*, commanded by Captain-Lieutenant Rodionov and with Captain Third Rank Fedorov aboard, suddenly launched two torpedoes at an enemy escort vessel at a range of 300 yards, 60 degrees on the port bow. Two minutes later, *TKA-205*, commanded by Lieutenant Direnko, attacked the other escort vessel, after which both cutters began to withdraw toward base. The cutters visually observed the explosions of their torpedoes and the sinking of the enemy ships. These undetected and successful attacks were made possible by the fact that the Germans' attention had been diverted by the actions of the torpedo boats of the first group. Both cutters returned to base at 0245.

During the combat engagements with the enemy of the cutters of the first and second groups, the third group, comprised of *TKA-226* and *TKA-244*, under the command of First Division's Second Detachment commander, Senior Lieutenant Palamarchuk, was conducting a search in the area of Petsamovuono Inlet and Kobbholmfjord. Orientating on the intercepted radio traffic of the first group's cutters, Senior Lieutenant Palamarchuk sought out the head of the convoy in the area of the entrance to Kirkenes. But, due to a faulty compass, he lost his position and could not find the convoy.

At 0122 on 12 October, the fourth group, consisting of torpedo cutters Nos. *114* and *116*, commanded by First Division's First Detachment commander, Hero of the Soviet Union Captain-Lieutenant Shabalin, set out to intercept the convoy under attack in the Cape Komagnes area. All attempts by *TKA-230* to vector the third and fourth groups to the convoy were unsuccessful, and at 0456 the brigade commander ordered all cutters to return to base. All cutters had arrived back at Pummanki by 0710.

As a result of all engagements during the search for the convoy moving to Kirkenes, the enemy losses were as follows: a transport displacing 6,000–8,000 tons (sunk by *TKA-238*), a transport displacing 4,000–5,000 tons (sunk by *TKA-230*), a transport displacing approximately 4,000 tons (sunk by *TKA-241*), and two escort vessels (sunk by *TKA-204* and *TKA-219*).

Attack on an Enemy Convoy in the Area of Cape Kibergnes on the Night of 20–21 October

During the day on 20 October, air reconnaissance detected the movement of an enemy convoy from Tanafjord to Varangerfjord. At 2205 of that day, on orders from the brigade commander, torpedo cutters Nos. *237* and *244*, commanded by Captain Third Rank Kholin, departed Pummanki for the Lille Ekkere Island area. Their mission was to search for the enemy close to the shoreline, attack them, and then vector subsequent groups of cutters into the target area. The zone of actions of this group extended to Havningberg.

Illumination aircraft flew out to the search area at the same time. At 2330, another group of torpedo cutters, Nos. *205*, *215*, and *230*, reached this same area, but bounded on the north by a line parallel to Cape Kibergnes. This group, commanded by Captain Third Rank Efimov on *TKA-230*, was equipped with a radar set.

Shortly after the arrival of the second group, the brigade command post received intelligence data that an enemy convoy consisting of a sailing vessel displacing 4,000 tons, with two tugboats, three transports, three minesweepers, and a number of small vessels, had set out from Bekfjord toward the north at 1930. Both groups of cutters were quickly vectored toward this convoy by radio.

At 0130 on 21 October, *TKA-230* detected the convoy on radar near Cape Kibergnes. There were seven large ships and 6–8 escorts, moving close to the shoreline. At the moment of detection, the torpedo cutters were 5.0–5.5 nautical miles distant from the convoy.

Captain Third Rank Kholin's group, lacking radar, searched for the convoy in the Vardo area. At 0145, cutters Nos. *205*, *215*, and *230* managed to execute an undetected sternward approach to the enemy convoy. However, the cutters were detected and attacked by enemy escort ships and cutters during their attempt to penetrate the escort screen.

Despite this, at 0148 *TKA-230* launched two torpedoes at an escort vessel from a range of 400–600 yards, sharply increased speed from 18 to 33 knots, threw off smoke dischargers, and moved out from under intensive enemy shelling at a zigzag. The radar set was disabled by a 37 mm hit on the cutter during this withdrawal. This prevented the subsequent employment of the radar for vectoring the remaining cutters to the convoy.

Close on the heels of *TKA-230*, Lieutenant Direnko's *TKA-205* fired torpedoes on the lead escort vessel or minesweeper and then also evaded pursuit. The cutter commanders observed their targets' sinking. Enemy ships, having mistaken one of their own escort cutters for our torpedo cutters, subjected it to intense interlocking fires.

TKA-215, commanded by Senior Lieutenant Kuznetsov, made three unsuccessful attempts to attack the enemy convoy. The enemy escort force was taking extremely active countermeasures. Shortly thereafter, the brigade command post ordered *TKA-215* to proceed to the Persfjord area and there link up with Captain Third Rank Kholin's group. Both of the other cutters returned safely to base by 0355.

TKA-215, proceeding toward the rendezvous with Kholin's group, at 0402 detected a convoy at a range of approximately 2,000 yards to seaward near Cape Bludshyut-udden. Senior Lieutenant Kuznetsov closed on the trailing ship, which he believed was a minesweeper, and attacked it at 0409 at a range of 300 yards. After the strike of its torpedo on the target, the cutter increased speed, covered itself with a smoke screen, and evaded the shells coming from the escort vessels that pursued it for 17 minutes.

At the same time, Captain Third Rank Kholin's group, *TKA-237* and *TKA-244*, had reached Cape Segludden. At 0410, it detected enemy ships moving into Persfjord. This was the convoy that had moved out of Bekfjord and had already been attacked by Captain Third Rank Efimov's group of cutters.

Ten minutes later, *TKA-244*, commanded by Lieutenant Todorov and with Captain Third Rank Kholin aboard, and right behind it *TKA-237*, commanded by Captain-Lieutenant Shulyakovskiy, attacked and sank two trailing transports. After the attack, the cutters were subjected to pursuit. But, employing their maximum speed and covering themselves with a smoke screen, they broke contact with the enemy and safely returned to port by 0435.

Thus, active measures by all five cutters that were conducting the search resulted in the sinking of two enemy transports and two minesweepers or escort vessels. Three successive successful attacks against the same convoy, conducted over the course of 2 hours 33 minutes, affirmed the effectiveness of placing several groups of torpedo cutters, with 3–4 boats in each group, along the convoy's general course.

In addition to these described incidences of attacks on enemy convoys, there was an attempt by a group of eight torpedo cutters to conduct a foray into Tanafjord on the night of 27–28 October. Reconnaissance had noted a large collection of combat vessels, including two light cruisers, and transports. The torpedo boat raid on Tanafjord, which was 120 miles from the Pummanki base, was carried out without success. The cutter crews were insufficiently trained for such operations, lacked precise information concerning the locations of the enemy ships, knowledge of operational procedures, and the aviation and surface vessel support essential for such operations. The cutters that were searching with radar sets for the enemy vessels were detected by enemy patrol craft, could not penetrate into Tanafjord, and were unable to carry out an inspection of several small fjords in which enemy ships were concealed.

C. ACTIONS OF RED BANNER SUBMARINE BRIGADE

The following missions were given to the commander, Submarine Brigade, for the operation:

- With 6–8 submarines deployed along the northern coastline of Norway from Vardo to longitude

20°00′ east, disrupt enemy sea lines of communication and protect the movement of Allied convoy *RA-61* against possible enemy surface fleet attack;
- Maintain two submarines at the main base in readiness to deploy as the fleet command's reserve.

In response to these assigned missions, and in accordance with his operational strength, the brigade commander decided to prolong the time at sea of earlier-deployed submarines *S-51* and *V-2*,[27] to the full extent of their provisions or until they had expended all their torpedoes. In addition, measures were taken for the preparation of other submarines for participation in the operation, to increase the number of vessels in positions to the quantity specified by the fleet commander.

The deployment of submarines in conjunction with the operational plan was begun on 8 October. During the period 8–28 October, the following submarines were deployed successively: *S-104*, *M-171* (two sorties), *S-102*, *S-14*, *V-4*,[28] *L-20*, and *S-101*. Six submarines from this list were deployed in the sector Cape Nordkin to Vardo, and a seventh (*L-20*) took up a position near the coast between 20° and 23° east longitude.

In this operation, Northern Fleet did not employ any new methods in command, control, and utilization of submarines that differed from those already developed in earlier periods of the war. Command and control of submarines at sea was totally concentrated in the hands of the brigade commander, located with his staff at the main base. A sufficiently broad maneuver zone was designated for each submarine deployed at sea. In the event a boat commander detected an enemy convoy or was closing in for an attack on the basis of intelligence data, he was given the right to enter his neighbor's maneuver zone.

The safety of a submarine from attack by our own vessels in its designated zone was achieved by a prohibition on attacks there against any detected submarines. Submarines were to launch their attacks only upon personal visual and hydroacoustical observation in their designated maneuver zone or based on data received from jointly operating air reconnaissance.

To receive air reconnaissance data in a timely manner, all submarines were instructed to proceed out of visual observation of the coast during daylight hours, maneuver on the surface, and conduct continuous monitoring of air reconnaissance radio channels. If for any reason they could not remain on the surface during this activity, the submarines were required to run submerged at antenna depth for the first 10 minutes of each hour, when shore-based radio transmitters would provide summarized intelligence data for them.

When air reconnaissance could not be conducted, the brigade commander directed the submarines toward the shore by special order to conduct independent searches for targets. This briefly described method of employing submarines, in combination with the excellent tactical training of boat commanders and their adequate knowledge of the area of their combat operations, permitted them to achieve good results in their efforts against enemy sea lines of communication.

The actions of each individual submarine are described below.

Submarine *S-51*, commanded by Captain Third Rank Kolosov, sailed to the Porsangerfjord area on 24 September 1944. The submarine patrolled in its designated area from 26 September to 11 October and returned safely to base on the morning of 13 October.

During his stay in this area, the commander systematically received information from air reconnaissance, both directly from the reconnaissance aircraft itself and from the brigade staff. However, he was unable to take advantage of the majority of this data, due to the great distance to the detected targets. Only one time did Captain Third Rank Kolosov make the decision to set course toward shore for a search and attack on a convoy. At 0103 on 7 October, he received a radio-telegram from the brigade operations staff duty officer, indicating that communications intelligence had detected an enemy convoy in the Sture-Ekkere area, moving east.

Upon its arrival on the coastal shipping lane, the submarine came up to a depth of 15 meters and, maneuvering at slow speed, began continuous acoustical watch. The sonarman detected the noise of enemy minesweeper screws three times between 0600 and 0755, but an inspection of the horizon in the periscope in visibility up to 4.0 nautical miles revealed nothing. The commander again submerged to a depth of 15 meters.

---

27 The *V-2* was the former British submarine *Unbroken*, turned over in Lend-Lease to a Northern Fleet crew in Newcastle on 30.05.44 [30 May 1944] and sailed to Murmansk. Berezhnoy, *Flot SSSR*, p. 18.—Translator

28 The *V-4* was the former British submarine *Ursala*, also turned over in Lend-Lease to a Northern Fleet crew in Newcastle on 30.05.44 [30 May 1944] and sailed to Murmansk. Berezhnoy, *Flot SSSR*, p. 19.—Translator

At 1135 the sonarman again heard the noise of a ship. This time, ascent to periscope depth and inspection revealed the silhouette of a ship. Visibility had lessened from 4.0 nautical miles to low visibility, due to the passage of a fog bank on the surface of the sea. The commander gave the signal for torpedo attack and began maneuvering to close with the believed enemy convoy.

Later, not one silhouette, but three enemy escort vessels were noted in the periscope. Temporarily losing contact with the enemy, the submarine continued to close, intending to attack not the escort vessels, but the more valuable targets in the suspected convoy.

The crew was unable to detect any other ships, however, and at 1214 the commander gave the order to stand down from the torpedo attack.

Dwelling for a moment on this partial example, one cannot but note that the commander conducted the entire search in this area in an extremely indecisive manner. The repeated detection of the sound of ship propellers evoked an exceptionally inert response from the commander.

His refusal to attack the three escort vessels, on the belief that more valuable targets would be detected, remains completely unconvincing, the more so because measures were not taken for an energetic search for the anticipated convoy. The submarine remained in the immediate vicinity of the escort vessels, the search for the convoy was called off, and the torpedo attack was canceled.

On the night of 9–10 October, after a period of charging batteries away from the coastline, the boat commander made the decision to move to the Laksefjord area and search there for the enemy in the coastal shipping lane. Upon arriving in the designated area, the submarine came up to a depth of 15 meters and, maneuvering across the fjord entrance at slow speed, began continuous hydroacoustic monitoring.

Visibility was 5.0 nautical miles at 0800, and the sea and winds were both at force 5.

At 0925, the sonarman detected the noise of the screws of a motorized launch. Eight minutes later, during a subsequent scanning of the horizon in the periscope, the commander observed a low-flying enemy aircraft of the *Arado* type,[29] on a bearing of 150 degrees.

A short time later, the sonarman again reported ship noises, and at 1014 an enemy minesweeper was seen in the periscope at a bearing of 258 degrees. There appeared to be a convoy immediately beyond the minesweeper. At 1018, the composition of the convoy was determined. There were two transports of 7,000–8,000 tons displacement each, destroyer escort, escort vessel, and minesweeper. The convoy was moving on a changing course, generally eastward, at a speed of 10 knots.

Having detected the enemy, the commander began to maneuver for a torpedo attack on the lead transport. At 1057, the submarine commander attacked the transport with four type *ET-80* torpedoes from a range of 1,500 yards, fired at an impact angle of 130 degrees with a time interval of 10 seconds. One minute later, two explosions were felt in the submarine, followed 45 seconds later by a third.

The commander of *S-51* raised his periscope seven minutes after launching his torpedoes. During an inspection of the horizon, he determined that the transport he had attacked was burning and, it appeared, dead in the water. The enemy destroyer escort was not visible on the surface. It was obvious that the first two torpedoes struck and sank the destroyer escort that was on the target line of the transport. The third torpedo had exploded in the hull of the transport.

The commander was unable to conduct a second attack on the convoy due to pursuit of his submarine by enemy escort vessels. The fate of the damaged transport remained unknown.

After this attack, *S-51* did not have any other enemy sightings. At 2127 on 11 October, the submarine received the brigade commander's order to return to base. *S-51* safely returned to Polyarnoye on the morning of 13 October.

Submarine *V-2*, commanded by Captain-Lieutenant Shchekin, set out for the Cape Nordkin–Cape Sletnes area on the evening of 30 September. This submarine remained in its designated area from 2 to 12 October, after which the brigade commander ordered it back to base.

During the patrol of its zone, the submarine received a large quantity of information by radio from the brigade staff concerning the movement of enemy convoys and individual ships. The commander attempted to take

---

29 This was probably an Arado Ar-196, a low-wing monoplane float plane, the standard shipboard-launched reconnaissance aircraft of the German Navy. It had a two-man crew (pilot, observer), and was powered by a 9-cylinder, air-cooled radial engine; the aircraft was thus made capable of 193 mph speed and a range of 670 miles. It was armed with two 7.92 mm machine guns and two forward-firing 20 mm cannons. It could also carry a 50-kilogram bomb load.—Translator

advantage of a portion of this information and based on it, set off for the suspected location of a convoy. Thus, for example, at 0615 on 9 October, when the submarine was in a holding position some 40 miles to the north of Cape Nordkin, the commander received a radio message concerning the movement of an enemy convoy in the Cape Nordkin area, on a southeastward course.

The commander made the decision to close with the enemy and attack him. His calculations showed that he could intercept the convoy only in the Vardo area.

Employing surface speed, the submarine reached the enemy's coastal shipping lane north of Vardo by 0336 on 10 October. Positioned in this area and maneuvering on changing course, the commander conducted a search until 0520 and, unable to find the enemy, set a course for return to his designated area.

He was unsuccessful in intercepting the convoy in the Vardo area, it seems, because the calculated speed of the enemy—eight knots—turned out to be considerably low. The submarine, on the other hand, could make only 10.7 knots, and therefore arrived at the intercept point too late.

On the morning of 11 October, *V-2* was positioned two miles from the shore in the Cape Nordkin area and maneuvering, awaiting the enemy at a depth of 50 feet. The boat was conducting continuous sonar watch. The commander was ascending to periscope depth at 10-minute intervals to inspect the horizon. The visibility was good; the sea and wind were up to force 4.

At 1014, the sonarman on duty reported the noise of ships' screws on a bearing of 143 degrees. The submarine ascended to periscope depth one minute later, and the commander observed an enemy convoy on the bearing noted by the sonarman. The convoy contained one transport, two escort vessels, two minesweepers, and one escort cutter. The convoy was moving eastward along the shore at a speed of 10 knots.

V-2 began to maneuver for an attack on the transport. The submarine took up a firing position 20 minutes after detecting the convoy, and the commander attacked with four torpedoes, [and] fired at the transport from the forward tubes with a time interval of seven seconds, an attack angle of 110 degrees, at a range of 3,000 yards.

Immediately after the attack, *V-2* began to maneuver to break off from enemy contact, and after two minutes the crew clearly heard the explosions of three torpedoes. They immediately initiated pursuit by enemy escort vessels prevented the *V-2*'s commander from visually observing the results of the attack.

He was able to raise his periscope at 1048, 13 minutes after firing the torpedoes. On the horizon he noted an enemy transport, a minesweeper, an escort vessel, and an escort cutter proceeding eastward. One minesweeper and one escort vessel were nowhere to be seen. Our air reconnaissance that was positioned in this same area reported the sinking of one escort vessel displacing 800 tons. The fact of the sinking of the minesweeper remained unconfirmed.

On the following morning, after a night of recharging batteries, *V-2* again approached the shore. Excellent visibility made observation by periscope possible, but complete calm forced the commander, as on the previous night, to hold a depth of 50 feet, conduct continuous hydroacoustic watch, and only periodically come up to periscope depth.

During the day, the sonarman reported the noise of the screws of single motor launches several times; however, a search of the horizon in the periscope revealed nothing. At 1555, during a routine raising of the periscope, the commander noted smoke and an aircraft above the horizon on a bearing of 110 degrees.

Twenty-five minutes later, the range to the convoy, which was proceeding eastward, had been reduced so much that it was already possible to make out in the periscope one transport displacing approximately 3,000 tons, one minesweeper, and one escort vessel. It was not possible to identify the convoy's other ships.

Enemy aircraft flew cover above the convoy, which in a calm sea significantly encumbered a submarine's actions. Having evaluated the situation, the *V-2*'s commander made the decision to delay the attack somewhat and take advantage of approaching nightfall.

At 1716, the submarine launched four torpedoes at the transport from a range of 3,600 yards, with a time interval of nine seconds, and a calculated impact angle of 100 degrees. After launching the torpedoes, the submarine lay on course for breaking contact with the enemy. Two minutes later, the explosions of two torpedoes were clearly felt, after which the noise of the transport's screws, which had been clearly distinguishable with onboard equipment, immediately ceased.

The commander was unable to verify the results of the attack by an inspection of the horizon, because even prior to the explosion of his torpedoes, the enemy aircraft and escort vessels had begun an intensive pursuit of his submarine. This pursuit continued until 1806.

During this time, the enemy dropped 43 depth charges, some of which inflicted insignificant damage to the submarine. *V-2* was able to elude the pursuit by maneuvering on changing speeds and courses at a depth of 50 feet, using its sonar gear to locate the enemy.

On the basis of the submarine crew's observation, and the effectiveness of the enemy's pursuit after the attack, one can project that the transport was probably sunk. However, no corroborating information was received. *V-2* did not have any other engagements after this attack on the convoy and returned safely to base on 14 October.

Guards Submarine *M-171*, commanded by Guards Captain-Lieutenant Kovalenko, carried out two combat sorties during the operation. *M-171* set out from the main base at Polyarnoye to the Cape Makkaur and Cape Harbaken area at 1900 on 9 October for action against the enemy's coastal shipping lane. The submarine was in its designated position by noon on 10 October. The commander began to search for the enemy, maneuvering submerged at a depth of 15–20 meters, periodically ascending to periscope depth to inspect the horizon. He maintained 2–3 miles from shore. The crew conducted continuous sonar watch while submerged.

The first day of searching bore no results. At 1644 on the second day, when the submarine was three miles east of Cape Harbaken, the sonarman reported the noise of ships' screws on a bearing of 292 degrees. Four minutes later, during a search of the horizon in the periscope, the commander observed the smoke of ships on that bearing. The convoy was moving on a southeast course, holding close to the shore. The commander of *M-171* began his attack.

At 1733 a transport was observed in the convoy, but the commander could not clearly identify other ships or the escort vessels, because the entire convoy was viewed against the backdrop of the high rocky coastline, and blended into it. Continuing to close in for the attack, at 1836 the commander noted that the transport and accompanying escorts were hiding in Syultefjord, toward which they had all made a sharp turn several miles earlier.

The submarine made no attempt to attack the enemy inside the fjord. Thirty minutes after the convoy entered Syultefjord, *M-171* departed the area and went out to sea to recharge its batteries. The hurried departure of the submarine from the Syultefjord area was entirely the fault of the commander. He should have remained near the fjord's entrance for at least two or three hours, anticipating that the convoy would remain in the fjord for a short time.

Upon completion of the battery recharge, *M-171* returned to the coastal area on the following morning and renewed its search. By 0500 visibility had reached 4,000 yards, and the wind was between force 1 and 2. Maintaining sonar watch, the submarine maneuvered at a depth of 15–20 meters, and periodically ascended to periscope depth.

At 0531, the sonarman reported the noise of screws of a patrol cutter on a bearing of 170 degrees. Five minutes later, a search of the horizon through the periscope revealed nothing in the predawn darkness. At 0646, the sonarman reported a new noise. This time he also heard a working diesel engine.

Although a search of the horizon did not yield results, the commander gave the order to prepare for a torpedo attack and changed course toward shore. A short time later, another look through the periscope revealed the silhouette of a ship on a bearing of 217 degrees. The commander began to maneuver the submarine into an attack position.

After 18 minutes of maneuvering, he was able to determine that an enemy convoy lay ahead of the submarine, traveling in two groups on a course of 320 degrees at a speed of eight knots. The first group was silhouetted against Cape Harbaken, and its composition could not be determined. The second group was clearly distinguishable and consisted of one transport and three escort vessels. The commander chose the transport as his target.

The submarine closed to within 2,000 yards of the target, and at 0726 fired two torpedoes with a time interval of 10 seconds at an angle of 110 degrees. At the moment he launched the torpedoes, the commander noted that the foremast of the transport was aligned with the aftmast of one of the escort vessels in the periscope.

After launching the torpedoes, the submarine did not hold at periscope depth, but began a steep dive. The commander took energetic measures to take the submarine down quickly while at reverse engines. The rapid descent and leveling did not permit the crew to immediately determine the results of their attack.

Only 12 minutes after launching torpedoes, *M-171* came up to periscope depth. On the surface they observed the transport and two escort vessels of the second group, proceeding on their previous course. The third escort vessel was not visible, perhaps sunk. The enemy escort vessels detected the submarine's presence and began a frantic pursuit of the *M-171*, periodically dropping depth charges. During the chase, which lasted until 1200, the enemy dropped as many as 50 depth charges, but did not inflict any damage.

By the morning of 13 October, the *M-171* had returned safely to base. The next day, after taking on torpedoes and replenishments, the submarine deployed on its second sortie to the same area. The commander twice observed the silhouettes of enemy ships on the morning of 16 October but could not launch torpedoes either time because of the large angle of attack.

With darkness already upon them as they were moving out to sea to their nighttime position, the crew of *M-171* received a radio message from brigade staff. A German convoy was moving to sea from Kirkenes harbor. The message indicated that the convoy of three transports, two escort vessels, and 12 escort cutters had departed the port at 1245, moving northward at a speed of 12 knots. The submarine, now out at sea, was ordered to attack the enemy convoy.

The commander of the *M-171* changed his earlier decision to move to the seaward side of his operating sector and decided to move as close as possible to shore. In this way, he could attack the enemy in conditions most favorable to himself. The submarine reached the shore area at 2022, and detected the convoy three minutes later. Remaining surfaced, the *M-171* took up a course to engage the enemy.

Having closed to within 2,000 yards of the enemy, the commander attacked with two torpedoes, launching them at a transport displacing 8,000–10,000 tons with a time interval of 10 seconds at an angle of 80 degrees. After launching torpedoes, the *M-171* turned about and rapidly flooded ballast tanks, not waiting for visual confirmation of the results of the attack. The boat's crew clearly heard the explosions of both torpedoes while submerging.

Although the sonarman heard the noise of ships' screws in the target area for a brief time, the submarine was not pursued. Bearing in mind that the torpedoes were launched toward the open sea, one must believe that the explosions were hits on the transport. It is likely, therefore, that the transport was sunk.

After the attacks on the convoy and the expenditure of its torpedoes, the *M-171* left its position and returned safely to Polyarnoye on 17 October.

Submarine *S-104*, commanded by Captain Second Rank Turaev, operated along the Norwegian coastline in the area from Tanafjord to Cape Sletnes from 10 to 22 October 1944. The submarine held 2–4 miles offshore at periscope depth during the day, but at night it moved closer to the shore, with only the conning tower above the surface. Captain Second Rank Turaev had two combat engagements with enemy ships and convoys during the period described.

At 1201 on 12 October, when the *S-104* was positioned near Cape Tanahorn, a convoy of two transports, [a] minesweeper, four escort ships, four cutters, and two self-propelled barges was observed through the periscope at 6.5 nautical miles. Four antisubmarine aircraft were escorting the convoy.

While the submarine was maneuvering into an attack position, our aircraft attacked the convoy from 1238 to 1240. After fending off these strikes, the convoy resumed movement on a course of 310 degrees. At 1305, the *S-104* lay on a course for attacking the lead transport. However, an escort ship, though it had not observed the submarine, interfered with the torpedo attack by its maneuvering. Diving beneath this ship, the *S-104* broke through the inner escort screen and at 1317 fired four noncontact torpedoes at the second transport, displacing 7,000 tons, and at an escort vessel from a range of 1,400 yards and an angle of 90 degrees with a time interval of eight seconds.

Eight minutes later, when the submarine ascended to periscope depth, there were remnants of the deck and mast, boats, and many men where the transport and escort vessel had sailed. Several minutes later, our torpedo bombers attacked the remaining part of the convoy. Their attack was again repelled by massed fires of the convoy's ships, and an antiaircraft battery from the Berlevog area.

At 1352, Captain Second Rank Turaev attempted to attack two escort ships that were conducting rescue efforts among the men of the sunken transport. He was unable to get into a firing position, and the ships increased speed and departed in the wake of the convoy.

The second meeting with the enemy took place on 15 October. At 0047, the *S-104* was maneuvering in the

Berlevog area on a course of 290 degrees with its conning tower above the surface. The submarine observed the silhouettes of three transports, a minesweeper, and three other ships, on a course 45 degrees to starboard at 1,000 yards moving toward the submarine.

The close distance and sharp course angle would not allow the use of the bow torpedo tubes. The submarine, maneuvering on electric motors, made a circular turn to the left to attack with the stern tubes. Coming to a course of 200 degrees, the commander fired a two-torpedo salvo at the lead transport from a range of 1,000 yards. The torpedoes missed the target. Captain Second Rank Turaev decided to catch up to the convoy and attack it again, but this time with bow torpedoes.

At 0103, the submarine was in position for the attack. At that moment, even before the command "Launch!" from the bow tubes was issued, the torpedo shot out of the tube. The transport, displacing 5,000 tons and apparently laden with ammunition, exploded with a great force and sank instantly.

A minute later, the S-104 was rapidly diving, and remained submerged until 0256, avoiding the pursuit of enemy escort vessels. Later the submarine surfaced and made its escape in conditions of low visibility. At 0957 on the following day, the submarine detected three enemy patrol vessels and a cutter at a range of five nautical miles, moving on a course of 310 degrees. The commander refrained from attacking due to the large angle of the enemy's course. After this, the S-104 had no further contact with the enemy and returned to base safely on 24 October.

Submarine S-14, commanded by Captain Third Rank Kalanin, arrived in the area bounded by Cape Kelsnering and Cape Nordkin on 15 October, where it remained until 20 October.

At 1301 on 16 October, while positioned 2.8 nautical miles from Cape Kelsnering, the submarine detected three enemy M-1 minesweepers, moving in a tight column formation on a course of 230–225 degrees. Several minutes later, the minesweepers lay on a course of 250 degrees. The S-14 began to maneuver for an attack, and at 1327 launched four torpedoes from a range of 1,200 yards, with an attack angle of 120 degrees and an interval of 10 seconds between torpedoes.

Through the periscope, Captain Third Rank Kalanin observed the strike of the torpedoes into two minesweepers, which quickly sank. The sounds of the torpedo explosions were heard throughout the boat. Following the sinking of the other two ships from the formation, the third minesweeper began to hunt for the submarine, dropping 30 depth charges over the course of two and one-half hours. At 1600 the submarine slipped away from its pursuer without damage.

The S-14 did not make any contact with the enemy over the next three days. At 1900 on 19 October, the commander was vectored by radio from base toward two convoys.

The first consisted of two transports, four escort vessels, and six unidentified ships, and had departed from Bekfjord at 1720 moving northward. The second convoy, consisting of a transport, two destroyer escorts, three escort vessels, a self-propelled barge, and two patrol cutters, was proceeding east and was detected by our air reconnaissance at 1650 at 70°55' north, 26°00' east.

The submarine was dispatched to the area where it would likely intercept the convoy. The S-14 twice heard the noise of screws at dawn on 20 October but could not make visual contact with any ships. At 0852, positioned 1.8 nautical miles northwest of Cape Nordkin, the submarine observed a transport displacing 3,000 tons on a bearing of 200 degrees, along with two escort minesweepers. The convoy was moving on a course of 60 degrees.

Having taken a good position, Captain Third Rank Kalanin attacked the transport at 0914 with four torpedoes, fired with a time interval of 10 seconds at an attack angle of 120 degrees from a range of 2,200 yards. A powerful explosion was felt in the submarine two minutes later.

There was no transport to be seen at 0922, when the submarine ascended to periscope depth. One minesweeper was busy picking up survivors, and the second began the pursuit of the S-14, which lasted until 1045. The submarine had no further enemy contact and arrived back at base at 0910 on 22 October.

Submarine V-4, commanded by Hero of the Soviet Union Captain Third Rank Iosseliani,[30] was positioned

---

30 Yarislav Konstantinovich Iosselani (1912–1978) entered naval service in 1934. He completed the Frunze Naval Academy in 1938 and a special course for submarine commanders in 1940. While commanding the *Malyutka*-class *M-111* of 3rd Division, Black Sea Fleet Submarine Brigade, he completed 11 combat sorties, having sunk 12 enemy vessels. He was awarded Hero of the Soviet Union on 15.5.44 [15 May 1944]. He participated in the receipt and passage of the Royal

in the Cape Nordkin–Cape Sletnes area for the six days from 17 to 22 October.

At 0030 on 18 October, while stopped at 71°08' north, 27°44.5' east to charge batteries with only the conning tower above the surface, the submarine detected the noise of screws with its sonar on a bearing of 70 degrees. Battle stations was quickly sounded, and without submerging, the commander began maneuvering to close with the enemy.

A tanker was observed three minutes later, moving eastward. At 0047, Captain Third Rank Iosseliani attacked it with four torpedoes at a range of 2,400 yards. One of the torpedoes did not leave the tube, for mechanical reasons. The other three torpedoes passed close by the target but did not strike it. The submarine commander maneuvered for a second attack.

At 0103, a salvo of two torpedoes was fired from a range of 1,400 yards, but again one of the torpedoes did not leave the tube, and the second passed by the bow of the tanker, missing it. Captain Third Rank Iosseliani again maneuvered for another attack, and three minutes later fired two torpedoes at the tanker, one of which stuck in the tube. The launch was conducted at a range of 1,200 yards, and attack angle of 134 degrees.

This time, the torpedo strike into the hull of the tanker was clearly observed by everyone on the bridge. After another two or three minutes, there was a powerful explosion on the tanker, as a result of which it quickly sunk.

On 19 October at 2113, the submarine came across an unidentified enemy ship, guarded by many escort vessels. The attempt to attack this ship was unsuccessful, due to the submarine's bad position and interference from the escorts.

At dawn on 20 October, the *V-4* was stopped at 71°6.3' north, 27°25.3' east to charge batteries and with only the conning tower above the surface. An enemy convoy suddenly appeared at 0444, on a bearing of 90 degrees and a range of 1,000 yards, consisting of four transports, two destroyer escorts, and two escort vessels, moving on a course of 285 degrees. The submarine quickly began to maneuver for the attack.

Because the range and attack angle were too small, the commander gave the order for full astern. At 0446,

---

Navy submarine *V-4* to Northern Fleet in April 1944, and during the Petsamo Operation sunk an enemy tanker and two transports. *GSS*, Vol. 1 (1987), p. 589.—Translator

Captain Third Rank Iosseliani attacked the lead transport with torpedoes, launched with an interval of eight seconds at 600 yards and attack angle of 80 degrees.

The left torpedo launched first, its shock wave pushed the *V-4*'s bow to the right, and the second (right) torpedo therefore sped away several degrees to the right of its intended course. Due to mechanical difficulties in the tube, the third torpedo did not launch.

Twenty-one seconds later, there followed an explosion in the midship of the 8,000-ton freighter. The transport immediately capsized and began to sink, engulfed in fire. Another four seconds later, the second torpedo struck the hull of another 6,000-ton transport, which was steaming behind the first. The transport began to burn, and less than a minute later lay on its port side and quickly sank.

The submarine submerged at 0448 and began to withdraw toward the shore, because after the attack the convoy turned toward the sea. Enemy vessels dropped 38 depth charges in a pattern from 0459 to 0507 but failed to damage the submarine.

The *V-4* received an order from the brigade commander by radio to return to base at 1906 on 20 October and arrived safely at Polyarnoye at 1100 on 22 October.

Submarine *S-101*, commanded by Captain-Lieutenant Zinovev, patrolled in the Cape Sletnes–Cape Nordkin area from 28 October to 10 November. On 30 October, the submarine twice attacked an enemy minesweeper of the *A-17* type, in a position favoring a torpedo attack. But because of stormy weather that made periscope operations extremely difficult, two attempts to attack the enemy were unsuccessful.

At 0738 on 31 October, while positioned in the Nordkin–Kelsnering area, the submarine detected the sound of screws with sonar. The commander ascended to periscope depth and at 0751 noted the silhouettes of three German destroyer escorts against the background of the shore, on a course of 240 degrees. The submarine moved closer, and at 0808 attacked the trailing minesweeper at a range of 2,600 yards. The commander wanted to fire three *ET-80* torpedoes with a time interval of 10 seconds at an attack angle of 90 degrees. But because of a fault in the air firing system of tubes Nos. 2 and 3, only one torpedo was launched, from tube No. 1. Having taken on ballast computed for the launching of three torpedoes, the submarine lost its equilibrium and began to dive quickly. At 0811, the crew in compartment 5 heard the torpedo's explosion.

Having reestablished equilibrium, the submarine ascended to periscope depth at 0829, and found no enemy ships in sight. Our air reconnaissance spotted a burning enemy ship two miles north of Cape Mekhavn at 0920. This was believed to be the destroyer escort damaged by submarine *S-101*.

At 1451 on this same day, when the submarine was positioned three miles northeast of Cape Kelsnering, the sonarman reported the sound of ships' screws to starboard. At 1506, a minesweeper moving on a course of 60 degrees was observed through the periscope. Three minutes later, another minesweeper was spotted trailing the first, along with an escort vessel, following a course of 240 degrees.

At 1515, having received the report from the sonarman that the enemy escort vessel had made sonar contact with the submarine, Captain-Lieutenant Zinovev fired two *ET-80* torpedoes at the second minesweeper at a range of 2,200 yards. The results of the attack were not visually monitored, but the crews in compartments 2, 5, and 7, as well as the sonarman, heard the explosions of the torpedoes minutes after the launch.

Enemy ships pursued the submarine for several hours, dropping approximately 150 depth charges. The *S-101* sustained minor damage, which the crew was able to repair immediately. In subsequent days, the submarine made contact with enemy ships in its operating area several times but could not engage them. In all cases, the enemy was detected too late, resulting in unfavorable conditions for an attack. The *S-101* returned to base on 11 November.

Submarine *L-20*, commanded by Captain Third Rank Alekseev, had the mission to emplace a minefield in Lopphavet near the northwest coast of Norway, conduct a search for enemy ships in Soroysund, and reconnoiter Lopphavet, which had not been visited by our submarines that year.

The *L-20* sortied for its patrol area at 1900 on 19 October and arrived in position at 0400 on 22 October. On 23 October, from 1850 to 1919, the *L-20* placed two rows of mines, five and nine respectively, in the enemy channel near the shoreline. During the operation, the rails in the right tube dislodged and became jammed. A rope broke during an attempt to discharge the mines by hand, and six mines remained in the tube, one of which was stuck in the outer door, preventing it from closing.

The commander decided to withdraw toward the northeast coastal shelf of Soroy Island, there to clear the torpedo tube. The *L-20* surfaced near Soroy Island at 1932 on 24 October and removed the jammed mine. The remaining mines were being knocked around in the tube by the surface waves, forcing the crew to flood the tube and close the outer door. On the following day, after the submarine had submerged, the tube was drained, and the mines were secured to prevent their movement.

The *L-20* remained near Soroy Island on 25 and 26 October, unsuccessfully searching for enemy ships. Captain Third Rank Alekseev attempted without success to contact fleet main base by radio from 2150 on 26 October, to submit a report concerning the minelaying. Finally, on the 11th attempt, at 0227 on 27 October, he received an acknowledgment of receipt of his message. The submarine, positioned in such a vital area, was forced by a problem with the fleet main base radio transmitter to waste five hours 10 minutes in sending a single radio message. It was only pure luck that the *L-20* was not detected by an enemy radio direction-finding station and taken under pursuit. The *L-20* returned safely to base at 0757 on 29 October without any interference from the enemy.

In addition to these described submarine activities on enemy sea routes, the combat sortie of submarine *S-102* must be mentioned. This submarine was positioned in the Makkaur–Berlevog area from 12 to 24 October. Our reconnaissance reported the movement of 11 convoys in this area during this time. The commander of the *S-102* did not, however, display sufficient perseverance in searching, and did not make any contact with the convoys.

On 24 October, the *S-102* detected an enemy escort vessel but did not attack it. The submarine moved at periscope depth on a parallel course with this vessel for 45 minutes without being detected or attacked. The fleet command judged this sortie as unsatisfactory. It should be noted that the submarine had been tasked to operate in cooperation with air reconnaissance.

But because the *S-102* was not equipped with a periscope antenna and could not use the standard antenna due to the recent weather (it tossed the boat about on the surface), the submarine could not receive radio reports from air reconnaissance. A table of the results of submarine attacks is shown at appendix 4.

D. ACTIONS OF THE NORTHERN FLEET AIR FORCES

Fleet Air Forces flew 243 sorties in reconnaissance of sea lines of communication during the operation for the liberation of the far north. Air reconnaissance aircraft detected 54 of the 69 enemy convoys observed by aviation in this theater in the entire fourth quarter of 1944. Of the 54 convoys, 17 were proceeding inside Varangerfjord and 37 were sailing between fjords, anchorages, and ports of northern Norway. These figures adequately demonstrate the intensity of movement of combat and transport vessels on enemy sea lines of communication during the operation.

The level of activity of German shipping during the operation demanded intensified combat activity from all types of fleet aviation. On selected days, the workload reached as many as four sorties from a single aircraft.

The mission to destroy enemy ships and shipping assets at sea and in ports was accomplished by units of the Fifth Mine-Torpedo, Sixth Fighter, and 14th Mixed Aviation divisions operating from main base airfields and from Pummanki.

The mission was executed by the conduct of a series of massed and successive air strikes on convoys at sea and in ports, as well as by single torpedo bombers cruising on distant shipping lanes, and groups of fighter bombers and attack bombers cruising on close-in shipping lanes. Harbors were also subjected to concentrated air strikes, with the goal to disrupt their normal port activities. Kirkenes harbor was a special objective of these attacks.

In addition to large transports, the enemy used several small ships and cutters for the evacuation of their troops. The *Kittyhawk* fighter bomber was used against these targets with great effect. *Kittyhawk* aircraft conducted their bombing attacks both independently and in cooperation with other types of air strikes.

In the case of the former, their actions took on the character of a "free hunt." *Kittyhawk* aircraft, in groups of three or four and not following a specific flight plan, flew to Varangerfjord or toward the northern shore of Varangerfjord, searched out a target for themselves, and attacked it. In most cases, the preferred method was to drop bombs at mast level. Singly or in pairs, the aircraft approached the target from a right angle, and dropped their bombs from a range of 250–200 meters and at an altitude of 20–30 meters, simultaneously strafing the target with machine-gun fire. When conditions were right, the fighters made two or three passes to strafe the target with their machine guns.

The other method of employing *Kittyhawk* aircraft was to incorporate them into larger formations of attack aviation. Proceeding to the target area in the general formation, the *Kittyhawks* moved out ahead 2–3 minutes prior to arriving at the target area and attacked the targets from a steep dive or at mast level.

Kittyhawk fighter bombers used various ordnance in their attacks on enemy shipping, depending on the nature of the target. They flew with two *FAB-100* [*fugasnaya aviatsionnaya bomba*–fragmentation aviation bomb, 100 kilograms] bombs or a single *FAB-250*. Altogether, *Kittyhawk* aircraft sank 40 and damaged seven enemy ships.

Attack aviation (*Il-2* aircraft) most frequently conducted their bombing runs on enemy combat and transport ships in coordination with bombers and torpedo bombers. They used the mast-level or diving method, the mast-level being the most effective, and dive bombing the least effective. This was due to the inadequate training of the young crews, inexperienced in this type of bombing tactic. The basic tactical formation for attack aviation was a group of 4–6 *Il-2* aircraft operating under the cover of 6–8 fighters. Two or three groups of attack aircraft, striking the target at time intervals of 1–2 minutes, was the standard attack method.

Attack aviation used *FAB-250* bombs, with delayed action fuses. As a result of their efforts, 67 enemy vessels with a total displacement of 23,000 tons were sunk, and another 31 ships were damaged.

Torpedo bombers (*A-20 Boston* and *Il-4* aircraft) operated against enemy shipping in torpedo-carrying, mine-carrying, and bomber variants. Low-flying torpedo bombers operated singly, as "hunters," and in groups. Three to five torpedo bombers under the cover of 6–12 *Airacobra*[31] fighters comprised a typical group.

---

31 The *Bell P-39 Airacobra* was a prewar designed air superiority pursuit (fighter) aircraft, distinguished by its tricycle landing gear and car-type doors. It was powered by a liquid-cooled *Allison V-12* positioned behind the pilot, which drove the propeller through a floor-mounted driveshaft to a differential gearbox below the propeller gear. In its most powerful variants, the N and Q models (with which by this time the Northern Fleet Air Force was largely equipped), it was capable of

Attacks on convoys by groups of torpedo bombers were supported by preliminary strikes against the same convoys by bombers and attack aircraft. In two cases, high-altitude torpedo bombers carried out the preliminary attacks, flying a total of seven sorties. The aircraft flying the supporting strikes against the convoys conducted their attacks several minutes prior to the main attack.

As a rule, torpedo bombers attacked a convoy from the flank, with the aircraft in trail at an interval of 200–300 meters between aircraft. These attacks were not always effective, because the torpedo bombers had inadequate support against enemy antiaircraft fires. In several cases, the aircraft flying in preliminary strike groups were late arriving at the target. As a result, torpedo bombers encountered heavy antiaircraft fire from escort ships, dropped their torpedoes from long ranges (up to 5,000 meters), and suffered heavy losses. To a significant degree this was explained by the absence of reliable coordination between the torpedo bombers and supporting aviation groups.

The activities of minelaying aircraft were limited also in the fact that they flew only nine sorties. They placed nine *AMG-1* mines: five were dropped into enemy waters on the approaches to the ports Petsamo and Kirkenes, and the other four into a lake, due to poor weather conditions and the inability to place them in the designated area.

A-20G Boston and *Il-4* torpedo bombers were also employed in bomber variants, mainly for strikes on ships in ports and at anchorages. In this case, the *Boston* carried two *FAB-500* bombs or one *FAB-1000*. Bombing strikes against enemy transports and other vessels and ports were conducted primarily in daylight, in groups of from 5 to 18 aircraft. A group was given a target and an aiming point. The ordnance was dropped in horizontal flight from an altitude of from 2,300 to 3,400 meters, upon signal of the lead aircraft. Bombers carried out their strikes in coordination with attack, fighter, and torpedo-carrying aircraft.

On the whole, these medium altitude bombing operations against enemy ships were less effective than other types of air strikes. One of the shortcomings in this method was the desire to use a larger bomb than was needed to destroy the target. A result of this tendency was a lower probability of striking the target. It was not necessary to drop a 1,000-kilogram fragmentation bomb against enemy transports and small ships, when a 250-kilogram or less fragmentation bomb would have been adequate to ensure their sinking.

Air reconnaissance played a significant role during the conduct of operations at sea. Continuous reconnaissance of the sea lines of communication was conducted along the northern Norwegian coast as far west as Hammerfest. The nature and intensity of enemy shipping, the location of their principal vessels, and the concentration areas of his transports and light vessels were known on each day of the operation.

As a rule, reconnaissance was conducted three times each day: in the morning (at first light), in the middle of the day, and just before nightfall. Continuous monitoring of shipping lanes prevented enemy convoys from secretly sailing from Varangerfjord ports to Hammerfest. Overall, it was reconnaissance aviation that flew illumination missions. In isolated cases, combat aviation units that conducted reconnaissance on close-in shipping lanes, enemy convoys, and single enemy ships were attached. Reconnaissance always preceded the actions of attack aviation against enemy convoys and ports. The crews that flew on the bombing runs always knew the exact location of the convoy, its composition, and its movement formation, which significantly contributed to the success of their attack.

A total of 105 group air sorties were flown against naval targets during the operation for the liberation of the far north, of these 14 with torpedoes and 91 with bombs.

Meteorological conditions were favorable for air activities. Altogether in October, there were 27 flying and limited-flying days, which were maximally utilized for air strikes against enemy shipping.

The quantity of strikes flown by fleet aviation against various targets on enemy sea lines of communication from 7 to 31 October 1944, the time of their execution, and the number of participating aircraft are shown in figure 5.13.

The following most typical examples are given to show the nature of fleet aviation activities against enemy sea lines of communication.

---

389 mph with a range of 525 miles. It was armed with a nose-mounted 37 mm cannon that fired through the propeller spinner, flanked by two Browning .50 cal. machine guns that fired through the propeller on interrupters. It also had a single .50 cal. machine gun mounted in each wing. It could carry a bomb load of 230 kilograms on fuselage and wing hangers. The USSR received 4,719 P-39s of various models, nearly half of Bell's total production of this aircraft. It was the aircraft choice of a number of leading Soviet aces and was used through to the end of the war on 9 May 1945.—Translator

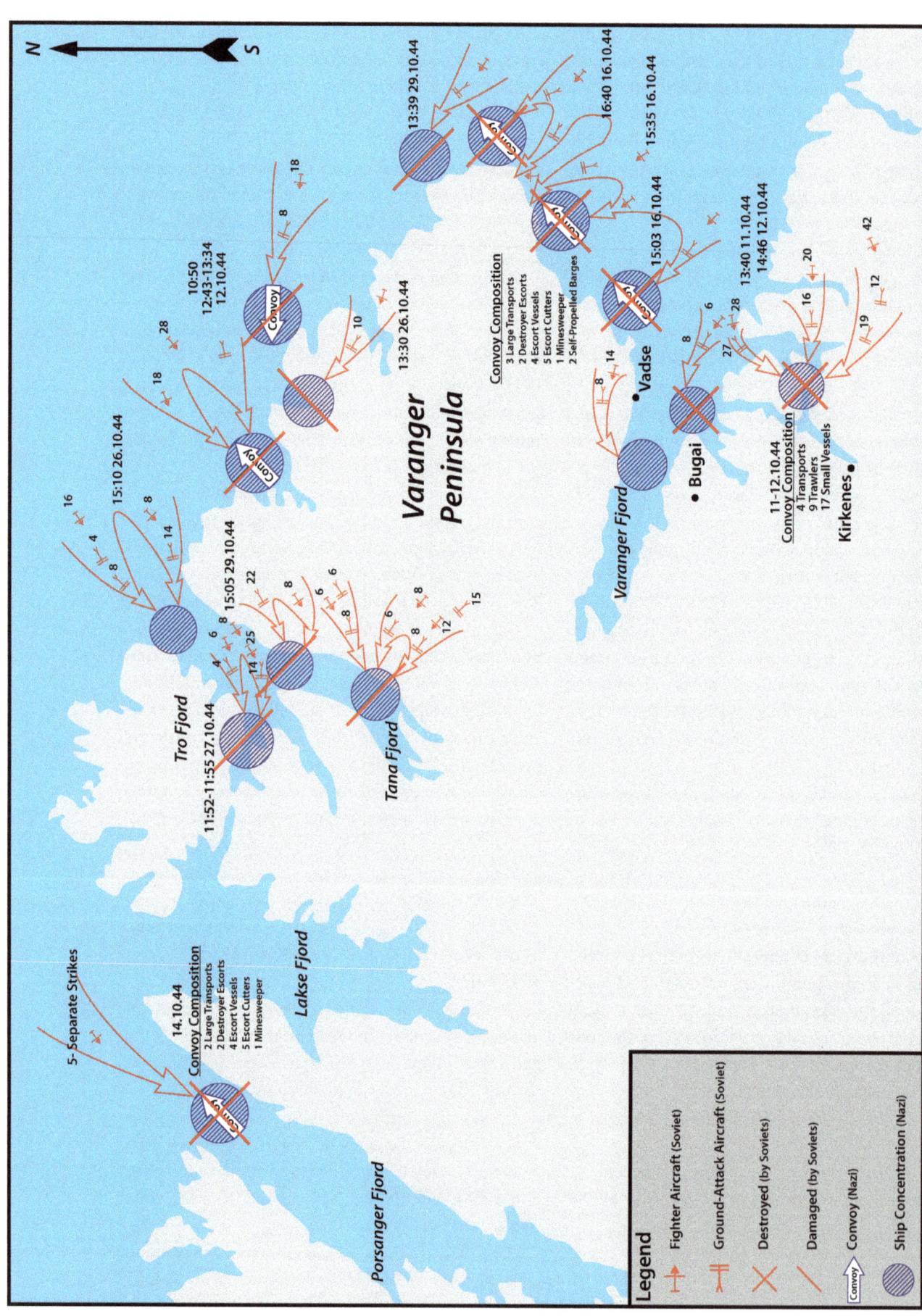

FIGURE 5.13. Northern Fleet Air Forces air strikes on enemy sea lines of communication

1. Attack against an enemy convoy by units of 14th Mixed Air Division near the entrance to Bekfjord on 11 October.

Careful reconnaissance of this area preceded the attack. By 11 October, four transports, one fast assault barge, and nine escort vessels were observed in Kirkenes port. Airfields at Kirkenes, Heybukten, and Salmiyarvi held 26 *Ju-87*, two *Ju-88*, four *Do-24*,[32] and 32 *Bf-109* aircraft.

With first light, at 0755, a reconnaissance aircraft detected a convoy in Jarfjord, consisting of three transports and 12 escort vessels, moving in the direction of Bekfjord at a speed of 7–8 knots. It was decided to carry out an attack on the convoy while it was moving. At the same time, it was considered that the presence of enemy fighters on nearby airfields could interfere with the attack. Therefore, a sizable group of fighters was designated to protect the attack group.

The division commander assigned the mission to the units at 0801, six minutes after the convoy was detected. Seventeen *Il-2* aircraft in three groups were designated as the attack force, and 28 fighters were selected for cover: 14 *Airacobras*, 10 *Yak-7s*,[33] and four *Kittyhawks*.

The strike was planned to be executed in the following manner. The first group–six *Il-2s*, each carrying six *FAB-100* bombs, under the protection of eight *Airacobras*, and the second group—seven *Il-2s*, each carrying four *FAB-100* bombs, under the protection of 10 *Yak-7s* and four *Kittyhawks* carrying two *FAB-100* bombs each—were simultaneously to conduct diving attacks from various directions with the goal to suppress and attract to themselves enemy antiaircraft fire. The third group—four *Il-2* mast-top bombers, carrying two *FAB-250* bombs each, under the protection of six *Airacobras*—were to attack and destroy two transports immediately following the dive bombers' attack. All the cooperating strike groups were ordered to attack the enemy with a time interval of from 30 to 60 seconds.

Because it was necessary to launch the mission right away to prevent the convoy from reaching Kirkenes port, time for preparation of the flying crews for the strike was limited. All coordination between the groups was accomplished by telephone. The departure time was designated as 0820, and the groups sortied exactly at that time. The flight to the target proceeded in an organized manner.

Seven minutes before arrival at the target, the attack aircraft observed the convoy. It was approaching Bekfjord. The leader of the first group designated the direction of attack by radio, assigned the targets, and properly positioned his group for the attack. At 0910, the first and second groups of strike and fighter aircraft attacked the convoy. The first group struck the convoy's tail, and the second group the head. Having observed the dive bombers' actions, the strike and mast-top bombers of the third group delivered their ordnance 20–30 seconds after the dive bombers' attack. The four *Kittyhawks* attacked the convoy's remnants 3–4 minutes after the strike bombers' attack (figure 14). This air attack destroyed the convoy. One transport displacing 6,000 tons, one transport displacing 2,000 tons, two escort vessels, and two escort cutters were sunk. One transport displacing 4,000 tons was damaged.

The attack aircraft and fighters did not have any losses, though several of them received damage from enemy antiaircraft artillery fire. This attack was characterized by close cooperation between dive bombers, mast-top bombers, and fighters. Competent tactical decisions by the leaders of the strike groups and precisely timed attacks with minimum time intervals contributed significantly to the good results. Good timing was particularly important in dispersing enemy antiaircraft fires and disorganizing the convoy's air defense system.

One should note as well that on this same day, units of 14th Mixed Air Division and 5th Mine-Torpedo Division carried out several other successful strikes against German ships. For example, at 1218 hours, seven *Il-2* aircraft with eight *Yak-7* fighters executed an attack on an enemy convoy in the Reney Island area.

At 1340, 12 *Il-2* aircraft covered by 14 *Airacobras* and four *Yak-7s* carried out an attack against enemy ships in Langfjord. Following this attack by strike aviation, 14 *Boston* bombers covered by 18 fighters conducted a bombing attack against the same convoy.

At 1445, five *Boston* aircraft covered by eight fighters carried out a bombing raid on enemy ships in Kirkenes

---

[32] The *Dornier Do-24* was a high-wing (strut-mounted) amphibian with three 9-cylinder air-cooled radial engines, designed for sea search and rescue. It was capable of a top speed of 210 mph with a cruise speed of 183 mph and range of 1,800 miles. It was armed with a 20 mm cannon in the dorsal turret, a 7.92 mm machine gun in the nose, and a second 7.92 mm machine gun in the tail.—Translator

[33] The *Yakovlev Yak-7* was a single-seat fighter, developed from the Yak-1. Its liquid-cooled, V-12 engine powered it to a maximum speed of 308 mph and a range of 400 miles. Its armament included a 20 mm cannon and two 7.62 mm machine guns or, in later models, 12.7 mm machine guns.—Translator

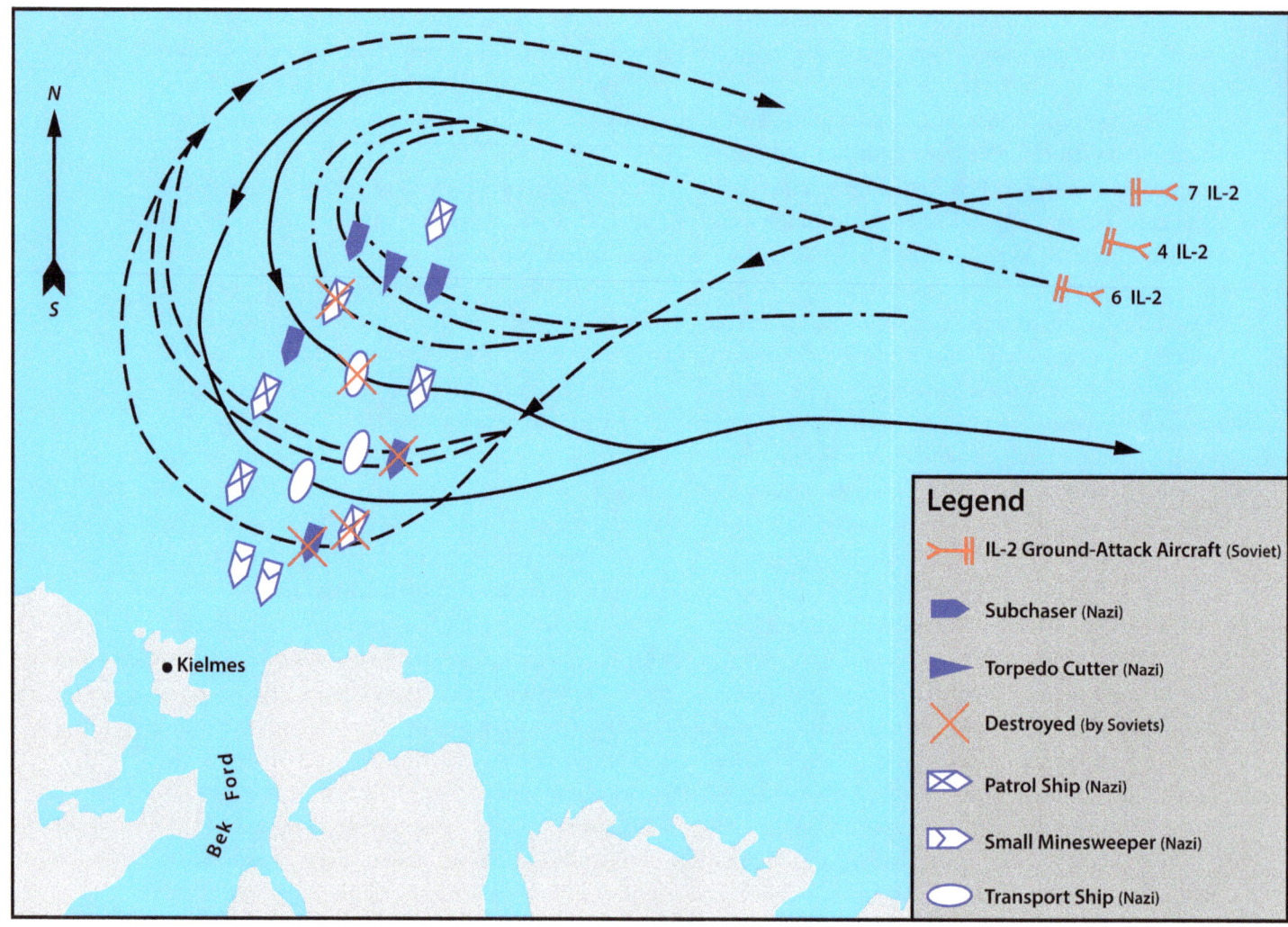

FIGURE 5.14. Air attacks on a convoy on 11 October 1944

harbor, and at 1610 four *Boston* aircraft protected by 12 fighters made a torpedo strike on an enemy convoy in the Batsfjord area.

Altogether on 11 October, 56 bombers and strike bombers, and 92 fighters participated in air strikes against enemy ships. As a result of these attacks, five transports with a total displacement of 17,000 tons, three escort vessels, two escort cutters, three barges, and two motor launches were sunk. Three transports with a combined displacement of 10,000 tons, two escort cutters, and one motor launch were damaged. Eight enemy aircraft were shot down in air-to-air combat, at a cost of five from Northern Fleet Air Forces.

2. On 12 October, Northern Fleet Air Forces conducted three successive strikes against enemy ships in Kirkenes port and on convoys at Berlevog and Kongsfjord. These strikes resulted in the sinking of one transport, one destroyer escort, one minesweeper, one escort vessel, three patrol cutters, two self-propelled barges, three motorized launches, and one unidentified vessel. Three transports and three motorized launches were damaged.

Altogether, Northern Fleet Air Forces flew 200 sorties on 12 October. A description of the course of events of an attack by torpedo bombers of 5th Mine–Torpedo Division on an enemy convoy in the Berlevog area follows.

At 0810, air reconnaissance observed a German convoy of two transports, one destroyer escort, one minesweeper, and two escort vessels in the Persfjord area proceeding at eight knots in a northeasterly direction. Four Boston aircraft, covered by eight *Airacobras*, flew out to attack the convoy. The torpedo bombers found and attacked the convoy at 1334. Three torpedo bombers in formation abreast attacked the trail transport

80 CHAPTER V: EXECUTION OF THE ASSIGNED MISSIONS

from a range of 600 meters at an altitude of 30 meters, and a single aircraft attacked the destroyer escort from a range of 1,500 meters. The destroyer escort turned away from the torpedo, but the torpedo struck the minesweeper following behind it. The minesweeper blew up and sunk. While on their torpedo runs, the aircraft took heavy, organized fire from the ships' antiaircraft weapons and from shore batteries.

All the aircraft received heavy damage. The lead plane sustained serious damage during its target run but did not alter course. Only after launching its torpedo did it break off from the attack and, barely controllable, fly back to its airfield accompanied by fighters. As a result of this skillful and daring attack, four torpedo bombers sank one minesweeper and damaged one transport of 4,000 tons displacement.

3. The most effective air strike by torpedo bombers against an enemy convoy took place on 14 October, in the Porsangerfjord area. At 0925, air reconnaissance reported a German convoy of two large transports, two destroyer escorts, four escort vessels, five escort cutters, and a single minesweeper in the Omgang area. Five *Boston* aircraft flew out without fighter escort to attack the convoy.

Having detected the convoy and reorganized into a formation abreast, at 1222 the aircraft attacked the ships. They dropped their torpedoes upon signal of the lead aircraft at a range of 500–700 meters. The weather in the target area, a heavy cloud ceiling at 300–400 meters, with a visibility of 4–5 kilometers and sea at force 4, enabled the aircraft to reach the convoy undetected and launch a surprise attack. The enemy opened fire on the aircraft only after they had dropped their torpedoes. One aircraft was shot down flying away from the target by shipboard antiaircraft fire, and the remainder received significant damage from shell fragments.

As a result of this sudden, daring, and skillfully conducted attack, all five torpedoes struck their target. Two transports with a combined displacement of 14,000 tons and one escort cutter were sunk.

4. 16 October was one of the most indicative days regarding the intensity and success of the Northern Fleet Air Forces against enemy shipping. Heavy losses in shipping assets had forced the enemy to accompany their transports with increased combat escort.

On this day, a convoy of three transports, two destroyer escorts, six escort ships, one minesweeper, two self-propelled barges, and 13 escort cutters departed Kirkenes port sailing northward. Two *Bf-109* fighters and one four-engined aircraft covered this convoy from the air. Despite intense counterfire, five successive strikes were made against this convoy.

Twelve *Il-2s* covered by 14 *Airacobra* fighters made the first attack on the convoy during its passage toward Ekkere. Their mission was to suppress antiaircraft fires from the escort vessels. As a result of the attack, the ships' antiaircraft defenses were somewhat suppressed, and one escort vessel was sunk.

The second strike was flown by 12 *Il-2s*, covered by 15 fighters. This group had the same mission as the first. The aircraft used dive bombing tactics, sinking one destroyer escort and two escort cutters. As in the first attack, during the second the enemy offered strong resistance, and shot down two *Il-2s* with shipboard antiaircraft fires.

After the attack bombers, two groups of 10 low-flying *Boston* torpedo bombers launched the third strike, covered by 14 *Airacobra* fighters. Ten enemy *FW-190* and *Bf-109* fighters attacked the torpedo bombers during and immediately after their runs, while the ships were firing at them with antiaircraft weapons. Two *Bostons* were shot down, one by a German fighter and the other by antiaircraft fire from a ship.

One transport, one escort vessel, one unidentified ship, and one escort cutter were sunk as a result of the torpedo attacks.

Five *Il-2s* covered by 10 fighters flew the fourth strike. The fifth air strike on the convoy, 10 low-flying *Boston* torpedo bombers covered by 14 *Airacobra* fighters, came in right behind the attack bombers. The torpedo bombers took heavy antiaircraft fires and were attacked by enemy fighters during their approach to the convoy. Three *Boston* torpedo bombers were downed by shipboard antiaircraft fires during their pull away from the torpedo runs. The air strike sank two transports, one minesweeper, one unidentified vessel, and one escort cutter.

The enemy lost 13 ships total as a result of the five successive air strikes on the same convoy: three transports, three escort vessels, one destroyer escort, two unidentified ships, and four escort cutters. Northern Fleet Air Forces flew 166 sorties against the enemy convoy, losing 11 aircraft in air-to-air combat and to shipboard antiaircraft fires. They shot down six enemy fighters in air engagements. Continuous monitoring of the convoy by air reconnaissance greatly facilitated the actions against it by the strike groups.

It should be noted that on this same day, simultaneous with these attacks on the convoy, Northern Fleet Air Forces was carrying out air strikes on enemy shipping assets in Persfjord and Kobbholmfjord, sinking one minesweeper and one self-propelled barge loaded with troops.

Altogether during the operation, Northern Fleet Air Forces sank 136 enemy vessels with a total displacement of 86,050 tons and damaged another 45 vessels in actions against convoys at sea or against ports. A total of 1,357 bombs were dropped on ships. Fifty-six enemy aircraft were destroyed in air-to-air combat, and our forces lost 55 aircraft.

5. Execution of the Mission to Transport Forces by Sea

The transport of Karelian *Front* forces and various types of supplies for them by sea was one of the missions the *front* commander assigned to Northern Fleet. Responsibility for the accomplishment of this mission fell upon Northern Fleet transportation units, which were tasked to provide the following:

- ferrying of Karelian *Front* units and formations that had arrived by railroad across Kola Inlet from Murmansk to Mishukov;
- transportation by sea of various classes of supply for units of the forces operating on the coastal flank as they moved westward;
- transportation of the wounded across Kola Inlet and by sea as the offensive progressed.

Troops and primarily equipment that had been concentrated in anticipation of the offensive were ferried to the western shore of Kola Inlet from 6 September to 1 October. Later-arriving troops were transported from the railhead across the bay from 1 to 17 October. A special loading ramp was constructed at Kabotazhnaya moorage, and the planking and timbering of the structure that supported heavier cargo were reinforced, to ensure the most appropriate and rapid loading and reliable transfer of the heavy combat equipment that was arriving. The deck of the lighter designated for transport of *KV* tanks and *JSU-152* self-propelled guns was also reinforced by additional planking and vertical braces.[34]

Altogether, from 6 September to 17 October, the following quantities of men and materiel were transported across Kola Inlet to its western shore: 5,719 men, 18 horses, 96 tanks, 19 self-propelled guns, three armored troop transporters and armored cars, 153 artillery pieces, 137 artillery prime movers, 197 wheeled vehicles, 74 wagons, 270 tons of ammunition, 33 tons of fuel, and 250 tons of assorted cargo.

Simultaneously with the transfer of Karelian *Front* forces across Kola Inlet, Northern Fleet assets transported supplies and cargo to the Northern Defensive Region from Kildin Island, the areas of Set-Navolok and Murmansk to Ozerko on Sredniy Peninsula. From 4 September to 7 October, the following items were moved: 6,000 personnel, eight tanks, five self-propelled guns, 12 artillery pieces, seven prime movers and wheeled vehicles, 42 wagons, 1,760 tons of ammunition, 1,520 tons of foodstuffs, 1,036 tons of fuel, 820 tons of wood, and 1,697 tons of assorted cargo. After Northern Fleet's amphibious landing captured Liinakhamari port and 14th Army forces occupied Pechenga, additional transport by sea was required in connection with the establishment of Pechenga Naval Base and for the movement of supplies for Karelian *Front* forces.

Transport associated with the establishment of Pechenga Naval Base was carried out in the main using minesweepers, fishing boats, and motor launches. On 16 October, the command and control elements of Pechenga Naval Base were first to arrive in Liinakhamari on two minesweepers and one dispatch boat. A naval garrison commandant also arrived in Liinakhamari to take charge of activities there. An inspection of the condition of port facilities in Liinakhamari revealed that the enemy did not succeed in completely destroying the docks, and indicated that with some repairs they could be used for cargo-handling operations.

Liinakhamari port was quickly able to receive all loads of supplies for Karelian *Front* units that were continuing the offensive toward the Norwegian border after the seizure of the Pechenga area. Transport ships of the Soviet Navy carried out the movement of supply

---

34 Depending on model, the *KV* tank weighed from 45 to 52 metric tons, and the *JSU-152* 47.3 metric tons.—Translator.

loads. The first of these transports to arrive at Liinakhamari with supplies was *Revolutsiya*, on 19 October.

The naval commandant in Liinakhamari had at his disposal two fishing boats, four or five motor launches, and one naval tugboat with two barges from Northern Fleet logistic units. Using light self-propelled assets, the naval commandant moved loads of supplies to advancing units along the Varangerfjord coastline during periods of darkness. Return runs were used to move the wounded.

These cargo movements were conducted in new, unfamiliar areas that had been heavily mined by the enemy. The transport of cargo and evacuation by sea for the Karelian *Front* and Northern Fleet from 7 to 30 October is shown in the data in table 5.2.

In addition, the following items were transported in connection with the establishment of Pechenga Naval Base: 2,488 personnel, 27 horses, 61 artillery pieces, six prime movers, 56 wheeled and special purpose vehicles, 1,165 tons of ammunition, 1,315 tons of foodstuffs, 1,155 tons of fuel, 270 tons of construction materials, 2,211 tons of assorted cargo, and 63 wagons.

Titovka settlement, on the southern shore of Motovskiy Bay, was one of the intermediate stops on the sea route. After the Germans abandoned it on 11 October, a fleet transportation mobile control team was sent there, along with a separate engineer construction platoon with a pontoon bridge set, floating docks, and construction materials for partial rebuilding of the burned-out docks. Six hours after the arrival of the engineer construction platoon in the settlement, all the approaches had been cleared of mines, and the floating dock made from *A-3* boats had been deployed. This dock could receive transports of the *Sosnovets* type, along with fishing and motorboats.

An evacuation hospital was delivered from Murmansk to Titovka, and the evacuation of wounded was planned to begin by 17 October. Altogether, 3,302 personnel were evacuated to Murmansk from Titovka during the operation, along with 484 from Liinakhamari, and 5,804 from Mishukov, a total of 9,630 troops.

6. Execution of the Logistic Support Mission

In connection with the fact that the greatest quantity of personnel and equipment came from the Northern

TABLE 5.2. Naval transport of cargo and personnel 7–30 October

Nature of Cargo	For the Karelian Front	For Northern Fleet
Troops	15,860	1,150
Tanks	7	–
Artillery pieces	–	4
Wheeled vehicles	–	20
Ammunition	4,015 tons	860 tons
Foodstuffs	8,168 tons	510 tons
Fuel	997 tons	445 tons
Assorted cargo	1,655 tons	385 tons
Firewood, lumber	950 tons	500 tons

Defensive Region, its logistic support units played a large role in providing logistic support to the operation. Reserve stocks of all classes of supply were delivered in requested quantities to the troops before the operation. The delivery of all these necessities to the troops was exceedingly difficult for Northern Fleet logistic support units because there was only one land road for this purpose, the Titovka–Porovaara Road.

In addition, the absence of direct communications between the brigade logistics chief and the staffs of his subordinate units could not help but complicate the work of the logistic units. Indeed, from the first day of the operation, the lack of roads and the naval infantry brigade logistic chief's lack of radio communications led to the situation where the logistic support units lagged their supported units and lost contact with them. The resupplying of units was accomplished in the first days by using up reserves carried by the troops and at battalion level, and the appropriate exploitation of stores captured from the enemy.

Logistic support units of 12th and 63rd Naval Infantry Brigade reached Kutovaya only on 12 October, but the Titovka–Kutovaya road was mined. In addition, all the brigades' artillery was moving along this same road. Only on the fourth day of the battle did brigade logistic support units catch up to their supported units. The initial preoperation disposition of logistic support units is shown in figure 4.2.

The absence of roads forced units to rely on the use of porters and reindeer sleds for the delivery of foodstuffs in several cases, 348th Separate Machine-Gun Battalion being an example. The delivery of provisions and ammunition to Captain Barchenko's composite reconnaissance detachment on Cape Krestovyy was accomplished with airplanes. Aircraft at Pummanki airfield had been prepared ahead of time, with ammunition packed in metal and wooden containers, and food in sacks, which were dropped into the detachment's position.

As a result of separation from their logistic support, 12th NIB units arrived at Cape Krestovyy on 14 October without provisions. This is indicative of the fact that the difficulties in the organization of supply movement had not been resolved during the advance of naval infantry units from the isthmus of Sredniy Peninsula to Porovaara.

The arrival of these units on the shore at Petsamovuono Inlet and the capture of Liinakhamari port immediately resolved the issue of supply movement by switching units from a land-based to a sea-based supply route. With this goal in mind, a Northern Defensive Region logistic support forward supply base was established in Liinakhamari. This was done in an efficient manner, considering that this had not been considered in the plan for the support of units during the operation.

Northern Fleet logistic command sea transport and combat vessels stocked the supply base in Liinakhamari with reserves by sea delivery from Pummanki.

The following data gives an indication of the supply deliveries to units from Northern Defensive Region supply dumps during the operation.

From this table, it can be seen that a large portion of the supply tonnage was moved by wheeled and animal-drawn transport. Keeping in mind that there was only a single road for this purpose—the Titovka–Porovaara Road—it was quite difficult to move these supplies. But the relatively short length of the land-based supply route of the Northern Fleet units in this operation before their arrival at the Petsamovuono shoreline, about 30 kilometers, and the short duration of the initial phase of the operation, altogether five days, did not lead to any delays in supplying the troops. The more so, because fleet logistic command undertook all necessary measures for the supplying of units by sea lines of communication in a timely manner. Just the same, units should have more carefully developed their supply plans during the planning for this operation, and not permitted the separation of logistic units of 12th and 63rd Naval Infantry Brigades, which occurred from 12 to 14 October.

Naval infantry units received the following supplies from fleet logistic storage facilities during the opera-

TABLE 5.3. Tonnage moved from Northern Defensive Region supply dumps during operation

	Wheeled and Animal-Drawn Transport	By Ship	By Aircraft	Total (tons)
Munitions	469	250	2.0	721.0
Food and fodder	227	63	0.5	290.5
Misc. supplies	47	8	–	55.0
Fuel	225	–	–	225.0
Total	968	321	2.5	1,291.5

tion: 500 tons of ammunition, 800 tons of food and fodder, and 58 tons of miscellaneous supplies.

Northern Fleet aviation logistic support elements provided supplies and spare parts for fleet aviation units designated to support the operation from Pummanki through 16th Aviation Base. The following supplies were delivered from fleet aviation logistic storage facilities to Pummanki during the operation: 182 tons of aviation gas, 160 tons of ammunition, and 550 tons of miscellaneous supplies. Other Northern Fleet air bases, such as Vaenga, Rost, Ura-guba, and others, provided approximately 1,500 tons of fuel, 1,000 tons of ammunition, and 1,200 tons of miscellaneous supplies to air units during the operation.

Logistic support for ships of the fleet was accomplished without any problems. The cutters were able to refuel from barges positioned near the piers at Pummanki prior to the start of the operation. Large submarine chasers did not require refueling in place, because they carried sufficient fuel on board for several days' operations.

The cutters received other classes of supply as they were needed from their brigade's storage facility in Pummanki. Large subchasers accomplished resupply principally at bases in Kola Inlet. The resupply of ships during the operation was adequately organized, and there were no difficulties in provisioning them with everything they required.

In the resupplying of Northern Defensive Region units, difficulties in the conduct of resupply by land were successfully resolved with unit stockage, efficient utilization of captured supply dumps, and rapid transition to employment of the sea lines of communication.

The great energy displayed in the supplying of every necessity to the 125th Naval Infantry Regiment detachment, which was formed in an extremely short time in Polyarnoye (10–12 hours), and which participated in the amphibious assault on Liinakhamari port, deserves mention in the work of logistic support units. Efficient and appropriate coordination between fleet staff and logistic support command, established during the conduct of the operation, and full and timely exchange of information about the situation made this possible.

7. Execution of the Medical Support Mission

Medical service support, prepared in an appropriate manner for the accomplishment of missions assigned to it, deployed its units from the first day of the operation. The first wounded began to arrive at *PPG-2215* [Forward Field Hospital No. 2215] at 0600 on 10 October. These were wounded men from 12th NIB units that were going into the attack on the isthmus of Sredniy Peninsula during the breakthrough of the enemy's defenses.

The greatest number of wounded passed through *PPG-2215* from 10 to 18 October, with from 140 to 210 patients arriving on 10, 11, 14, and 15 October, and from 20 to 40 patients on 13, 16, and 17 October. The total number of patients received at *PPG-2215* from 10 to 18 October was 896, of these 849 wounded, 44 shell-shocked, two burned, and one frostbitten.

In contrast to army field mobile hospitals, *PPG-2215* was immobile, because it did not have transportation assets. Therefore, a mobile surgical detachment, which served as an intermediate stage between *PPG-2215* and the naval infantry brigade medical service companies, was created prior to the operation as a reinforcing group. At the beginning of the operation, the 12th NIB's medical service company was located 4–5 kilometers from forward units. Between it and forward units was a surgical point, at which the wounded received first aid. After that, as the medical service company advanced behind the attacking units, the mobile surgical detachment took its place, with the goal to be the intermediate stop on the evacuation route of the wounded to the hospital.

This disposition of medical treatment facilities during the land battle was planned to provide the following division of treatment responsibility for the

TABLE 5.4. Northern Defensive Region unit wounded

12th Red Banner Naval Infantry Brigade	307
63rd Naval Infantry Brigade	239
Machine-gun battalions	52
614th Separate Punishment Company	106
589th Separate Punishment Platoon	5
Total	709

TABLE 5.5. Northern Defense Region casualties

125th Naval Infantry Regiment	48
Reconnaissance Detachment of HQ, fleet	8
Red Banner Torpedo Cutter Brigade	7
Fleet Air Forces	7
Red Banner Submarine Brigade	1
Remaining units	178
Total	249

wounded: Battalion aid stations were to stop bleeding temporarily, treat for shock, apply bandages, immobilize, and document the wounded; brigade medical service companies were to stop bleeding definitively, bring patients out of shock, immobilize patients more securely, conduct field amputations, and evacuate patients; the mobile surgical detachments were to treat the wounded so as to prevent their deaths during evacuation as a result of untimely and incorrect medical treatment.

During the westward movement of the naval infantry brigades as they pursued the retreating enemy, and corresponding dislocation of medical service companies behind the brigades, the mobile surgical detachment reached the area of Hill 388.9. Here it took up positions in the half-destroyed German hospital and provided not only medical treatment to the wounded but also hot meals.

Northern Defensive Region units suffered the greatest number of wounded during the operation. Table 5.4 has some figures on individual units.

In addition, 323 were killed and seven missing in action in the Northern Defensive Region.

Table 5.5 shows losses in wounded for other Northern Fleet units and formations.

Of the total number of 958 Northern Fleet personnel who were wounded, 92 were officers, 214 were sergeants and petty officers, and 652 were soldiers and sailors. Their wounds can be categorized as shown in table 5.6.

TABLE 5.6. Northern Fleet casualties

Projectile	211	22.0%
Artillery shrapnel	188	19.6%
Mortar shrapnel	426	44.5%
Grenade shrapnel	52	5.4%
Bayonet, knife	4	0.4%
Concussion	49	5.1%
Burns	5	0.4%
Frostbite	2	0.2%
Unspecified causes	21	2.4%

Shrapnel wounds were for the most part received in 12th NIB units during the breakthrough of the enemy's defenses on the isthmus of Sredniy Peninsula. Projectile wounds predominated in the later days of the operation, and were primarily among the soldiers of 63rd NIB, those at the head of the combat formations pursuing the retreating enemy.

Seven hundred sixty-two operations were conducted during treatment at main hospitals, 410 of those at *PPG-2215*. Of the total number of surgeries, 711 were done in initial treatment, 36 were to remove foreign objects, 16 were surgeries of the skull, 30 were abdominal surgeries, and so on. More than 60 percent of the surgeries done in initial treatment were done at *PPG-2215*. All the instances of immobilization by splints (463) were done at stages of evacuation before the *PPG*, but plaster casts (627) were made only at base hospitals.

Twenty-four of the wounded taken to hospitals died, three of these from the Red Army. Sixteen personnel died at *PPG-2215*, four at *GVMG* [Main Naval Hospital], one at 74th *VMG* [Naval Hospital], and three at 71st *VMG*. All the dead were from among the seriously wounded. Ten casualties at *PPG-2215* died from shock as a result of puncture wounds of the stomach, pelvis, [and] cranium, and extensive fractures of large bones. All the shock fatalities died shortly after their admission to the hospital. Two personnel died from gangrene associated with septicemia.

The evacuation of wounded from the battlefield to *PPG-2215* was done in accordance with established procedures. Combat medics brought the wounded to the battalion aid station on litters and makeshift means. The wounded were evacuated from the battalion aid stations to *PPG-2215* by the naval infantry brigade medical service companies in wheeled vehicles. Two large submarine chasers evacuated 120 casualties to 74th *VMG* in Murmansk, and air transport delivered 29 seriously wounded Red Army casualties to 71st *VMG*.

The same fishing boats that were used to evacuate Northern Fleet wounded—*PMB-87* and *PMB-88*—were used to move 323 personnel from Titovka and 1,132 personnel from Cape Mishukov to Murmansk. In addition, Red Army casualties were transported from Titovka on the passenger ship *Sosnovets*, which was designated for this purpose. Altogether, 1,569 personnel were delivered to Murmansk on this ship. Wounded personnel received qualified medical treatment at all stages of their evacuation.

The reception of wounded at base hospitals was organized in the following manner. Those brought in for treatment were examined in a receiving area by a doctor, who determined the nature of their wounds. They received necessary medical care, including treatment for shock and X-rays. After this screening, they were directed to an area for bandaging or surgery. The *GVMG* admitted and treated 410 personnel, 74th *VMG* admitted and treated 485 personnel, and 71st *VMG* admitted and treated 198 personnel.

Blood transfusions played a significant role in providing medical treatment. Blood supplies maintained for this purpose in Northern Fleet treatment facilities were increased by 38 kilograms of additionally prepared preserved blood. During the combat operation, 78 kilograms of blood were issued for transfusions, 51 kilograms to Northern Defensive Region units, and 27 kilograms to *GVMG*. Seventy-first and 74th *VMG* were provided with blood for transfusions by the Murmansk city blood bank and did not experience any problems in this area.

Medical treatment for the wounded during this combat operation was so rapid and comprehensive that the number of complications and infections after surgical treatment was insignificant. There were relatively few incidences of shock and death from shock, thanks to the widespread use by medical personnel of blood transfusions to the wounded.

Base hospitals noted the arrival of wounded from the Northern Defensive Region with appropriate documentation, good immobilization, and surgical treatment. Thanks to the latter, there were only five cases of infection. It is important to note that in the entire course of the operation, the sanitary and epidemiological status of the Northern Fleet operating units remained excellent.

CHAPTER VI

Organization of Command and Control for Combat and the Accomplishment of Coordination

1. The Fleet Commander's Decision as a Basis for the Organization of Combat Command and Control

The fleet commander's decision, adopted after he received information from the commander of 14th Army concerning the upcoming Karelian *Front* offensive operation for the liberation of the Soviet far north, became the basis for the actions of all Northern Fleet units that would participate in the operation. The essence of the fleet commander's decision was a breakthrough of enemy defenses on the isthmus of Sredniy Peninsula, with a preliminary amphibious landing on the coastline of Maattivuono and Motovskiy Bays (on the flanks of the defensive line), as well as actions against enemy sea lines of communication.

The decision determined the operational goals of fleet units designated to participate in the operation and became the basis for the organization of coordination between them for the accomplishment of their assigned missions. Operational coordination between fleet and ground forces considered the actions of Karelian *Front* forces on land and of the Northern Fleet naval infantry forces on the coastline, along with the actions of ships at sea.

At the same time, the combined actions of the naval infantry brigades with artillery, aviation, and ships of the fleet necessitated tactical coordination of the Northern Fleet's forces for the resolution of common problems. Initial data for the development of the fleet commander's operational decision included an evaluation of the situation, presented by the fleet chief of staff, based on evaluation of our own and the enemy's capabilities.

In connection with the *Front* commander's 29 September specification of the fleet's missions, the operations plan underwent minor modifications, and the combat directive was replaced by a new one (No. 0052/*op*). It is important to note that in his directive the fleet commander, anticipating the flow of the operation, ordered the Northern Defensive Region commander to "keep in mind an offensive on Petsamo after linking up with 14th Army units." By this order, he oriented the Northern Defensive Region commander toward actions to be taken as the operation developed successfully, and thus established a basis for the decision during the operation to pursue the enemy toward Pechenga.

The fleet commander's decision served as a foundation for the staff's efforts to organize combat command and control during the operation and for the organization of coordination between the units participating in the operation.

2. Development of the Decision

The fleet commander's decision was developed by the fleet staff and published in the form of the following basic combat documents: operations plan, organizational order No. 0048/*op* (appendix 1), and combat directive No. 0052/*op* (appendix 2). The operations plan, approved by the fleet Military Council, contained initial data for the conduct of the operation, including the composition of forces, their organization, and coordinating instructions, and was an internal staff document.

To preserve the security of the preparation for the operation, only a small group of staff assistants, each of whom worked only on specific issues assigned to him, took part in the development of the plan. No single participant in this group knew the composite plan. The chiefs of staffs of the formations participating in the operation prepared materials for the fleet staff that supported subordinate unit plans. This was accomplished simultaneously with the development of the fleet staff's documents.

The outlined procedure made it possible to determine precisely the composition of forces and to specify all issues that required coordination between various units during the preparation for the operation. The fleet's principal staff specialists worked out the necessary measures for their own areas of responsibility for support of the implementation of the decision and prepared the appropriate documents.

3. Combat Documents

During the preparation for the operation, the fleet staff and most of the staffs of participating formations developed the minimally required quantity of combat documents. A list of these documents was included in the chapter concerning the preparation for the operation. The largest group of documents (15) was prepared by the staff of the Northern Defensive Region, and six documents concerned the organization of communications. Such a large quantity of documents was not necessary.

In the combat documents prepared by the fleet staff, those stand out in which the chain of command sometimes not only specified the unit missions of a formation but also designated which unit would accomplish the given mission. This cannot be considered appropriate, since in these cases the formation commander only had to repeat in his own order that which had already been decided by the chain of command. This was the case in the Northern Defensive Region commander's order No. 0014/*op* (appendix 3). There are no observations to make concerning the remaining fleet staff documents. They were carefully prepared and clear for the participants.

Documents prepared by the formation staffs were also well done. It should be noted that all formations gave much attention in their documents to the issue of organizing communications. In addition, commanders of all formations that were participating in the operation attempted to give a combat order or directive to their formation. This was done even in such formations as the Surface Squadron, from which only two destroyer escorts were tasked for naval gunfire support. The dispatch of these two ships for this mission could have been accomplished with separate instructions. But Surface Squadron staff prepared a combat directive, a fire plan, and a fire-planning table.

During the preparation for the operation, along with written documents, fleet staff and the formation staffs widely employed individually issued warning orders, mainly oral. This was done particularly regarding the sequence of preparation of ships, air assets, and ground force units, and logistic support of their combat operations.

The Northern Defensive Region commander issued one combat order during the operation. This was order No. 0015/*op*, signed at 1400 on 10 October, that is, when 12th NIB units had broken through enemy defenses on the isthmus of Sredniy Peninsula and were linking up with 63rd NIB units that had landed on the Maattivuono coastline. In essence, this order only specified the mission to the units to encircle the enemy and prevent them from reaching Pechenga on the Titovka–Porovaara Road. It simply reaffirmed the same goal for the naval infantry brigades that had been established by order No. 0014/*op* on 3 October.

This order could have created a new grouping, and instructions to the units for uninterrupted pursuit of the enemy, so that his units could not break contact. The Northern Defensive Region commander limited himself to designating the attack in the zones of 347th and 348th Separate Machine-Gun Battalions and did not assign a single unit to pursue the enemy. It should be added that 12th and 63rd NIB units did not receive an order to continue combat operations at night that had been initiated during the day. Thus, the opportunity to pursue the enemy was wasted, and the enemy succeeded in breaking contact with attacking Northern Defensive Region units during the night of 10–11 October. The commander of the Northern Defensive Region did not give the order to pursue the enemy, and units acted in accordance with individual orders received during the operation.

So that they could remain informed of the combat situation, the fleet commander and staff received battle reports and operational summaries concerning the locations of units and their activities during the operation. On instructions of Karelian *Front* staff, beginning on 8 October combat reports were to be submitted daily by 0400, 0700, 1200, 1900, and 2100, with an operational summary by 0200. Fleet staff passed this instruction to the chief of staff of the Northern Defensive Region, who was tasked to present the combat reports and operational summary to the operations group of Karelian *Front* staff, the staff of 14th Army, and the Northern Fleet staff.

The experience of the first two days of the operation clearly showed that combat reports and operational summaries submitted in coded form lost their value to influence combat because of the length of time required for transmission and the rapidly changing situation. Therefore, for this operation it was decided to transmit reports and information in clear text, encoding only the unit designations. This method was widely employed during communications of ground forces and cutters with aircraft. The transmission of reports in clear text had been avoided in the operation's preparatory period, and during previously conducted operations. Experience showed that in this offensive operation the use of open text for transmission of information by telegraph or radio fully supported the success of combat activities, permitting the rapid exchange of information on the situation between units and formations.

A. OPERATIONAL *MASKIROVKA* FOR THIS OPERATION[35]

Measures were taken in support of operational *maskirovka* during the preparation for the operation, principally to conceal the time of the conduct of the operation and the commander's concept. These measures included the following:

- preparation for the operation was conducted so that it did not differ from the fleet's daily activities, especially in that the fleet formations were prepared in exercises and war games, and in the course of combat training for the conduct of the amphibious landing operations;
- even the fleet major formation commanders were not informed of the time of the beginning of the operation until the last moment;
- repositioning of ships, units, and air assets to concentration areas was conducted only at night;
- by their systematic activities, our forces distracted the enemy as to the defense of his lines of communication;
- normal daily routing radio traffic was maintained.

Thanks to these measures, the activities of the Northern Fleet units and ships remained a tactical surprise to the Germans. Confirmation of this fact was the absence of enemy resistance during the amphibious landing on Maattivuono coastline.

4. Organization of Combat Command and Control

Northern Fleet staff gave special attention to the organization of combat command and control in the operation. The anticipated offensive activities demanded coordination of the work of all levels of organized combat formations, and most of all coordination between ground forces and aviation, between ships and aviation. It was determined that command and control should be such that coordination was precise and uninterrupted and would permit the rapid concentration of the combat power necessary for striking the enemy. At the same time, it was considered best to command and

---

35 *Maskirovka* is a complex of measures directed at leading the enemy to false conclusions relative to the presence and disposition of troops, ships, military facilities, and command plans. It includes camouflage and concealment, demonstrative actions, simulation, and disinformation.—Translator

control from a location that permitted observation of the course of combat activities, rapid evaluation of the situation, the making of decisions, issuing of combat missions, and oversight of timely accomplishment of these missions by subordinate units.

Bearing in mind that the fleet commander reserved to himself control of the forces participating in the operation, he decided that during the operation he would be in direct proximity to the area of combat activity—on Sredniy Peninsula. Collocated with the fleet commander was his mobile staff, consisting of two officers from the operations section, chief of the intelligence department, chief of the force composition section, chief of the general support section, chief of communications, one operator-engineer, one officer of the fleet personnel section, and one officer for encoded communications.

Rear Admiral Pavlovich, chief of the faculty of general tactics of the Naval Academy, who at this time was at the Northern Fleet, was named chief of the mobile staff. Rear Admiral Pavlovich departed after the conduct of the first phase of the operation (the amphibious landing on the coastline of Maattivuono Bay), turning over his responsibilities as chief of the mobile staff to Captain Second Rank (now Captain First Rank) Rigerman.

The fleet main staff remained in Polyarnoye, maintaining communications with the staffs of the Karelian *Front* and 14th Army, with Main Naval Staff [Moscow], and collecting its own reports concerning the situation of advancing Karelian *Front* forces. Fleet staff also collected data concerning all the sea sectors of the Northern Fleet.

These two command and control nodes permitted the management of all combat activities that could arise in this sector during the operation.

For the same purpose of direct observation of the course of combat activities, command posts of the commanders of formations participating in the operation were located at short distances from operating units. They were positioned with consideration for the best observation and ease of communications with subordinate units, with formations with which coordination was required, and with staffs of formations higher in the chain of command.

As a result of these efforts, the fleet commander, who commanded this operation, reliably and successfully exercised combat command and control during the operation through formation commanders who were positioned close to him.

It should be noted that during the amphibious landing on the coastline of Maattivuono Bay, the landing commander (commander of Sea Approach Defenses of Main Base) was located on Sredniy Peninsula at the same command post as the commander of the Northern Defensive Region. This permitted observation from the shore of the movement of the amphibious landing forces to the landing sites, allowed them to see the landing area, and, most importantly, to render timely fire support from Northern Defensive Region artillery in the event it was needed to counter enemy batteries that may have opposed the amphibious assault.

The experience of this operation showed that in each situation, it is fully possible for a landing commander to organize combat command and control of an amphibious assault from a shore-based command post.

The Northern Defensive Region staff organized command and control of the ground forces by designating an operations group from among the staff officers. They performed their duties at the Northern Defensive Region commander's command post, initially located on Hill 342.0, then on Hill 146.0, and as the forces moved, on Hill 388.9 and beyond.

For quite some time, the main staff of the commander, Northern Defensive Region, remained on Hill 342.0, gathering all information on the situation for coordination with Karelian *Front* units, aviation, and Northern Fleet ships.

Fleet Air Forces staff organized command and control of the Northern Fleet air assets. They sent an operations group of staff officers to Fleet Air Forces alternate command post on Hill 200 on Sredniy Peninsula, near Pummanki. From this location they were able to organize and monitor all flights from Pummanki airfield. From here they could also observe the air strikes on main enemy strongpoints on the isthmus of Sredniy Peninsula and on shore batteries on the coastline of Petsamovuono Inlet.

The main staff of the Northern Fleet Air Forces remained at the fleet main command post, along with fleet staff, with the chief of staff in charge for the collection of information regarding the situation in all sectors, and for management of air activities conducted from airfields at Vaenga, Ura-guba, Rost, and Kildin.

At the beginning of the operation the chief of rear services was collocated with the fleet commander on Sredniy Peninsula for command and control of fleet logistic elements supporting the operation. All orders that pertained to the logistic effort were sent to the command post at Polyarnoye. From there, the orders were retransmitted to the rear services command post or to the deputy chief of rear services in Murmansk. Brief summaries were transmitted to the rear services command post through the fleet command post to keep the logistics command current on the combat situation. Care was taken to keep documents brief, in order not to overburden the communications system used to transmit them. The chief of rear services familiarized himself with the situation at fleet headquarters daily, and this permitted him quickly and rationally to react to all changes in the situation and take appropriate measures.

5. The Organization of Coordination

During the preparation for this operation, the headquarters of all the formations gave special attention to the organization of coordination. The breakthrough of the enemy's defenses on Sredniy Peninsula and strikes against enemy convoys in Varangerfjord were organized and conducted based on operational coordination between the forces of the Karelian *Front* and Northern Fleet. At the same time, the Northern Fleet protected the forces of the Karelian *Front* from an enemy attack from the sea based on operational coordination.

Air reconnaissance of the battlefield, roads leading to the forward area, and enemy reserves; air and artillery strikes on defensive fortifications; and air strikes in support of ground forces during the pursuit of the enemy and to defeat any resistance the enemy offered were organized and executed based on tactical coordination. Tactical coordination between torpedo cutters and air assets participating in the operation was organized and executed with the goal of covering the torpedo boats' actions against enemy sea lines of communication with air support, and of employing illumination aircraft to conduct night searches for enemy convoys.

Coordination between cutters during the amphibious landings took the form of mutual orientation concerning the tactical situation, and in support by fire and smoke screen coverage during the penetration of the enemy's defensive fires.

Coordination was achieved first by the establishment of precise agreement in actions between formations participating in the operation, especially between the staffs of Fleet Air Forces, the Northern Defensive Region, and Torpedo Cutter Brigade. Also important was the presence of the absolutely required quantity of documents pertaining to coordination.

Liaison officers played an important role in the accomplishment of coordination. Their principal duty was to report the situation as it developed in the operating area of the formation to which they were attached. For example, liaison officers from Fleet Air Forces attached to naval infantry were to inform the Northern Fleet Air Forces staff about the situation in the Northern Defensive Region's sector, amplify the defensive region commander's plan for employment of air assets, and determine the air taskings and their sequence for the following day. They also ensured the timely marking of the forward line of friendly troops, conducted target designation, and directed air strikes.

Using radios, liaison officers established communications with their aircraft overhead, vectored them to targets, and adjusted their strikes. Coordination was organized so that air strikes against the enemy could occur synchronously from various directions. This was done, for example, during the breakthrough of enemy defenses on the isthmus of Sredniy Peninsula, when air strikes had to be synchronized for both the amphibious landings and the breakthrough of enemy defenses by naval infantry units.

In addition, for the purposes of coordination, officers of the operations group with Northern Fleet Air Forces commander occasionally went out to the Northern Defensive Region command post and conducted face-to-face discussions with the naval infantry brigade commanders.

In the interests of coordination with artillery, rifle unit and subunit commanders down to company level, the ground commanders received photo reproductions of the positions and sectors of terrain that the artillery would fire on. These were prepared by the artillery staff before the start of the operation. In addition, long-range artillery sent out forward observer teams to ensure coordination between their units and the infantry. Each naval infantry brigade received three artillery fire coordination teams, one of which was located with the brigade commander, and the other two with first-echelon battalion commanders. Naval infantry brigades received a single forward observer team from the coastal artillery battalion, and another went with Captain Barchenko's composite reconnaissance detachment [Cape Krestovyy raid]. Artillery designated for direct support of infantry sent two forward observer teams to the battalions of 12th NIB and one forward observer team to Fourth Battalion of 63rd NIB. Altogether, 14 artillery forward observer teams provided reliable coordination between infantry subunits and their supporting artillery units.

The coordination of artillery with naval gunfire support was provided by the presence of the Surface Squadron gunnery officer at the command post of the artillery staff and the dispatch of one naval gunfire forward observer team to the sound-ranging platoon of the separate artillery reconnaissance battalion. Coordination between artillery and aviation forward air controllers was also established prior to the start of the operation. The procedure for calling in air strikes, call signs, and radio frequencies were worked out. There were, however, some difficulties during the execution of this type of coordination. The ability of a forward air controller to fly depended in each instance on the presence at the airfield of a fighter aircraft not tasked for another mission. Also, forward air controllers did not have their own dedicated cover aircraft.

Thus, thanks to precise organization of coordination, there existed every opportunity to inflict strikes on the enemy that were coordinated as to a time and place that in a given situation were the most dangerous to him.

6. Command and Control During Combat

Careful preparation led to a relatively easy achievement of success in the initial period of the operation. All elements that were considered ahead of time in the plan were accomplished. The development of success and subsequent purposefulness of the offensive demonstrated by the forces participating in it completely depended on the ability of the commander of the operation and his formation commanders to exercise combat command and control of their attacking forces.

One of the conditions that favored this was that the commander of the operation was himself positioned in the immediate vicinity of the combat area, at an auxiliary command post. This enabled him personally to accomplish several tasks: make necessary decisions; establish new missions for his subordinates; with the help of the staff officer group that accompanied him, to keep track of the development of combat actions; study the situation; remain informed about adjacent units; and confidently exercise leadership of the offensive activities, thus increasing the force of the strikes against the enemy.

Thus, for example, the fleet commander was able personally to observe the amphibious landing of 63rd NIB on the coastline of Maattivuono Bay and the breakthrough of the fortified defenses on the isthmus of Sredniy Peninsula by 12th NIB units on the night of 9–10 October. The fleet commander also personally observed the course of combat actions during the breakthrough of the cutters into Petsamovuono Inlet for the capture of Liinakhamari port. This was initially accomplished from the command post of Torpedo Cutter Brigade, and later from the command post of 113th Separate Artillery Battalion.

Also of substantial significance for combat command and control during the operation was the fact that the fleet commander was continuously informed about the offensive of Karelian *Front* forces and about the situation in the other sectors of the Northern Fleet. Thanks to favorable communications conditions, he had the ability in a timely manner to receive data from the fleet chief of staff collected by the fleet main staff at the command post in Polyarnoye, and in turn to inform the fleet chief of staff concerning the situation in the operations area.

At the same time, the fleet commander was able to report on what was happening directly from his location to the commander-in-chief, Red Navy, in Moscow, through the Main Naval Staff representative, Captain First Rank Pilipovskiy, who was collocated with the fleet commander during the operation.

The command's knowledge concerning the actions of the attacking naval infantry units was sufficiently complete and timely. Only the mistake in the determination of his location by the commander of First Battalion, 63rd NIB, in the first two days of the attack, somewhat disoriented the brigade commander and caused him to send the reserve battalion to a place other than where it was needed. If the battalion commander had correctly determined his location (while near Hill 268 it was very favorable in respect to the threat from enemy units retreating to Porovaara) and had confirmed his judgment by reconnaissance of the route, he would have come out deep in the rear of the enemy, who was continuing to hold on in the area of Hill 388.9. It would have been possible to cut off the enemy's sole path of retreat.

The battalion did not take advantage of this good position, and the enemy, preventing First Battalion of 63rd NIB from reaching the Titovka–Porovaara Road, covered their own withdrawal to the west along this road with other units. It should be assumed that if the Northern Defensive Region commander had known about and correctly evaluated how favorable First Battalion's position was blocking the enemy's withdrawal routes, he would have taken measures for a more energetic movement of units in a westward direction for pursuit of the enemy. The movement of the Northern Defensive Region commander with a group of staff officers to the lead units for the purpose of commanding and controlling them from a place closer to the battle did not accelerate the tempo of the pursuit of the Germans.

The defensive region main staff moved from Hill 342.0 to Hill 388.9, where information was being collected concerning the situation, and where operational summaries and reports were being assembled. From here, command and control was exercised by means of radio and telephone transmissions of fragmentary combat orders.

For the success of the energetic pursuit of the enemy, the naval infantry had access to vital information from air reconnaissance as a result of coordination with Fleet Air Forces and were able to receive timely assistance from aviation when needed. During the operation, this was accomplished in the following manner.

Basic coordination issues for the first three or four days of the offensive were worked out by the staffs of the Northern Defensive Region and Fleet Air Forces ahead of time, obviating the need to do this daily. At the end of each day, ground units were required to outline their air support needs for the following day, so that aircraft and sorties could be scheduled depending on the ongoing battlefield changes. Liaison officers from air units passed information about the situation of naval infantry units and their activities to the Fleet Air Forces command post and made requests for air sorties. It is important to note that in doing this daily coordination, the staffs did not use encoded messages or map designators, and all conversations were conducted in clear text.

However, not a single instance was noted where the enemy was able to use these clear-text conversations for their own purposes. The attacking forces were the benefactors of this, because without question the time required to encode and decode was saved.

Thanks to this, aircraft could prepare more quickly for their sorties, and there was no misunderstanding about what was said in the message traffic.

An officer of the operations group of the auxiliary command post verified the situation with the Northern Defensive Region staff concerning the accumulation of data at Fleet Air Forces command post on ground force requests for air support. After this, the Fleet Air Forces commander evaluated the situation and decided on the employment of his air assets. Then the necessary instructions were published.

Air units operating from Pummanki airfield received missions for support of ground forces through an officer of the operations group of Fleet Air Forces staff, who came to the airfield and personally worked out the mission details with the crews of tactical groups that would be flying the mission. In this manner, the crews received more complete information, which had a positive impact on the effects of the air strike and protected their own units from being shot down for failure to be recognized by friendly forces.

An evaluation of the effectiveness of close air support was conducted during the battle, principally the reports of air crews who were sent out to adjust the strikes, and from the reports received from the naval infantry unit commanders in whose sectors the air strikes were conducted.

When time permitted during the operation, the Fleet Air Forces commander conducted a study with his subordinate commanders of the most typical combat episodes. This study emphasized both good and bad points of each tactical group, so that the lessons could be incorporated into their flight activities on subsequent days. This was an excellent means to make quick use of experience gained in combat.

The difficulty of commanding and controlling air activities by a close air support strike group was once again affirmed during the conduct of the operation. Once again, due to the use of clear-text radio communications, one of the air liaison officers with 63rd NIB was able to call a group of aircraft that was flying over his brigade's position and give them a target that was preventing the brigade's accomplishment of its combat mission.

Also confirmed was the utility of sending out an aircraft for prestrike reconnaissance of a designated ground target, and the use of that aircraft to vector the strike group to the target.

To a significant degree, the successful employment of aviation during the conduct of the operation was a consequence of all actions at the auxiliary command post and the designating of air missions by the Fleet Air Forces commander. In other words, a centralized method of combat command and control was employed. The constant feeding to the Fleet Air Forces commander of complete information concerning the situation in all sectors of combat actions had great significance. The close proximity of the fleet and Fleet Air Forces command posts, along with the good work of liaison officers, facilitated the process.

Combat command and control of actions on the sea were accomplished by management of the daily combat service of ships, units, and formations, and also by leadership of their combat actions during the conduct of the operation. It was especially important for the fleet commander to know the situation and how the offensive of the Karelian *Front*'s forces was progressing, and where the combat formations of our attacking forces were located. With this goal, liaison officers from the fleet staff with the Karelian *Front* and 14th Army were continuously updating fleet staff on the actions and locations of *Front* units. This was accomplished by transmitting by telephone excerpts from 14th Army combat reports, which were sent under the signature of a liaison officer to the fleet staff with the note "for the sailors." Liaison officers and fleet staff officers conversed by telephone for the same purpose.

In connection with the fact that at the beginning of the offensive the fleet staff did not have the communications cipher for army units, information concerning the course of combat activities and unit locations had to be passed along by supplementary transmissions. Although the cipher was quickly received, the need for it was minimal, since clear text was often used for radio and land line transmissions concerning the activities of the troops.

Sometimes, liaison officers from 14th Army staff not only discussed the actions of Karelian *Front* forces, but also anticipated command decisions in their reports. Colonel Ostrikov, the liaison officer with 14th Army staff, made such reports on 16, 17, and 20 October. This was not the proper thing to do, since it might disclose the commander's intentions. But the enemy, disorganized and retreating under the pressure of our forces, could in no way interfere with their accomplishment.

Timely information from 14th Army concerning the next day's activities enabled the fleet commander and his staff to carry out precisely those actions on the sea and the Varangerfjord coastline that would most quickly and best support the accomplishments of the ground command in the combined operation. Knowledge of the situation on land and its correct evaluation by the fleet commander suggested to him the most favorable time for the conduct of the amphibious assault for the capture of Liinakhamari port.

The fleet commander had formed the intent to execute this landing earlier but did not include it in a single document during the preparation for the operation, in the interests of security. But from the fact alone that on the first day of the operation the composite reconnaissance detachment was sent to Cape Krestovyy to capture the shore batteries there (these batteries could conduct sustained fire on boats coming into Petsamovuono Inlet), one can judge about the fleet commander's foresight in developing the operation, leading to the necessity to capture Liinakhamari port from the sea.

Therefore, having already decided to conduct an amphibious assault on Liinakhamari port, after 63rd NIB's amphibious landing on the coastline of Maattivuono Bay and the breakthrough of the enemy's defenses on the isthmus of Sredniy Peninsula were successful, the fleet commander made his decision on 10 October concerning the formation of the amphibious landing force. He ordered the commander of Torpedo Cutter Brigade to be prepared to enter Petsamovuono Inlet on the night of 12–13 October for the amphibious landing in Liinakhamari port.

The 349th Separate Machine-Gun Battalion from the Northern Defensive Region commander's reserve, and a detachment from the 125th Naval Infantry Regiment, which was forming up in Olen Inlet, were designated as the amphibious landing forces reserve. Since member of the Northern Fleet Military Council Admiral Nikolaev and Chief of the Northern Fleet Rear Services Engineer Rear Admiral Dubrovin went from Sredniy Peninsula to Polyarnoye to participate in the most rapid preparation of the detachment (selection of the troops and issuing all necessary items to them), the organizing of the latter detachment was conducted in an efficient manner.

In the subsequent course of the operation, command and control of actions on the sea and along the coastline were executed with consideration for the development of the Karelian *Front*'s offensive. The fleet commander's decisions made provision for actions against enemy warships and transports that were observed on sea lines of communication, and successive amphibious landings on the Varangerfjord coastline in consonance with the forward progress of 14th Army units toward the Norwegian border.

Direct leadership of the amphibious landings was vested in the commander of the just-formed Pechenga Naval Base. The timely conduct of successive amphibious landings on the southern coast of Varangerfjord and the actions of the torpedo cutters and aviation against enemy convoys detected by air reconnaissance attest to the energy of the combat command and control at this phase of the operation.

All the actions flowed out of the situation as it unfolded, and their success was ensured by close mutual communications between the fleet commander's auxiliary and main command posts. Actions against enemy shipping were carried out with the granting of considerable initiative to the Fleet Air Forces commander and the commanders of Torpedo Cutter and Submarine Brigades.

Logistic support during the operation was executed by representatives of the fleet logistic command, including the chief of rear services, who was located in the combat area and who personally resolved all issues concerning supply.

7. Organization and Work of Communications Units

Combat command and control in the operation were supported by reliable and organized communications. The preservation of the daily communications operating system and existing fleet documentation was the guiding principle in this effort. The main communications nodes were served by several redundant channels of communication and by various types of equipment.

The communications plan and necessary implementing documents for the operation were prepared only for the operation's first phase—the period of the conduct of the amphibious landing on the coastline of Maattivuono Bay and the breakthrough of German defenses on the isthmus of Sredniy Peninsula. The organization of communications and orders for the subsequent period of the operation were developed during its course.

Wire communications were set up for the most part using existing permanent telephone and telegraph lines. The communications plan is shown in figures 6.1 and 6.2.

The communications plan was developed by fleet staff before the operation was approved on 11 September. It considered the establishment of the fleet commander's auxiliary command post on Sredniy Peninsula. The need for this facility was identified immediately prior to the start of the operation. But, despite this, the fleet staff chief of communications, Captain Second Rank Polozok, who was on Sredniy Peninsula to supervise the preparation of the communications system, was able to create a supplementary communications center for support of command and control from the fleet auxiliary command post using spare equipment consisting of a mobile transmitter and 100 kilometers of cable. Special attention was given to providing radio communications for coordination with 14th Army in the organization of fleet staff communications and the orders generated before the operation. Three radio nets (one reserve) were assigned to the Northern Defensive Region for this purpose. The station "Prima" was assigned to the defensive region's chief of communications for work in one of these nets (figure 6.2 shows the organizational structure).

When units approached each other on the battlefield, they were to use "coordination (regiment-battalion) radio communications for converging units" to establish their identity and coordinate their combat actions.

Encode/decode tables and message formats were developed for telephone and telegraph messages. The work of liaison officers was not discussed in the instructions that were developed, and the chief of communications did not even know who the liaison officers were and to where they would be sent. This must be acknowledged as a substantive shortcoming in the working out of communications issues for the operation.

In addition to schematics, tables of coded signals were developed for Northern Defensive Region coordination between units, with ships, and with Fleet Air Forces. These tables contained a list of the signals in use, of coded signals for use on the radio or telephone and for signal rockets and lights, and of who was to

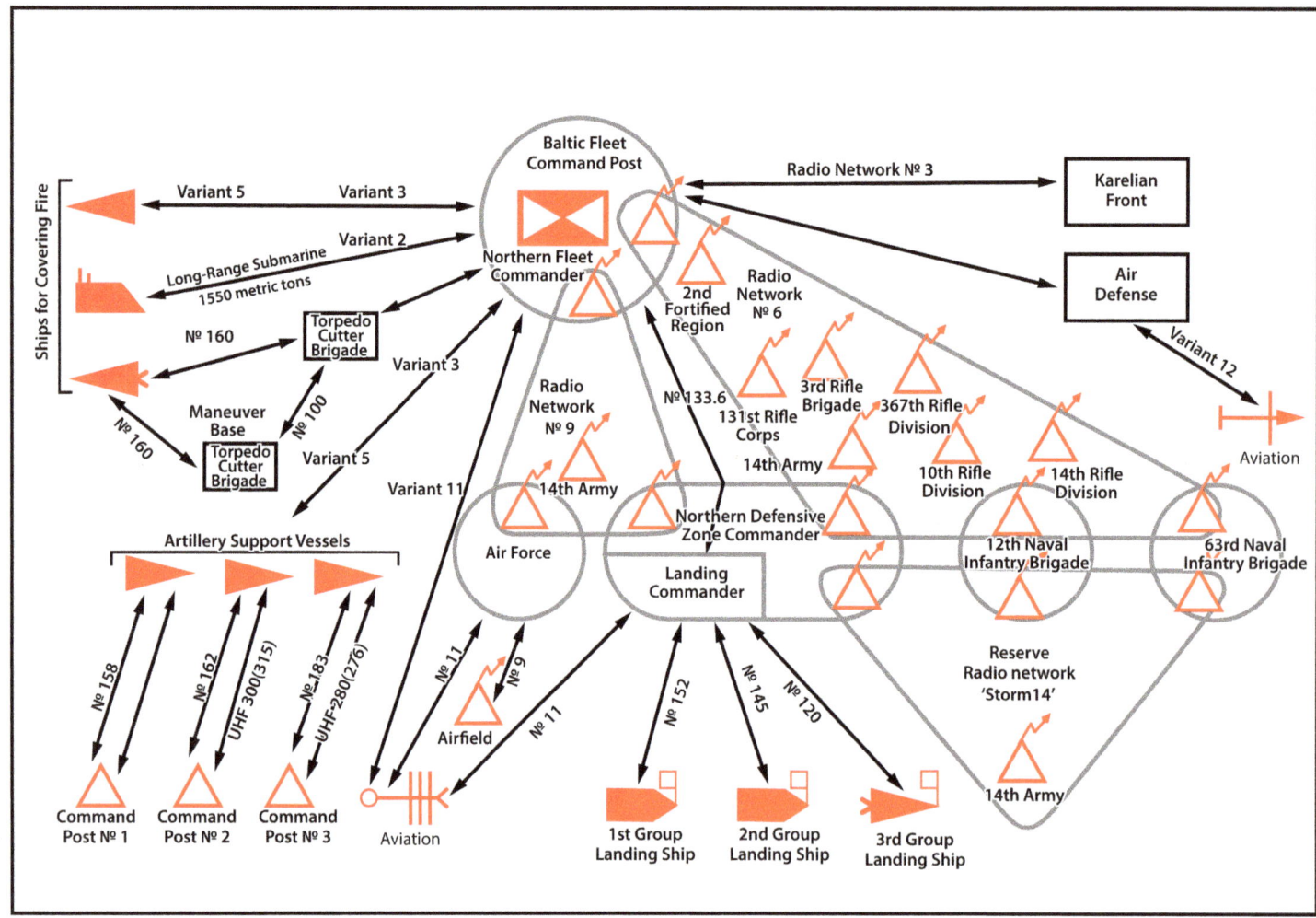

FIGURE 6.1. Organization of radio communications

initiate the signal. A call sign table was also developed for the officer component.

Appropriate communications schematics and instructions were also developed in organizing Fleet Air Forces communications, in the naval gunfire support detachment, and for the amphibious landing force commander. In addition, the amphibious landing commander had a table of 43 coded signals prepared for his use.

Communications support for combat command and control during the operation was at all times so good that there were never any concerns. As the operation proceeded, communications were provided at those positions designated by the fleet commander. Thus, for example, when the commander moved to the Pummanki area after the breakthrough of the enemy's defenses on the isthmus of Sredniy Peninsula, there was a need to provide communications at the new location. The radio sets of two observation and communications posts and Torpedo Cutter Brigade were used, and telephone lines were run to the command post.

Communications for support of the amphibious assault on Liinakhamari were prepared in the following manner. The fleet chief of staff assembled the communications chiefs of the landing units in Pummanki and gave them instructions on their work during the landing, designated the radio frequency already in use by Captain Barchenko's composite reconnaissance detachment, specified radio call signs, and distributed the available equipment.

Following this, he also confirmed their understanding of the organization of communications that had been established and clarified all questions that arose. He did not issue any written instructions. Communications were organized so that during the landing in Liinakhamari, the torpedo boats could talk openly

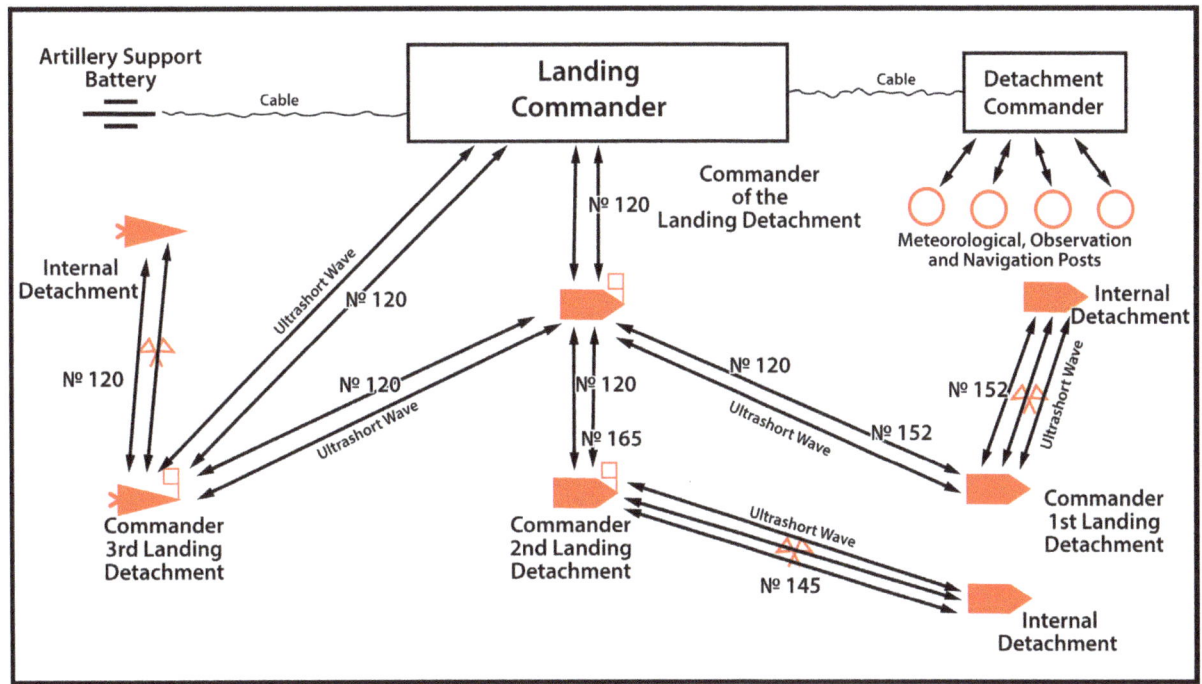

FIGURE 6.2. Organization of communications for the amphibious landing

using VHF, and the fleet commander could monitor the traffic. He could also hear the explosions of shells and shore battery fires.

After the occupation of Liinakhamari port, the escort vessel *Uragan* was brought to Liinakhamari and used to provide communications for the fleet commander. Its radio transmitter exchanged traffic with the Northern Defensive Region's main transmitter, and they could also patch through using the observation and communications service net. Dispatches traveled by telephone and telegraph from these locations to fleet headquarters in Polyarnoye.

The following data from tables showing the quantity and quality of coded message traffic from 7 to 31 October gives a representative indication of the work of communications assets during the operation. The distribution of messages prepared by fleet headquarters communications center, by priority, was as follows: IMMEDIATE—6.7 percent, URGENT—25.1 percent, PRIORITY—26 percent, and ROUTINE—42.2 percent.

Communications assets were heavily utilized during the operation, reaching their greatest peak on the day of the breakthrough of the defenses and the amphibious landings. The number of URGENT messages grew significantly during this period, from the normal 14 or 15 percent to 25 percent. The average time for the processing of a message through the communications center was satisfactory. A reduction in the processing time for reconnaissance summaries and combat reports from formations was achieved by transmitting them in clear text, encoding only unit designations using telegraph and telephone call signs, and their locations using a coded map.

A. MUTUAL RECOGNITION

Mutual recognition of ships between each other, with Fleet Air Forces, and with observation and communications service posts was accomplished using fleet operating instructions. Ground troops marked their positions for aviation by signaling, "Here is our forward trace" and "We are your troops." Much use was made of rocket flares and firing of tracer rounds for purposes of recognition. In addition to recognition signals, a five-round semaphore signal of the following colors was established to identify specific vessel types at sea: white for torpedo boats, green for small submarine chasers, and red for large submarine chasers.

General Lessons

A. Concerning Unit Actions During the Breakthrough of the Defenses on the Isthmus of Sredniy Peninsula and Pursuit of the Enemy

1. Twelfth Red Banner Naval Infantry Brigade accomplished its assigned mission and broke through the enemy's well-prepared and deeply echeloned defenses. The secrecy of the preparation and suddenness of the attack, as well as 63rd NIB's amphibious landing, made possible the rapid capture of the strongpoints on the left flank of the enemy's defenses. The development of the success that was achieved during the breakthrough led to the enemy's expulsion from the defensive zone, but not to their encirclement with subsequent capture or destruction of the strongpoint garrisons.
2. The pursuit of the retreating enemy was not sufficiently energetic. This is explained by the low degree of maneuverability of naval infantry units and their indecisive actions during periods of darkness.

    Pursuit of the enemy also was not rigorously undertaken after the naval infantry brigades reached Titovka–Porovaara Road. They delayed there, rather than quickly moving forward to the west and preventing the enemy from withdrawing their units. This must be acknowledged as the principal deficiency in the actions of the naval infantry units. The training of the soldiers for orientation on unfamiliar terrain during the transition to night conditions was weak, as a consequence of which night movement was curtailed. This enabled the enemy to break contact rapidly.

    Only the reconnaissance detachments of the Northern Defensive Region and headquarters, Northern Fleet, which executed the successful march to Cape Krestovyy in extremely difficult terrain conditions, were well prepared for night operations.
3. The actions of Northern Defensive Region engineer units did not support the construction of improved routes from the breakthrough area to Hill 146 and beyond toward Lake Tie-yarvi, as a consequence of which tanks and artillery units were forced to conduct a march by a longer route through Kutovaya, Titovka, and Hill 388.9. The slow clearing of mines and the restoration of the road from Kutovaya to Hill 388.9 and Porovaara caused a lengthy delay in the movement of artillery and their supply vehicles, and their falling behind infantry units.

B. During the Amphibious Landings

1. The amphibious landing on the coastline of Maattivuono Bay was conducted successfully and, thanks to tactical surprise, was a significant contribution to the breakthrough of the defenses on the isthmus of Sredniy Peninsula.

    The success of the landing was a result of transport of the landing force on fast-moving and shallow draft vessels, and strong artillery and air support. These made it exceedingly difficult for enemy shore batteries to fire upon the landing force during their activities.

    The landing site was well chosen. The absence of coastal roads prevented the enemy from rapidly bringing up the forces necessary to counter the landing. In addition, skillful and energetic actions by the boat and landed unit commanders enabled our units to capture a beachhead in a short time.

    A deficiency of the landing was that the commander did not have any reserve landing craft, and during the transit large subchasers considerably lengthened the formation. They also engaged in unnecessary radio conversation, and near the shore intermingled with the detachment in front of them, frequently disrupting the landing plan.

2. The success of the amphibious landing in Liinakhamari was achieved by its unexpectedness to the Germans, the momentum of the boats in breaking into Petsamovuono Inlet, and the coordinated and tactically sound employment of smoke screens. The actions of the amphibious landing force ashore were also energetic and decisive, which led to their success in overcoming more than one enemy counterattack.

3. The landings of assault forces on the southern coastline of Varangerfjord, which coincided with the forward advance of Karelian *Front* units in Pechenga Oblast toward the Norwegian border, were accomplished successfully. The landing areas were chosen with consideration for occupying sectors of the coastline on the enemy's flank and rear, thus more effectively supporting attacking 14th Army units. The good training of the troops and vessel crews, which they received in earlier landings, benefited them here.

    Northern Fleet Air Forces successfully accomplished all missions assigned to them for direct support of the attacking forces' actions. Their operations were correctly focused on suppression and destruction of artillery and mortar batteries, on strongpoints, and on enemy troops and vehicles on Titovka–Porovaara Road.

C. Concerning Actions on the Enemy's Sea Lines of Communication

1. Northern Fleet ships and aviation made a significant contribution to the success of the Karelian *Front*'s offensive and the amphibious landings by uninterrupted activities on the enemy's sea lines of communication in the area from Hammerfest to Varangerfjord. As a result of these operations at sea, the enemy was deprived of the ability to use their vital paths of communication in a planned manner, and suffered enormous losses in ships, men, supplies, and equipment.

2. Operational coordination was achieved by all participating forces during the battle on the sea lanes. Air strikes on enemy convoys were complemented by torpedo boat and submarine attacks. Most submarine attacks were carried out based on air reconnaissance. Several convoys were successively attacked by air strikes and then submarines. Such examples are indicative of the efficacy and genuine opportunity not only of operational, but also of tactical coordination of submarines and aviation, which the operations plan had not foreseen.

3. Radar equipment, present on type-V submarine acquired in England, was not employed during night search activities. No doubt this reduced the effectiveness of these vessels' actions.

4. The countless instances of failure of torpedoes to launch from the tubes of Type-V submarines attests to the fact that by the time of the conduct of this operation, the crews of these submarines had not fully mastered their new equipment. This negatively influenced the success of their attacks.

5. Northern Fleet Air Forces were sufficiently active on enemy sea lines of communication, and inflicted losses on the enemy. The most effective air assets were fighter-bombers, which employed the mast-top bombing technique. The attack bomber strikes were also successful in most cases.

    Among the shortcomings of air activities were the absence of necessary coordination between tactical groups, and the violation of established time intervals between attacking groups. This led to a concentration of the convoys' antiaircraft fires on each group separately, and subsequent significant losses.

    In addition, the weak determination and inability of some group leaders to arrive precisely at the target were revealed. The attacks of torpedo bombers, which in some cases launched their torpedoes against convoys from great distances and without aiming, were shown to be of little effect.

6. The following causal factors contributed to the success of the operation:
   - air superiority of our air forces, which prevented the enemy air forces from interfering with the concentration of forces or with their actions during the accomplishment of their missions;
   - precise work of political organs in support of the operation, as a result of which the enlisted ranks displayed unexampled bravery, a high degree of fighting spirit, and determination in the execution of their assigned missions;
   - the good work of rear service units in providing logistic support and materiel, and in rendering medical treatment.

D. Concerning Command and Control and the Accomplishment of Coordination

1. The organization of command and control and the work of staffs during the conduct of the operation fully supported combat command and control by the fleet major commands, in conditions of a rapidly changing situation. The fact that the fleet commander, Fleet Air Forces commander, Northern Defensive Region commander, and Torpedo Cutter Brigade commander were located at command posts positioned quite close to each other and to the area of combat activities to facilitate combat command and control was a great contributor to this success. This gave them the ability to react quickly to changes in the situation and influence the course of battle in a timely manner with appropriate instructions.

2. The success gained in the operation was a result of well-organized and rationally executed coordination of all participating forces, united in a single effort for the accomplishment of the assigned mission. The appropriately organized coordination between forces of the Karelian *Front* and Northern Fleet, and within the latter between its individual formations, permitted them to carry out their combat actions in a manner coordinated as to time and place.

3. The successful accomplishment of coordination in the operation was achieved by close mutual communications between staffs and the correct assigning of liaison officers. The quality of coordination greatly facilitated systematic staff control over the actions of subordinate formations and units, and as well the understanding of the fleet commander's plan and intent by all formation commanders. Each responsible individual staff leader clearly assumed his proper role in the operation.

4. The accomplishment of coordination was possible only because of continuously operating communications. Communications worked well during this operation. To a large degree, this was a result of the fact that the communications organization and written instructions for the operation were based on fleet standing operating procedures.

   Along with this the necessity was revealed to have a mobile, adequately equipped communications center at the disposal of the fleet chief of communications. Such a center was required for providing service to the fleet commander's auxiliary command post, which was deployed in the area of combat activities.

   During the conduct of the operation, ships and units of the amphibious landing force used the method of unciphered radio traffic for combat command and control while landing and consolidating ashore. It was possible to use uncoded radio messages during offensive actions in conditions of rapidly unfolding events, which demanded particularly rapid information concerning the situation and the issuing of urgent instructions. In these conditions, the enemy ordinarily was unable to interfere with the intentions of the attacker.

Conclusion

In this manner, Northern Fleet successfully accomplished its assigned mission for joint actions with Karelian *Front* forces in the liberation of Pechenga Oblast and the Soviet far north. All the combat actions were accomplished by Northern Fleet in close operational coordination with the forces of the Karelian *Front*.

The fleet's successful actions in the operation for the liberation of the Soviet far north received high praise from the Supreme High Commander, Comrade Stalin.

On 15 October 1944, by order of the Supreme High Commander, Northern Fleet formations and units that distinguished themselves in battles for the capture of the town Pechenga were granted the title "Pechenga." The following units received this honorific title in accordance with this order:

12th Red Banner Naval Infantry Brigade
104th Red Banner Cannon Artillery Regiment
113th Red Banner Separate Artillery Battalion
6th Fighter Aviation Division
2nd Safonov Guards Fighter Aviation Regiment
Red Banner Torpedo Cutter Brigade

On 1 November 1944, by order of the Supreme High Commander, the following Northern Fleet formations and units that distinguished themselves in battles for the capture of the town Kirkenes were granted the honorific title "Kirkenes:"

63rd Red Banner Naval Infantry Brigade
Order of Ushakov Brigade of Submarine Chasers
5th Red Banner Torpedo Bomber Aviation Division
118th Red Banner Air Reconnaissance Regiment
9th Guards Red Banner Torpedo Bomber Aviation Regiment
20th Fighter Aviation Regiment

For exemplary accomplishment of combat missions during the operation, the following fleet formations and units were awarded combat orders.

Order of Ushakov, 1st Class
Red Banner Submarine Brigade
Red Banner Torpedo Cutter Brigade
Brigade of Submarine Chasers

Order of the Red Banner
63rd Naval Infantry Brigade
5th Torpedo Bomber Aviation Division
6th Fighter Aviation Division
14th Mixed Aviation Division

118th Separate Air Reconnaissance Division
27th Fighter Aviation Division
46th Red Banner Attack Aviation Regiment
78th Fighter Aviation Regiment

Glossary of Abbreviations Used in Appendixes

The appendixes to this document consist of military orders and reports, and thus contain abbreviations of unit designations, tactical measures, and pieces of equipment. These abbreviations are retained in this translation in order to preserve the original terse and succinct military style of these documents. This glossary contains all the abbreviations used in the appendixes, with both their Russian and English meanings.

Abbreviation	Transliterated Russian	English
A	armiya	army
AD	artilleriskiy division	artillery battalion
APBr	avia-polevaya brigada	airfield brigade
APP	artilleriya podderzhki pekhoty	infantry support artillery
BA	beregovaya artilleriya	coastal artillery
BFKP	beregovoy flagmanskiy komandnyy punkt	shore main command post
BO	bolshoy okhotnik [BO BO—plural]	large submarine chaser
BrMP	brigada morskoy pekhoty	naval infantry brigade
BTKA	brigada torpednykh katerov	torpedo cutter brigade
ChF	Chorniye Flot	Black Sea Fleet
DD	dalnego deystviya	long-range
DES	desant	amphibious assault landing
DZ	dymovaya zavesa	smoke screen
GB	glavnaya baza	main base [Polyarnoye environs]
GO	gidrometeorologicheskoye obespecheniye	weather-meteorological support
KBrMP	krasnoznamennaya brigada morskoy pekhoty	red banner naval infantry brigade

continued on next page

Abbreviation	Transliterated Russian	English
KBPL	krasnoznamennaya brigada podvodnykh lodok	red banner submarine brigade
KOAD	krasnoznamennyy otdelnyy artilleriskiy division	red banner separate artillery battalion
KOM	kamnemet	explosive device that hurled stones, used by engineer troops to clear lanes in obstacles
KP	komandnyy punkt	command post
KPAP	krasnoznamennyy pushechnyy artilleriskiy polk	red banner cannon artillery regiment
M	minonosets [M M—plural]	destroyer escort
MD	minometnyy division	mortar battalion
MO	malyy okhotnik [MO MO—plural]	small submarine chaser
MSO	mediko-sanitarnyy otryad	medical detachment
NP	nablyudatelnyy punkt	observation post
NSU	neopoznannoye sudno	unidentified ship
OAB	otdelnaya artilleriskaya brigada	separate artillery brigade
OIB	otdelnyy inzhenernyy batalon	separate engineer battalion
OIBr	otdelnaya inzhenernaya brigada	separate engineer brigade
OKhV	otdelnyy khimicheskiy vzvod	separate chemical platoon
op	operativnyy prikaz	operations order
OP	opornyy punkt	strongpoint
OPB	otdelnyy pekhotniy batalon	separate infantry battalion (German)
OPBMP	otdelnyy pulemetnyy batalon morskoy pekhoty	separate naval infantry machine-gun battalion
ORAD	otdelnyy razvedyvatelnyy artilleriskiy	separate artillery reconnaissance battalion division
OShB	otdelnyy shtrafnoy batalon	separate punishment battalion
OShR	otdelnaya shtrafnaya rota	separate punishment company
OVR	oborona vodnogo rayona	defense of seaward approaches
PAKP	pushechno-artilleriyskiy krasno-znamennyy polk	red banner cannon artillery regiment
PL	podvodnaya lodka [PL PL—plural]	submarine
PLO	protivolodochnaya oborona	antisubmarine defense
PP	pekhotnyy polk	infantry regiment (German)
PSO	posledovatelnoye sosredotocheniye ognya	successive fire concentration [artillery fire technique]
PVO	protivovozdushnaya oborona	antiaircraft defense
RO	razvedyvatelnyy otryad	reconnaissance
RTS	radiotekhnicheskiye sredstva	radio technical means [radar]
SB	strelkovyy batalon	rifle battalion
SF	severnyy flot	Northern Fleet
ShSF	shtab, severnogo flota	headquarters (staff), Northern Fleet
SIDR	sapernaya inzhenernaya desant-naya rota	sapper engineer assault company
SKA	storozhevoy kater [SKA SKA—plural]	patrol cutter(s)
SKR	storozhevoy korabl	escort vessel
SO	sosredotochennyy ogon	concentrated fire [artillery]

continued on next page

Abbreviation	Transliterated Russian	English
SOR	severnyy oboronitelnyy rayon	Northern Defensive Region
TA	torpednaya apparatura	torpedo tube or apparatus
TAD	tyazhelyy artilleriskiy division	heavy artillery battalion (German)
TKA	torpednyy kater [TKA TKA—plural]	torpedo cutter(s)
TR	transport [TR TR—plural]	cargo vessel(s)
TShch	tral'shchik [TShch TShch—plural]	minesweeper(s)
VMF SSSR	voyenno-morskoy flot soyuza sovetskikh sotsialisticheskikh respublik	Navy of the Union of Soviet Socialist Republics
VOSO	sluzhba voyennykh soobshcheniy	military transportation service
VVS	voyennovozdushnyye sila	air forces
VZR	vpyshko-zvukovaya rota	sound-flash company [artillery]
ZA	zenitnaya artilleriya	antiaircraft artillery
ZAP	zenitnyy artilleriskiy polk	antiaircraft artillery regiment
ZKP	zapasnyy komandnyy punkt	alternate command post

APPENDIX 1

Order of the Commander, Northern Fleet

08 September 1944 No. 0048/*op* Headquarters *SF*–Polyarnoye

Top Secret
Copy No.

Contents: Organization and composition of *SF* forces for Operation "West," being conducted jointly with 14 A for the defeat of the German Western Litsa [River] grouping.

I designate the following composition and organization of forces for Operation "WEST," being conducted jointly with 14 A for the defeat of the German Western Litsa grouping by amphibious landing and attack in their rear and a breakthrough from the front of the enemy's defenses on the isthmus of Sredniy Peninsula.

1. *Group of Ground and Amphibious Assault Forces*
   a. Commander of ground and amphibious assault forces is Major General Dubovtsev.
   b. Deputy commander for political affairs is Colonel Vagudin.
   c. Chief of staff is Captain First Rank Tuz.
   d. Ground forces are *12 KBrMP*, at full strength.
   e. Amphibious assault forces are *63 BrMP*, with *RO ShSF* and units attached to *SOR*; commander of the amphibious assault force is Colonel Krylov, commander of *63 BrMP*; deputy commander for political affairs is Colonel Fomin; controlling headquarters of the amphibious assault force is *63 BrMP* headquarters.
   f. Artillery units are *113 KOAD* and *104 KPAP*.
   g. Aviation component is Pummanki air operations group, consisting of 8–10 ground attack *Il-2s* and 16–20 fighters; three forward air controller aircraft provided by *VVS SF*.

2. *Forces for Landing Amphibious Assault*
   a. Landing commander is Rear Admiral Mikhaylov, commander of *OVR GB SF*; deputy landing commander for political affairs is Captain Second Rank Shulyak; the landing force commander will designate the landing force headquarters.
   b. Landing force vessels are the ships of *OVR GB SF*, consisting of 10 or 11 *BO* and 8–12 *MO*; 10–12 *TKA* from *BTKA* are placed in operational subordination to the landing force commander.
   c. Landing ship detachments:

1st Detachment: 8–12 *MO*;

2nd Detachment: 10–11 *BO*;

3rd Detachment: 10 *TKA*;

Detachment commanders and headquarters are as designated by landing force commander.

d. Commander of embarkation base and chief of engineer service for landing and billeting are as designated by commander, *SOR SF*;

commandants of embarkation and landing points are as designated by landing force commander.

e. Commander of navigational support detachment is Captain Third Rank Shelgunov, and commanders of three navigational support posts are as designated by chief, *GO SF*.

3. *Covering and Supporting Forces*

   A. **NAVAL GUNFIRE AND COVERING DETACHMENT.**

   a. Detachment commander is Captain First Rank Fokin, commander of the Northern Fleet Surface Squadron; detachment headquarters is Surface Squadron Headquarters.

   b. Naval gunfire support group: two type "G" *M*; group commander as designated by commander, Surface Squadron *SF*.

   c. Covering group: three or four type "G" *M*; commander is commander, Surface Squadron *SF*.

   B. **AVIATION.** All available torpedo, bomber, attack bomber, fighter, and reconnaissance aviation of *GB SF*, excluding assets in operational subordination to commander, *SOR* commander, *VVS SF* is commanding.

   C. **TORPEDO CUTTERS.** Attack group 10–12 *TKA*. Captain First Rank Kuzmin, commander, *BTKA*, is commanding.

   D. **SUBMARINES.** Attack group is 8–10 *PL*. Captain First Rank Kilyshkin, commander, *KBPL*, is commanding.

   F. **SHORE DEFENSE.** *BO GB SF* in existing composition. Major General Kustov, commandant of *BO GB SF*, is commanding.

   G. **FORCES AND ASSETS OF OVR.** All *OVR* assets not occupied in the amphibious landing are supporting defense of Kola Inlet. Officer designated by commander, *OVR GB SF*, is commanding.

4. *Transportation and Supporting Detachments*

   A. **FLEET TRANSPORTATION DETACHMENT.** Militarized ships of *VOSO SF* and auxiliary ships of *SF* Logistics Command. Captain Third Rank Sablin, chief, *VOSO SF*, is commanding.

   B. **RESCUE DETACHMENT.** One rescue tugboat and two rescue boats. Captain Second Rank Georgi is commanding.

   C. **EVACUATION DETACHMENT.** Two fishing boats of *MSO* and steamer *Sosnovets*. Commander of *MSO SF* ship detachment is commanding.

5. *Liaison Officers*

   with Headquarters, Karelian *Front*: Lieutenant Colonel Kazanovskiy;

   with Headquarters, 14 Army: Lieutenant Colonel Ostrikov;

   with staff of commander, *SOR*: Captain First Rank Meshcheryakov;

   with staff of landing force commander: Captain Third Rank Sutyagin.

6. *I am Commander of Overall Operation*

Commanders of landing force are subordinated to commander, *SOR SF*, Major General Dubovtsev.

My *BFKP* is at Polyarnoye, *ZKP* is at Pummanki.

Appendixes: schematic of chain of command on one sheet (overlay).

Commander, Northern Fleet	Member of *SF* Military Council
Admiral (*Golovko*)	Vice Admiral (*Nikolaev*)

Chief of Staff, Northern Fleet
Rear Admiral (*Platonov*)

APPENDIX 2

Combat Directive No. 0052/*op* of Commander, Northern Fleet

(FOR OPERATION "WEST")

Top Secret
of special importance
Copy No.
  To: Commander, Northern Defensive Region *SF*;
      Commander, *SF* Air Forces;
      Commander, Northern Fleet Surface Squadron;
      Commander, Defense of Main Base Seaward Approaches *SF*;
      Commander, Torpedo Cutter Brigade *SF*;
      Commander, Red Banner Submarine Brigade *SF*;
      Commandant, Shore Defenses Main Base *SF*.
Copies to:
      Commander in Chief, Karelian *Front*, Army General Comrade Meretskov
      Chief of Main Naval Staff *VMF SSSR*, Admiral Comrade Alafuzov
      Commander in Chief, 14 Army, Karelian *Front*, Lieutenant General Comrade Shcherbakov
      Headquarters Northern Fleet, Polyarnoye
      1430, 01.10 44 [1 October 1944]
      Maps:
          a. naval nos. 1434, 1320, 2513
          b. joint operations No. 2452
          c. topographic, 50,000 and 100,000

1. The enemy continues to support naval shipping between the ports of Narvik, Hammerfest, and Varangerfjord with his fleet and air assets. He is attempting to disrupt the movement of Allied convoys in the Barents with submarines, and to contest the transit of our ships and convoys in the Kara and southwestern portion of Barents Seas. He has strengthened his air reconnaissance of the front line on the Murmansk axis, trying to determine the grouping of our forces and defensive system. Ground forces of XIX Mountain Corps "Norway" are defending on the Murmansk axis, with the goal of holding on to currently occupied positions.

    In connection with Finland's exit from the war, as well as under pressure of Karelian *Front* units, German Twentieth Army units are withdrawing in the southern sector of the front. The concentration of the German 20th Army in northern Finland and in Pechenga Oblast is possible. Attempts to withdraw forces of the Western Litsa grouping into Norway are possible. During the withdrawal of enemy forces from northern Finland and Petsamo Oblast onto Norwegian territory, the evacuation of the forces themselves and their combat assets by sea through Varangerfjord ports is possible.

2. 14 Army, on special order of Commander, Karelian *Front*, intends to go over to the offensive in cooperation with Northern Fleet, with the mission to defeat the enemy's Western Litsa grouping.

3. [I order] **Northern Fleet**:
   a. To prevent evacuation of enemy troops by sea through Varangerfjord ports in the sector from Kirkenes to Hammerfest, and to destroy all enemy shipping assets in his attempt to withdraw by sea;
   b. With group of ground and amphibious landing forces of *SOR*, consisting of two infantry brigades with attached units, with support and cover by Fleet Air Forces and surface vessels, to break through the western sector of enemy defenses on isthmus of Sredniy Peninsula. Simultaneously to land by amphibious assault in rear across Maattivuono, bypass left flank of enemy defenses and, reaching Titovka–Petsamo Road in area of Rasvatunturi Hill, firmly hold it and prevent enemy from withdrawing forces along road to Petsamo.

   I order:

   A. Commander, Northern Defensive Region *SF*, with attached amphibious landing ships and operational air group, to be prepared on my special order to execute the following missions:
   a. **immediate**: Seize shoreline of Maattivuono Bay in area of Cape Punaynenniemi and Cape Akhkioniemi with amphibious assault by *63 BrMP* and reinforcing units. Conduct attack into rear of enemy defenses in the western sector of isthmus between mainland and Sredniy Peninsula.
   b. **subsequent**: Break through and destroy enemy defenses in the western sector of isthmus between mainland and Sredniy Peninsula by joint actions of *12 KBrMP* from the front and *63 BrMP* from the rear, with support of *SOR* artillery and Fleet Air Forces.
   c. **follow-on**: *12* and *63 BrMP* with attached units, supported by *SOR* artillery and Fleet Air Forces, to reach Titovka–Porovaara Road. Hold it firmly, prevent enemy from using road to withdraw his forces to Petsamo. Keep in mind attack on Petsamo after linking up with 14 Army units.
   d. With *SOR* artillery, operationally attached aviation, and in conjunction with Fleet Air Forces, to support landing and movement of landed forces, breakthrough of enemy defensive zone, and subsequent infantry movement to Titovka–Porovaara Road.
   e. With *ZA* assets and operationally attached aviation, to provide protection of assault forces and ships in concentration areas and in southern portion of Pummanki Bay.
   f. Be prepared to move reserves by sea for amphibious assault and to execute its withdrawal, depending on situation.

   B. [I order] Commander, *VVS SF*
   a. Suppress enemy shore batteries at entrance to Petsamovuono Inlet with bombing strikes to support landing of *63 BrMP*.
   b. Support breakthrough of enemy defenses by *SOR* units by bombing strikes on enemy artillery *OP*, his reserves, and command posts.
   c. Paralyze enemy air activity by bombing strikes on enemy airfields at Luostari and Salmiyarvi.
   d. Prevent bringing up of reserves to area of actions of *SOR* ground units and withdrawal of enemy forces from Titovka by bombing strikes on enemy forces in Titovka area and on Titovka–Petsamo Road.
   e. Maintain observation of enemy troops, air assets, and ships by systematic air reconnaissance or roads in Titovka–Tana region, of airfields at Heybukten, Luostari, Salmiyarvi, and bases at Kirkenes, Vadso, and Vardo.
   f. Continue to destroy enemy convoys and ships on Kirkenes–Hammerfest shipping lane, in Kirkenes, Vardo, and Vadso harbors and, jointly with *TKA TKA*, in Varangerfjord.
   g. Place an air operations group of 16–20 fighters, 8–10 attack aircraft, and three forward air controllers on Pummanki airfield, operationally subordinated to commander, *SOR*.

   C. Commander, *OVR GB SF*
   a. With *BO BO* and *MO MO* and attached *TKA*, covertly land amphibious force of *63 BrMP* with attached units in area of Cape Punaynenniemi and Cape Akhkioniemi on order of commander, *SOR*.
   b. Keep vessels in state of readiness to extract amphibious landing force in event of withdrawal under pressure or superior enemy force, and designate a portion of vessels to provide support to amphibious force after landing.

D. Commander, Brigade *TKA SF*

a. On my special order, place 10 *TKA* in operational subordination of commander, *OVR GB SF* in Pummanki for landing amphibious force.

b. Disrupt enemy sea lines of communication in Varangerfjord with attack group of 8 to 10 *TKA*, operating independently and jointly with air forces.

c. Cover transit and landing of amphibious force against enemy surface vessels from Varangerfjord by *TKA TKA* patrol on line Kobbholmfjord to Aynov Island.

E. Commander, Red Banner Submarine Brigade, *SF*

a. Disrupt enemy lines of communication with torpedo attacks and mine emplacement against his convoys with six to eight *PL*, deployed on my special order near enemy coast between Vardo and meridian 20°00.

b. Maintain two *PL* in reserve at *GB*.

F. Commander, Surface Squadron *SF*

a. Suppress enemy batteries in area of Hill 195.8 with naval gunfire of two destroyer escorts from Motovskiy Bay to support breakthrough of enemy defenses by *SOR SF* units and their subsequent forward movement.

b. On my special order, destroy bridge on Titovka River and destroy defenses of enemy *OP Oberhof*.

c. According to situation, on my special order, cover landing of amphibious force against enemy surface vessels with four *M*. Be prepared to conduct strikes against enemy convoys on Vardo-Nordkin shipping lane with these same vessels, independently in nonflying weather, and under air cover in event of flying weather. Maintain *M M* at readiness level No. 2 at Kil'din Inlet.

G. Commander, Shore Defenses *GB SF*

While the operation is being conducted, strengthen readiness for defense of *GB SF* from sea and cover departure of ships to operation from Kola Inlet and return with *BO* batteries.

H. To commanders of all major fleet formations:

a. 4 October 1944 is the time of unit preparedness to conduct operation. After 4 October 1944, units will be prepared to conduct operation on 24 hours' notice. Action will begin on my special order.

b. Observe strictest secrecy during preparatory period for operation, and do not disclose its concept by preparatory measures. Assign limited number of officers, related to operations work, to development of operation, under personal responsibility of formation commanders and chiefs of staff.

c. My location will be *BFKP* Polyarnoye. *ZKP* is at Pummanki.

4. I rescind my combat directive No. 0049/*op* of 08.09.44 [9 August 1944].

Enclosure: Planning Table for operation "West" in 3 pages.

Commander, Northern Fleet	Member of Military Council *SF*
Admiral (*Golovko*)	Vice Admiral (*Nikolaev*)

Chief of Staff *SF*
Rear Admiral (*Platonov*)

Approved		Top Secret
/s/ Commander, *SF*	/s/ Member of Military Council *SF*	of special importance
Admiral (*Golovko*)	Vice Admiral (*Nikolaev*)	Copy No. ____

/s/ Chief of Staff *SF* Rear Admiral (*Platonov*)
/s/ Chief of Operations Section *ShSF* Captain Second Rank (*G. Ivanov*)

TABLE A2.1. Planning table for operation "West," a joint operation with 14 Army to defeat Western Litsa Group of German forces

Actions of Fleet Forces

Phases	Amphibious Assault Landing and Breakthrough Forces	Breakthrough Forces	Artillery	Amphibious Assault Landing Vessels	Naval Gunfire Support Vessels	Screening Vessels	Fleet Air Forces
Third day prior to breakthrough of enemy defenses			Along with aviation, suppress enemy shore batteries at Petsamo Inlet				Suppress enemy shore batteries at entrance to Petsamo Inlet
Second night prior to breakthrough of enemy defenses			Maintain suppression of shore batteries at entrance to Petsamo Inlet				Maintain suppression of shore batteries at entrance to Petsamo Inlet
Second day prior to breakthrough of enemy defenses			Along with aviation, suppress enemy batteries, targets nos. 1, 7, 8, 25				Suppress enemy batteries, targets nos. 1, 7, 8, 25
First night prior to breakthrough	Concentrate in loading areas	Execute passages in obstacles	Continue suppression of batteries at entrance to Petsamo Inlet	Concentrate in loading areas	With naval gunfire of two M, suppress targets 1, 25. Destroy OP *Oberhof*, bridge on Titovka River. Support PLO with 2 MO (RTS).		Maintain suppression of batteries at entrance to Petsamo
First day prior to breakthrough			Destroy enemy defensive fortifications in breakthrough sector. Suppress shore batteries at entrance to Petsamo Inlet.				PVO of DEC ship and troop concentration. Suppress enemy shore batteries at entrance to Petsamo Inlet. Destroy enemy defensive fortifications and command and control by strikes on enemy *KP* and reserves.
Night of DEC landing, breakthrough of enemy defenses. Uploading of DEC to 2100	Load ships at Pummanki as per loading plan			Upload amphibious landing force per loading schedule		1. *TKA* group conducts patrol on line Kobbholmfjord—Aynov Island	

continued on next page

TABLE A2.1—continued

	Actions of Fleet Forces					
Transit by sea to 2300 Landing of DEC to 2400	Move on amphibious assault ships to landing areas at Capes Punaynenniemi and Ahkioniemi	Concentrate in departure areas for attack. Execute passages in enemy obstacles.	Continue suppression of batteries at entrance to Petsamo Inlet. APP-63 group be prepared to suppress enemy in landing area. Destroy defensive fortifications in breakthrough sector.	Transit in three echelons (detachments) to landing area: 1 ech.-10 MO 2 ech.-11 BO 3 ech.-10 TKA	1. M M suppress artillery batteries targets nos. 1, 25. Secondary targets—Titovka River bridge and OP Oberhof. Two MO (RTS) or two D-3 TKA support PLO.	2. M M at readiness level 2 in Kildin Inlet. 3. PL PL deploy on special order near enemy coastline. 4. TKA TKA strike group be prepared for actions against enemy convoys and ships.	Suppress enemy defenses in Petsamo area (bomb strikes)
					2. Demonstration assault group: two D-3		
Arrival of DEC in rear of enemy defenses to 0330	Attack toward Lake Selkyayarvi, south shore of Lake Mustayarvi to reach rear of enemy defenses		APP-63 group support movement of landing force with PSO. Destroy defensive fortifications in breakthrough sector.	Return to Pummanki and GB. Detachment six MO and two BO remain in Pummanki to provide supplies to DEC. TKA TKA go to Dolgaya Bay, BO BO to Pala Bay, 2–4 MO to Pala Bay.	TKA, one RTS, 2–3 motor launches demonstrate DES in Motovskiy Bay from 2300 at Cape Pikshuev, Cape Mogilnyy using machine-gun fire, smoke screens, firing of rockets, launching of one torpedo in feint toward Titovka. Group depart Vladimir port on signal.	Varangerfjord. From moment of departure of DES, move from Vladimir port to Pummanki.	

continued on next page

TABLE A2.1—continued

	Actions of Fleet Forces			
Artillery preparation [0330] to 0500	Concentrate at attack positions, support flanks and rear	Concentrate at attack positions	All artillery conduct prep fires as per artillery preparation plan	TKA TKA group withdraw from patrol to base	
Attack at 0500	Attack enemy OP on Hill 260 with portion of forces and destroy defenders. Hold line south shore of Lake Selkyayarvi, reference point 203.	Attack enemy OP on Hill 146 and destroy defenders	Shift fires to enemy defenses on Yaukhonomantunturi Ridge to suppress defense and prevent movement of reserves		Continuous suppression of artillery batteries—targets nos. 1, 7, 8, 9, 25, and deny reserve movement by attacks on roads and troop areas around Hill 388.9
First day of battle. Fighting in depth of defenses to 1800	12 and 63 BrMP reach south shore of Lake Selkyayarvi, reference point 203, west shore of lake at reference point 64	Support movement of infantry. Do not fire at targets serviced by aviation, to protect aircraft safety.			
Second day of battle	Reach line Rasvatunturi Hill, Lake Ustoyarvi	Support movement of infantry. Reposition artillery units to areas where infantry units are operating same as previous day.			
Third day of battle	Reach				

1. During the three days prior to the beginning of the operation (landing of the amphibious assault force), aviation conducts reconnaissance of the forces in SOR sector: along Titovka–Petsamo Road; Luostari, Heybukten, and Salmiyarvi airfields; enemy shipping lanes and ports. It also operates against enemy convoys, being careful to avoid attacks on our forces designated for suppression of enemy firing positions in support of the amphibious landing and those confirming the enemy defensive zone. Combined air attacks on convoys with TKA TKA, and on enemy airfields are to be conducted upon order of the fleet commander depending on the situation.

2. The inclusion of navigational support assets for the movement of the demonstration amphibious assault force (in Motovskiy Bay) is by order of the landing force commander.

APPENDIX 3

Combat Order No. 0014/*op*, Headquarters Northern Defensive Region *SF*

Top Secret
Copy No.

3.10.44 [3 October 1944] 1700 Hill 159.0 ground forces maps: 50,000; 100,000—1941 naval maps: No. 1320, No. 2452 (joint operations)

1. Enemy is defending with forces of *503 APBr*, *199 PP*, *10* Chemical Mortar Battalion, and artillery reinforcements in the sector Peuravuono Bay–Titovka Bay. According to unconfirmed data, enemy defense is reinforced by *13* and *14 OPB*. Coastline of Peuravuono Bay and Pitkyavuonofjord is defended by separate strongpoints of *1/503 APBr*, *1/193 PP* is defending Mustatunturi Range, and *2/* and *3/503 APBr* are defending Yakhonokan-tunturi Hill and Hill 109.0. Enemy defense has developed system of engineer fortifications and obstacles. Use of flame throwers by enemy is possible.

2. The Northern Defensive Region has been assigned the following missions:
    a. **Immediate**: Capture Maattivuono Bay coastline in sector Cape Santerinniemi–Cape Akhkioniemi by amphibious assault of *63 BrMP* and attached subunits; move into flank and rear of enemy defenses in Mustatunturi Range.
    b. **Subsequent**: Bypassing his flank, break through and destroy enemy defenses in Mustatunturi Range by joint actions of *12 KBrMP* from front and *63 BrMP* from rear with support of *SOR* artillery and *SF* air forces.
    c. **Follow-on**: *12 KBrMP* and *63 BrMP*, with attached subunits and support of *SOR* artillery and *SF* air forces, reach Porovaara–Titovka Road, firmly hold it, prevent enemy from using road to withdraw his forces to Petsamo.

3. Units of 14 Army are to destroy enemy's Western Litsa grouping.

4. I have decided:
    a. Having landed amphibiously at night in the area of Cape Santerinniemi and Cape Akhkioniemi, *63 BrMP* is to bypass left flank of enemy defenses in Mustatunturi Range, capture shore battery on Cape Krestovyy with forces of *RO SOR* and *RO ShSF*.
    b. After *63 BrMP* reaches flank and rear of enemy defense in Mustatunturi Range, *12 KBrMP* is to break through enemy's fortified

position in sector Ivari–Mustatunturi Range. Together with *63 BrMP*, destroy enemy forces defending in area of Hill 146, Hill 260, and reach road Lake Ustoyarvi–Mustatunturi Range.

    c. Subsequently, attacking along road from Lake Ustoyarvi to Mustatunturi Range, *12* and *63 BrMP* are to reach Porovaara–Titovka Road in area of Rasvatunturi Hill, Hill 276, and Hill 388.9. Holding road firmly, prevent enemy's use of road for withdrawal of his forces.

    d. Defend sector Ivari–Kutovaya with forces of *347* and *348 OPBMP*.

    e. Maintain *4/12 KBrMP*, *349 OPBMP*, and tank company in reserve.

5. *63 BrMP*, with attached *RO SOR*, *RO ShSF*, one sapper company of *388 OIB*, *506 SIDR*, *OKhV*, comprise the amphibious assault force. Commander, *63 BrMP* is the assault force commander.

    Immediate mission: To be landed in sector Cape Santerinniemi–Cape Akhkioniemi to destroy enemy units in landing area. Loading sites: No. 1-pier *NORD-1* (Pummanki); No. 2-pier *NORD-2* (Porokharyu Hill); No. 3-pier *NORD-3* (floating). Ten *MO*, ten *BO*, ten *TKA* are set aside for transporting the landing force. Uploading is from 2000 to 2200, landing from 2230 to 2400.

    Subsequent mission: To reach the area of Lake Selkyayarvi–Lake Mustayarvi, bypassing the enemy's defenses in Mustatunturi Range from rear, with a portion of forces acting with *12 KBrMP* to destroy enemy forces defending in area of Hills 146 and 260. With remaining forces, to prevent the approach of enemy reserves to breakthrough area from south along road Lake Ustoyarvi–Mustatunturi Range, holding the line of antitank ditch in area of Lake Selkyayarvi.

    Follow-on mission: To reach area of Rasvatunturi Hill, Hill 276, Hill 299; get firmly astride Porovaara–Titovka Road and, in cooperation with *12 BrMP*, prevent enemy from moving forces along road. Reconnaissance detachment *SOR* and reconnaissance detachment *ShSF* are to land on coastline of Punaynen-lakhti Bay north of Hill 141 with mission to capture 150 mm enemy battery on Cape Krestovyy (grid square 2836-9), holding *OP* until arrival of brigade units.

    Supporting units: *104 PAKP*, *113 KOAD*, *SOR* aviation operational group. Boundary with *12 KBrMP* is Cape Akhkioniemi, east shore of lake at reference point 114, south shore of Lake Mustayarvi, Hill 348, Hill 299, Hill 231.

6. *KBrMP* minus *4 SB* with attached *614 OShR*, *589 OShB*, *1 SOR* Obstacle Detachment, one sapper company of *388 OIBr*, *717 OKhV*.

    Immediate mission: In cooperation with *63 BrMP*, to break through enemy fortified position in sector Hill 146, Hill 260. Artillery preparation is from 0330 to 0500. Attack is at 0500. *104 PAKP*, *113 KOAD*, artillery of *63 BrMP*, *347*, *348*, *349 OPBMP*, and air operations group *SOR SF* are supporting during the breakthrough.

    Subsequent mission: Reach area Lake Suormusyarvi, Hill 388.9, Hill 326.5, get firmly astride Porovaara–Titovka Road. Firmly hold road from Ustoyarvi to Mustatunturi Range to support delivery of provisions to *63 BrMP* and *12 KBrMP*.

    Follow-on mission: In cooperation with *63 BrMP*, prevent enemy from moving forces along Titovka–Porovaara Road.

    Supporting units: *104 PAKP*, *113 KOAD*, *SOR SR* air operations group.

7. *347 OPBMP* with attached *348 OPBMP* are to defend sector Ivari–Kutovaya.

    Mission: Prevent enemy from breaking through across isthmus of Sredniy Peninsula. Support breakthrough of *12 KBrMP* in area Ivari—west slopes of Mustatunturi Range with active measures. Combat outpost line is as before. Be prepared to move right flank of combat outposts to southern slopes of Mustatunturi Range.

8. *SOR* artillery: *DD* is *104 PAKP* minus *284 AD*; *VZR* 225 *ORAD*, artillery section of *SOR*

    [forward air controllers, see para. 9e below]. *BA* is *113 KOAD* with attached *858 OAB*.

    APP-12 is *12 KBrMP AD* and *MD*, *284/204 PAKP*; two batteries *348 OPBMP*.

    APP-63 is *63 BrMP AD* and *MD*, one battery *347 OPBMP*, three batteries *349 OPBMP*.

Missions:

    a. Destroy command and control of enemy defense with powerful artillery barrage on *KP* in area of Hill 388.9.

    b. During the transit by sea and landing of *63 BrMP* amphibious force, suppress artillery batteries of enemy's *517 TAD*, targets nos. 71, 75, 76, 78 with *DD* and *BA* groups. *APP-63* is to destroy enemy troops and firing assets in brigade's landing area.

c. Support *63 BrMP* movement into rear of enemy defenses in Mustatunturi Range with successive fire concentrations on centers of resistance in depth of defense.
   d. Destroy enemy fire system and engineer fortifications on western and southern slopes of Mustatunturi Range with concentrated strike of all artillery means during breakthrough of enemy defenses.
   e. Together with Northern Fleet Surface Squadron destroyer escort group, suppress enemy artillery batteries, targets nos. 1, 2, 7, 8, 9, 25.
   f. Support movement of *12 KBrMP* and *63 BrMP* units to Titovka–Porovaara Road with successive fire concentrations on centers of resistance in depth of enemy defenses. Groups *APP-63* and *APP-12* are resubordinated to brigade commanders upon arrival of *12 KBrMP* units to line of lake with reference point 235, Lake Mustayarvi.

9. Missions of air operations group:
   a. Suppress enemy batteries at Ristiniemi, Numeroniemi, and Liinakhamari by bombing attacks combined with *SOR* artillery strikes.
   b. Disrupt command and control and prevent maneuver of enemy forces during breakthrough of their defenses with air strikes on enemy *KP*s and reserves in area of Hill 388.9.
   c. Destroy enemy reserves and retreating forces with air strikes on enemy forces on Porovaara–Titovka Road.
   d. Conduct systematic reconnaissance of movement of enemy forces on Porovaara–Titovka Road.
   e. Support adjustment of artillery fires of *104 PAKP* with forward air controllers. Sorties for this purpose will be on my command.
   f. In cooperation with *189 ZAP*, prevent enemy air strikes in concentration area of amphibious forces and means in southern portion of Pummankivuono Inlet.

10. **Missions** to amphibious landing commander: Land amphibious forces of *63 BrMP* in area of Cape Santerinniemi–Cape Akhkioniemi; land reconnaissance detachment on coastline of Punaynen-lakhti north of Hill 141. Support *63 BrMP* with provisions and movement of ammunition and evacuation of wounded until its linkup with *12 KBrMP* and clearing of enemy from road from Mustatunturi to Lake Ustoyarvi. Uploading of amphibious force is in southern portion of Pummankivuono Inlet. Upload points: No. 1–pier *NORD-1* (Pummanki), No. 2—pier *NORD-2* (Porokharyu), No. 3—pier *NORD-3* (floating). Uploading is from 2000 to 2200, landing from 2230 to 2400. *SOR* artillery covers concentration, uploading, transit by sea, and landing of amphibious force on shore.

11. **Mission** of 189 Antiaircraft Regiment: In coordination with air operations group, prevent air strikes by enemy aircraft on following areas: concentration areas of amphibious forces and means in southern portion of Pummankivuono Inlet; *12 KBrMP* troop concentrations and *SOR* artillery firing positions in western and southern portions of Sredniy Peninsula; Pummanki airfield and *SOR* logistic supply facilities. Opening of fire is at your discretion.

12. My reserve: *4/12 KBrMP* and *349 OPBMP* with attached tank company. Commander of *349 OPBMP* is reserve commander. On my signal, concentrate in area of Korabel'nyy stream. Be on one hour's notice to arrive at Titovka–Porovaara Road for combined actions with *12* and *63 BrMP*.

13. Time for preparedness of all units to execute missions is 2400, 5.10.44 [5 October 1944], 24 hours after my special order.

14. My *FKP* is at Hill 342; auxiliary on southern slope of Hill 342.
    Communications: Radio, telephone, runners. Submit reports: First—concerning the concentration at departure positions for attack and uploading; second—at commencement of landing and attack; third—upon completion of landing and breakthrough of enemy defenses. Subsequently, every three hours. Operations summary is to be submitted daily by 0700 and 1900.

15. Second in command—commander, *12 KBrMP*.
16. My order No. 0013/*op* is rescinded.

Commander *SOR SF*   Chief of Staff
/s/ Major General *Dubovtsev*   /s/ Captain First Rank *Tuz*

Approved   Top Secret
Commander, *SOR SF*   Copy No. ___
Major General *Dubovtsev*

TABLE A3.1. Planning table for Operation "West-2" (appendix to combat order 0014/op)

Actions of Fleet Forces

Phases	Amphibious Assault Forces (63 BrMP)	Breakthrough Forces (12 KBrMP)	Defense Forces (347 OPBMP)	Artillery	Ships	Fleet Air Forces	Engineer and Chemical Units
Third night prior to attack		Reconnoiter western slopes of Mustatunturi range, observe enemy defenses	Reconnoiter area of Hill 40.1. Defensive activities	Continue movement to firing positions. Barrage on Hill 122. Reconnoiter enemy batteries.			Reconnoiter and create passage lanes in friendly obstacles, establish KOM and smoke pots
Second day prior to attack	Conduct observation of enemy defenses in landing area	Company commanders reconnoiter breakthrough area, observe enemy defenses	Defensive activities	Destroy targets evenly across entire front. Reconnoiter enemy mortar batteries. Destroy batteries at target no. 76.		Destroy batteries of 517 TAD (Petsamo), destroy batteries vicinity Hill 195.8	Conduct observation. Organize chemical observation and notification of troops. Establish DZ for artillery in Kutovaya area.
Second night prior to attack	Concentrate in uploading area, observe enemy defenses	Reconnoiter OP No. 1. Observe enemy defenses. Reconnoiter departure positions for attack. Organize guides for passage through obstacles.	Reconnoiter area of Hill 122. Defensive activities	Barrage on Ristiniemi battery. Reconnoiter enemy mortar batteries	Concentrate in Pummanki Inlet		Reconnoiter and make passage lanes in enemy obstacles. Complete set up of KOM, smoke pots, and pole charges.
First day prior to attack	Observe enemy defenses	Observe enemy defenses	Conduct defensive activities	Destroy targets evenly across entire front. Destroy batteries on Numeroniemi and Ristiniemi. Prepare for night firing.	PVO of anchorage	Destroy batteries vicinity Hill 195.8. Destroy strongpoints in breakthrough area. Air strikes on enemy KP and reserves.	Conduct observation

continued on next page

TABLE A3.1—continued

Actions of Fleet Forces

Night of amphibious landing and preparation of attack (to 0500)	Upload from 2000 per upload schedule. Transit by sea and landing from 2230 to 2400. From 0000 to 0500, reach area of Selkyayarvi and Lake Mustayarvi.	From 2000 to 0300, move to attack positions as close to enemy as possible. Dig in, organize observation and communications. Enlarge passage lanes in enemy obstacles. Staffs control arrival at attack positions.	From H-1:30, participate in artillery preparation for attack. After barrage on Yaukhonokantunturi Hill and Hill 122, reconnaissance groups move from strongpoints 5 and 6.	From 2200 to completion of amphibious landing, 113 KOAD and APP 63 be prepared for rapid suppression of enemy batteries and fire support in landing area. Fire artillery prep per fire plan from H-1:30 to H. Suppress enemy mortar and artillery batteries, smoke OPs.	Upload from 2000 per uploading schedule, departure of 1 echelon at 2100, move until 2230, landing until 2245; 2 and 3 echelons follow successively behind 1, with 30-minute interval. MM group begin suppression of enemy artillery batteries in area of Hill 195.8 at 2330, hold in continuous suppression.	Be prepared for flight operations at dawn	Detonate pole charges uniformly across front at H-1:50, KOM at H-1:45. Sappers operate in infantry combat formations. Chemical units establish smoke screens at H-30 along entire forward edge and maintain until H-hour. Conduct chemical reconnaissance, observation, and reporting to forces on chemical threat.
Attack, battle for capture of enemy strongpoints in first defensive line until arrival of 12 KBrMP at like of lake with reference point 35, Lake Mustayarvi, until 0700	With portion of forces, attack mortar battery on west shore of Lake Mustayarvi, 150 mm battery on west shore of Lake Tie-yarvi. Reach south shore of Lake Selkyayarvi and antitank ditch area, then consolidate.	Battalions fire from march, throwing grenades at enemy. Destroy their troops, move forward without halting. With attacks in flank and rear, defeat resistance of enemy garrisons, destroy their troops and weapons.	Reconnaissance groups attack enemy positions	Continue to suppress mortar and artillery batteries and smoke enemy OP. Employ SO method to suppress enemy positions and hinder their movement. Prevent enemy counterattack. From area of south slopes of Mustatunturi, conduct interdicting fires parallel to brigade path of movement.	Amphibious assault vessels anchor in Pummanki, conduct PVO of anchorage. MM group suppress enemy batteries in area of Hill 195.8.	Suppress enemy mortar and artillery batteries that interfere with movement of our infantry with systematic air strikes in sector of Hill 109, lake with reference point 64.0. Provide air cover for infantry.	Sappers operate as obstacle-clearing groups and assault groups, prepare passage lanes in enemy obstacles. Chemical subunits reconnoiter and observe enemy, support movement of infantry with smoke screens.

continued on next page

TABLE A3.1—continued

Actions of Fleet Forces

Battle in depth of enemy defenses	Attack Rasvatunturi Hill, Hill 342. Reach road south of Hills 276, 299.	Attack toward Hill 388.9. Reach Titovka–Porovaara Road.	On special order, move right flank to south slopes of Mustatunturi Range; occupy defense there	Continue to suppress artillery batteries, smoke on OPs. Use PSO method. When infantry reach line Lake 235.0—Mustayarvi Lake, APP element is subordinated to brigade commander. Prepare for dislocation of artillery formations.	Amphibious assault vessels anchor in Pummanki, conduct PVO of anchorage. M M group suppress enemy batteries in area of Hill 195.8.	Prevent movement of enemy reserves from area of Hill 388.9 with systematic air strikes. Continue to suppress artillery and mortar batteries. Provide air cover for infantry.	Sappers operate as assault groups. Support reinforcement of occupied positions. Mark trail from Ivari to juncture with Mustatunturi–Lake Mustayarvi road.
Transition to defense on Titovka–Porovaara Road	Defend sector Rasvatunturi Hill to Hill 276, Hill 299, Hill 342, facing southwest	Defend sector from juncture with troops of defense to Lake Ustoyarvi, Hill 388.9, facing east and south	Move right flank to south slopes of Mustatunturi Range. Pin down opposing enemy with active measures.	With nightfall, part of artillery move to area of operations of naval infantry. Support naval infantry brigades with artillery fire from previous positions.	Amphibious landing vessels depart at nightfall for GB, leaving behind MO division (six units). M M continue to suppress enemy batteries.		Support reinforcement of occupied positions. Build trail from Ivari to road on northern shore of Lake Tie-yarvi.

Chief of Staff, *SOR SF*, Captain First Rank Tuz

APPENDIX 4

Results of Submarine Attacks

TABLE A4.1. Table of results of submarine attacks

Submarine	Attack Location	Time of Attack	Reported Target	Torpedoes Fired, Range	Results of Attack
S-51	Kellefjord	1057, TAT	Convoy: two *TR*, *M*, *SKR*, *TShch*; course east	4 type *ET-80* torpedoes at 1,500 yards	8,000-ton transport damaged and 600-ton patrol vessel sunk
V-2	Nordkin	1048, 11.10.44	Convoy: *TR*, two *TShch*, *SKA*, two *SKR*; course east	4 torpedoes at 3,000 yards	600-ton patrol vessel sunk
V-2	Nordkin	1840, 12.10.44	Convoy: *TR*, *TShch*, *SKR*, *SKA*; course west	4 torpedoes at 3,600 yards	3,000-ton transport and 600-ton minesweeper damaged
M-171	Syultefjord	1205, 12.10.44	Convoy: *TR*, three *SKR*, course west	2 torpedoes at 2,000 yards	600-ton patrol vessel damaged
M-171	Syultefjord	2232, 16.10.44	Convoy: two *TR*, three *M*, four *SKR*; course west	2 torpedoes at 2,000 yards	8,000-ton transport damaged
S-104	Tanafjord	1413, 12.10.44	Convoy: two *TR*, *TShch*, four *SKR*, two self-propelled barges, four *PLO* aircraft; course west	4 torpedoes at 1,400 yards	7,000-ton transport and 800-ton patrol vessel sunk
S-104	Tanafjord	0105, 15.10.44	Convoy: three *TR*, *TShch*, several other vessels, course east	3 torpedoes at 1,200 yards	First attack with stern *TA* misses. 5,000-ton transport sunk in follow-on attack.

continued on next page

TABLE A4.1—*continued*

Submarine	Attack Location	Time of Attack	Reported Target	Torpedoes Fired, Range	Results of Attack
V-4	Nordkin	0106, 18.10.44	Unescorted tanker, course west	5 torpedoes at 2,500 and 1,200 yards	Attacked three times, first two resulted in misses. 3,000-ton tanker sunk in third attack.
V-4	Nordkin	0509, 20.10.44	Convoy: four TR, two M, two SKR, and several NSU	2 torpedoes at 600 yards	8,000-ton and 6,000-ton transports sunk
S-14	Kelsnering	1327, 16.10.44	Three TShch type M-1, course west	4 torpedoes at 1,200 yards	600-ton minesweeper sunk
S-14	Nordkin	0914, 20.10.44	TR, two TShch	4 torpedoes at 2,000 yards	3,000-ton transport sunk
S-101	Nordkin	0808, 31.10.44	Two M type Z-17 and NSU	1 ET-80 torpedo at 2,600 yards	1,800-ton destroyer escort damaged
S-101	Kelsnering	1515, 31.10.44	Two TShch and SKR	2 ET-80 torpedoes at 2,200 yards	600-ton minesweeper believed sunk

Sixteen attacks were conducted in all, of these three unsuccessful (V-4 and S-104). Forty-one torpedoes were fired, of these seven of the ET-80 type.

Follow-on attacks were conducted following misses on two occasions. Two targets were attacked on five occasions. [Dates are all in day.month.year format.]

TRANSLATOR'S APPENDIX 1

Excerpted from Study No. 38, *Intelligence Support of the Northern Fleet in the Great Patriotic War (1941-1945)*

Excerpted from Study No. 38, *Intelligence Support of the Northern Fleet in the Great Patriotic War (1941–1945)* (Moscow: Naval Press of the Ministry of the Navy of the USSR, Moscow, 1950).

Chapter VI: Northern Fleet Intelligence Support in the Pechenga Operation

The largest in scale operation in the north during the Great Patriotic War was the combined operation of the forces of the Karelian *Front* and Northern Fleet for the liberation of Pechenga oblast, conducted from 7 to 31 October 1944.

A detailed discussion of this operation has already been published.[36] Therefore, this section only summarizes, with special attention given to issues of intelligence support to the operation.

---

[36] The operation is named the *Petsamo-Kirkenes Operation* in Soviet historiography. The editor's note here cites *Collection of Materials on the Study of War Experience No. 20*, published by the Directorate for the Utilization of War Experience of the General Staff of the Red Army, 1945, pages 24–47; and *Collection of Materials on the Experience of Combat Activities of the Naval Forces of the USSR No. 27*, published by the Main Naval Staff of the Soviet Navy, 1945.—Translator

The mission for the liberation of Pechenga oblast was assigned to the Karelian *Front* by a directive of *STAVKA* of the Supreme High Command of 26 September 1944. The situation that had developed by this time in the north favored the accomplishment of this mission. The situation of the German forces in the north had worsened significantly with Finland's withdrawal from the war in August 1944. Striving to hold on to the northern Norwegian ports and the nickel mine in the Pechenga area, the Germans continued stubbornly to defend in the Murmansk sector. But, at the same time, the enemy began to withdraw a portion of their forces northward from the Ukhtinsk, Kandalaksha, and Kestenga sectors of the front.

After 15 September 1944, we began to receive information concerning the concentration of a large quantity of transports in northern Norwegian ports, about the increased movement of vehicles with German troops along the Finnish-Swedish border toward the northwest, and about the emptying out of corps-level storage depots of military equipment in the Kandalaksha area.

These reports gave a basis to suggest that the enemy was preparing to evacuate a portion of their forces and military equipment from northern Finland. But at the same time, reports surfaced concerning the enemy's increasing of their ground and air forces on the Murmansk axis, about the reinforcement of his forward lines of defense. In the second half of September, Bicycle Reconnaissance Brigade Norway arrived in the Murmansk sector from northern Norway, in the Luostari–Lake Chapr area; [and] 163rd Infantry Division, 13th and 14th Separate Infantry Battalions [arrived] from the Kandalaksha axis. At the same time, 2nd Mountain Division units occupied defenses in the Lake Chapr area.

These facts demonstrated that, despite the evacuation of troop units and equipment, the Germans were taking all measures to hold Pechenga oblast as long as possible.

By 7 October 1944, the Germans had more than 60,000 men on all sectors of their ground front (isthmus of Sredniy Peninsula, Western Litsa River, Lake Chapr area). Our reconnaissance counted approximately 300 guns of calibers 37–211 mm, up to 30 antiaircraft guns, more than 400 mortars in calibers from 50 to 105 mm, and approximately 80 flame-throwers. The approaches to Pechenga Inlet were defended by four batteries of 150–210 mm guns, and 25 antiship and antiaircraft pieces. Kirkenes harbor, the German's man naval base in northeastern Norway, was protected by seven shore batteries of 75–240 mm guns and 14 antiaircraft artillery batteries.

The intensity of naval shipping between Varangerfjord ports and northwest Norwegian ports sharply increased in September 1944. One or two convoys arrived and departed daily, moving nickel ore and troop units westward. Enemy convoys, especially on the transit from the west into Varangerfjord, were accompanied by significant escort forces which, besides escort vessels and cutters, included destroyer escorts. The enemy increased their patrols in Varangerfjord.

Prior to our forces' offensive actions, enemy aviation increased its reconnaissance of the front, sea lines of communication, and antiaircraft defenses of our bases and convoys. German air strength was increased on the coastal flank by 108 aircraft redeployed from the Kandalaksha sector. A large portion of enemy air assets were repositioned to airfields closer to the line of ground defenses. In addition, there were 57 combat aircraft, among them 14 bombers, on airfields at Rovaniemi and Kemiyarvi, which could be quickly moved to airfields on the Murmansk axis.

1. INTELLIGENCE COLLECTION DURING NORTHERN FLEET'S PREPARATION FOR THE OPERATION

Issues of intelligence support occupied a significant place in the work of the Northern Fleet staff, as well as the staffs of major fleet units during Northern Fleet's preparation for the Pechenga operation.

Having received the commander's guidance to prepare for the operation, and taking into consideration the situation that had evolved in the theater by this time, the disposition and nature of the activities of enemy naval forces, and also the combat missions assigned to the fleet, Northern Fleet staff developed a detailed plan of intelligence support of the fleet and its major commands for the upcoming operation. The following intelligence collection missions for major fleet commands devolved from this plan:

- to Fleet Air Forces staff—systematic air reconnaissance of the forward edge, roads, rear areas, airfields, naval bases, and sea lines of communication;
- to Northern Defensive Region staff—reconnaissance of the forward edge of the enemy's defenses in the breakthrough area on the isthmus of Sredniy Peninsula;
- to the Surface Squadron staff, the staffs of Submarine, Torpedo Cutter, and Subchaser Brigades—reconnaissance of enemy sea lines of communication.

The conduct of communications intelligence collection, the gathering, sorting, and analysis of data about the enemy in the theater were tasked to the fleet staff intelligence department.

Practical preparation for the operation to liberate the Soviet far north was begun on 3 September, when all the combat activities of the fleet were directed to implementing measures that would lead to the weakening of enemy forces, interruption of their sea lines of communication, disruption of normal activity in their bases and ports, and destruction of firing points on the forward edge and in the depth of the enemy defenses. Simultaneously, information was gathered on the nature of the anti-landing defenses of the enemy-occupied coast. The front in the north had been stable through most of the war, and fleet intelligence collection organs had had the opportunity to obtain complete and accurate information concerning enemy order of battle and the nature of their activities. Therefore, the main effort of intelligence collection during the preparation for the operation was directed to pre-reconnaissance, to clarify and verify information obtained earlier.

The INTELLIGENCE DEPARTMENT OF FLEET STAFF was involved in the following activities during the preparation for the operation.

Fulfilling the tasks assigned by the command, in the early days of September the intelligence department gathered and developed all available materials about the enemy's defensive system in the areas of proposed amphibious landings, and in sectors where the breakthrough of their defenses would occur. The most attention was devoted to defining strongpoints; forward edge of the defenses; mine situation in the area of proposed actions; disposition of ground units; and location of enemy air assets, ships, and reserves. All processed materials were immediately distributed to interested major commands and units that had been designated to participate in the operation.

Information gleaned from air reconnaissance was widely utilized in the period of preparation for the operation. The intelligence department published 50 copies of aerial mosaics of the enemy defenses from Kutovaya Bay to Tulli-vuono Inlet, with the goal of more widely familiarizing the officer component of units and commands participating in the operation with the enemy's system of defense, engineer preparation of the forward edge, location of strongpoints, and so on. At the same time, informational materials on the defenses of the enemy coastline from Cape Pikshuev to Pechenga Inlet were illustrated by photographs and panoramas.

In the second half of September, the intelligence department compiled and sent to staffs of the brigades of escort vessels and torpedo cutters a special estimate of the mine situation in the amphibious landing areas. In addition, a large-scale map was sent to the escort vessel brigade showing the current situation in the enemy defenses in front of the Northern Defensive Region.

In addition to the intelligence materials and documents that were distributed, several of the fleet officer leadership were familiarized in greater detail with the most important issues in the intelligence department.

By order of the intelligence department, vertical and oblique aerial photography of the forward edge of the enemy defenses, Liinakhamari harbor, and areas designated for amphibious landings was conducted on 8, 12, and 16 September for the purpose of amplification and supplementation of data obtained earlier. The photographic products thus gathered were rapidly processed and sent to interested commands and units.

Several days prior to the start of the operation, aerial confirmation photography was conducted for the purpose of pre-reconnaissance of enemy defenses in amphibious landing areas and centers of resistance in the depth of the defenses. This information was used to prepare sketches and maps of the location of enemy defenses and firing assets in the forward edge. These maps and sketches were provided to all commanders of Northern Defensive Region units and subunits down to company (battery) level. All information on Liinakhamari, Kirkenes, and Vardo harbors was republished, and the available intelligence maps and descriptions of the enemy coastline from the isthmus of Sredniy Peninsula to Kirkenes port were corrected over a brief period.

The number of copies of published intelligence documents was set to provide the maximum support of fleet commands and units designated to participate in the operation.

Liinakhamari harbor, for example, where a rapid amphibious landing was planned, had special importance to the Torpedo Cutter Brigade command. Despite the fact that the description of this harbor had detailed information about its defenses and the route into the harbor, intelligence department officers held additional consultations with the command component of Torpedo Cutter Brigade, including the brigade commander himself, several days before the beginning of the operation. In addition, the brigade was provided with a large quantity of various photographs, plans, and maps with marked positions of shore batteries and anti-landing firing positions, with notes on the believed density of fire and sectors of fire along the routes into the harbor.

Parallel with providing participants in the operation information on the situation in the theater, the intelligence department systematically informed major fleet commands and units on the current situation with daily intelligence summaries and separate informational papers, which included all new intelligence reports on the enemy.

Throughout the preparatory period for the operation, the intelligence department maintained close contact and mutual intelligence not only with the intelligence organs of major fleet commands and units but also with the intelligence department of headquarters, Karelian *Front*. Intelligence data exchange with the latter was accomplished primarily through liaison officers.

COMMUNICATIONS INTELLIGENCE was tasked, in addition to the daily radio intercept mission, to conduct continuous monitoring and intercept of enemy radio traffic in Varangerfjord during the preparatory period for the operation. To accomplish this mission, all standing monitoring and intercept tasks were reviewed on 1–2 October. Additional shifts were organized by taking personnel from secondary tasks; single shift watches were replaced by double shift watches, and five reserve watches were set up in case the enemy began using new frequencies and it became necessary to establish additional monitoring of them. The most critical watches were staffed and reinforced with the best radio operators on 3–4 October. Simultaneously, a special group of radio direction finders was assigned to operate against enemy radio transmitters located in the Varangerfjord area. From 5 October onward, a permanently manned duty staff composed of the best trained officers was appointed and given assistants from the operations section. An additional land line was added to the existing lines connecting the direction-finding stations.

In the preparatory period of the operation, in addition to the accomplishment of tasks projected by the intelligence collection for September and October, **air reconnaissance** conducted numerous missions to photograph Liinakhamari and Kirkenes harbors, and enemy defensive engineer fortifications and firing positions in front of Northern Defensive Region units. Air reconnaissance conducted systematic observation of the following:

- enemy troops, frontal and rear area roads, with the goal to discover their groupings and the road movement of troops;
- airfields at Luostari, Salmiyarvi, Kirkenes, Hoybuktmoen, Banak, and Billefjord, with the mission of determining enemy aviation groupings;
- the harbors at Liinakhamari, Kirkenes, Vardo, and Vadso, with the goal of discovering possible unloading of enemy troops and equipment.

Fleet Air Forces intelligence department staff personnel prepared more than 3.000 photo mosaics and photographs of various enemy objectives during the preparatory period for the operation.

Photographs of enemy facilities that were the planned targets of bombing raids were duplicated in sufficient quantity that every crew designated to participate in the operation received copies.

Northern Fleet Air Forces conducted a total of 360 sorties during the preparatory period for the operation. Of these, more than 100 were conducted to reconnoiter and photograph enemy objectives. In addition to aircraft of the 118th Air Reconnaissance Regiment, strike and fighter aviation were assigned air reconnaissance tasks.

Four aircraft from 118th Regiment were sent from their permanent base to Pummanki airfield to provide the most rapid delivery of data gained about the enemy to the command.

On the whole, the actions of NORTHERN DEFENSIVE REGION INTELLIGENCE ORGANS in the preparatory period were devoted to pre-reconnaissance and clarification of data obtained earlier. The first order of business was to reconnoiter and elaborate on the following:

- the grouping of enemy forces in front of the Northern Defensive Region;
- principal enemy centers of resistance on their forward edge and in the depths of his defenses in the breakthrough sector;
- quantity and caliber of the weapons of artillery and mortar batteries on the southern slopes of Mustatunturi Ridge;
- system of fire, engineer fortifications, and approaches to the forward edge in the breakthrough area;
- and the amphibious landing sites.

All the intelligence forces and means of Northern Defensive Region units were dedicated to the accomplishment of the assigned tasks. In just the period 1–10 October, NDR scouts conducted 36 reconnaissance patrols and 10 ambushes. This activity exposed the approaches to the forward edge and enemy firing positions and established the presence and nature of antitank obstacles along the forward edge of the enemy defenses.

Northern Defensive Region artillery reconnaissance assets were concentrated on the breakthrough sector to accomplish pre-reconnaissance of enemy firing positions. The pre-reconnaissance located six enemy artillery batteries and the probable sites of individual mobile guns along the road in the sector Lake Ustoyarvi–Selkyayarvi. The positions of 15 mortar batteries were determined in the sector from Ivari to Kutovaya. In addition, systematic monitoring of enemy artillery registration was accomplished.

All the information that was obtained concerning the enemy's defense of their forward area was passed along to the intelligence department of fleet staff, where it was utilized to assemble maps and sketches. These sketches were provided to the entire officer complement assigned to participate in the breakthrough of the enemy's defenses, down to battery commanders.

The activity of NDR engineer unit scouts was directed at pre-reconnaissance and further clarification of data obtained earlier concerning engineer preparation of the enemy's forward area. Prior to the start of the operation, six reconnaissance parties with a combined strength of 236 men prepared 37 lanes in barbed wire obstacles, removed more than 800 mines, and neutralized five pressure-activated demolition devices in the breakthrough sector.

The actions of NDR reconnaissance forces and assets uncovered the entire enemy system of defense in the breakthrough area, which to a significant degree facilitated the successful offensive of NDR units and major commands in the course of the operation.

SUBMARINE INTELLIGENCE COLLECTION during the preparatory period for the operation was conducted in conjunction with their combat mission. Submarines conducted nine combat sorties for actions against distant enemy sea lines of communication during the preparatory period. From their positions at sea, submarines reconnoitered the movement of convoys, convoy defenses, changes in convoy sailing patterns, and so on.

Intelligence collection on the enemy's sea lines of communication in the Varangerfjord area was accomplished by surface ships and most of all by torpedo and escort cutters. Torpedo boats made 19 group sorties during this period, in which they had six encounters with individual enemy transports and naval vessels.

2. INTELLIGENCE COLLECTION DURING THE OPERATION

Carrying out the order of *STAVKA* of the Supreme High Command, units of the Karelian *Front*, after an artillery barrage, began a decisive offensive in the sector between Lakes Chapr and Bolshoy Karikvayvish on 7 October. In two days of bitter combat, *Front* troops broke through the first and second enemy defensive belts on the axis of the main attack, forced the Titovka River, and created the threat of encirclement of the German main grouping. Attempting to avoid encirclement, the enemy waged stubborn defensive battles in the Luostari area, and began to withdraw toward Pechenga in the remaining sectors of the front.

In responding to his mission for a joint offensive with the forces of the Karelian *Front*, the commander of the Northern Fleet ordered his forces to break through the enemy's defenses on the isthmus of Sredniy Peninsula and seize the Titovka–Porovaara Road in the Rasvatunturi Hill area, thereby cutting the enemy's path of withdrawal to Pechenga. Northern Defensive Region's 12th and 63rd Naval Infantry Brigades were assigned this task. The 12th Red Banner Naval Infantry Brigade, with the support and protection of naval vessels and air forces, was to break through the enemy defensive positions on the isthmus of Sredniy Peninsula. The 63rd Brigade, with the composite reconnaissance detachment of fleet staff intelligence department and the Northern Defensive Region, was to land on the south coast of Malaya Volokovaya Bay and strike the defending enemy in the rear. The amphibious landing was to precede the attack of 12th Brigade units.

A screen of three torpedo cutters was placed in Varangerfjord to cover the amphibious landing, and a detachment of support ships consisting of two fleet destroyers was designated to support the breakthrough of the defenses on the isthmus of Sredniy Peninsula from the sea.

Missions to interrupt enemy sea lines of communication were assigned to aviation units and the submarine and torpedo cutter brigades. In addition, it was also intended to employ fleet surface ships for these purposes if the weather was good. Fleet Air Forces was also assigned the tasks to support the NDR units' attack, protect ships at sea, and conduct air reconnaissance in theater.

The initiation of combat activities by Northern Fleet major commands and units in cooperation with the Karelian *Front* operation occurred in the following sequence. The 63rd Naval Infantry Brigade with attached units landed on the southern coast of Malaya Volokovaya Bay from 2300 on 9 October to 0110 on 10 October. After a three-hour artillery preparation,

12th Naval Infantry Brigade units launched their offensive on the isthmus of Sredniy Peninsula at 0500 on 10 October. The forces designated for actions against enemy sea lines of communication began their activities in the preparatory period for the operation.

With the operation's commencement, the work of all Northern Fleet intelligence organs was directed totally to support of the combat actions of fleet major commands and units participating in the operation.

The composite reconnaissance detachment, consisting of 181st Reconnaissance Detachment of Headquarters, Fleet, and the reconnaissance detachment of Headquarters, Northern Defensive Region, played an especially important role in supporting the combat actions of 63rd and 12th Naval Infantry Brigade units, particularly in the capture of Liinakhamari harbor. This composite detachment landed on the southern coast of Malaya Volokovaya Bay together with 63rd Brigade units. The brigade units landed, left one battalion to secure the landing site, and quickly began their movement inland to link up with 12th Brigade units that had broken through enemy defenses on Sredniy Peninsula. At the same time, the composite reconnaissance detachment began its cross-country movement toward Cape Krestovyy to execute its mission to capture the coast artillery batteries located on this cape.

Having conducted difficult movement across extremely rugged terrain over the course of 10 and 11 October, the detachment reached the isthmus of Cape Krestovyy at 0200 on 12 October. It attacked the four-gun 88 mm enemy antiaircraft artillery battery at dawn and captured it after a brief fight. Three functioning guns and three prisoners were captured. The remaining battery personnel were killed or fled. After the successful storming of the antiaircraft battery, the detachment began the fight to capture the 150 mm shore battery that covered the entrance to Petsamovuono Inlet and the immediate approaches to Liinakhamari harbor by fire. By this time, two German assault groups totaling 100 men had landed to support the battery garrison. The reconnaissance detachment was forced to go over to the defense.

The scouts courageously fought off the enemy attack using the guns of the captured antiaircraft battery. On request of the detachment commander, a group of *Il-2* aircraft and fighters carried out a series of air strikes against the enemy garrison on the afternoon of 12 October. It must be noted that, thanks to good communications with the aviation, the air strikes were executed with great precision and did not injure any of the reconnaissance detachment personnel, despite the great danger of this. Altogether, 43 sorties were flown in support of the reconnaissance detachment over a period of four hours. A significant number of enemy officers and soldiers were destroyed, two barracks and a pier were set ablaze, one motor launch and two other boats were damaged, and two antiaircraft batteries at Numeroniemi and Liinakhamari were suppressed as a result of these air strikes.

Simultaneously with the conduct of air strikes on the enemy garrison, an *A-20G* from Pummanki airfield dropped ammunition and provisions to the reconnaissance detachment on the western portion of Cape Krestovyy. Five cargo parachutes were dropped in two sorties. Despite the low ceiling, all the cargo was successfully delivered by the aircraft and received by the scouts. The parachute delivery of ammunition and provisions was continued on 13 October.

Help came to the composite reconnaissance detachment at 0800 on 13 October in the form of the reconnaissance company of 63rd Brigade, reinforced by a submachine gun platoon and a sapper platoon. Fifty soldiers mistakenly landed on the eastern shore of Petsamovuono Inlet from the amphibious assault force that had landed on the night of 12–13 October in Liinakhamari harbor linked up with the detachment at 1500 that day. With these reinforcements, the scouts increased the pressure on the enemy position, and by the evening of 13 October had forced it to surrender. The detachment captured 63 prisoners, documents, one functional 150 mm gun, 1,200 shells, 12 machine guns, 100 rifles, tens of thousands of cartridges, and two caches of provisions as a result of the battle for the second battery. The enemy group that had landed to support the battery garrison was almost destroyed.

By its capture of these two enemy batteries on Cape Krestovyy, which blocked the entrance to Petsamovuono Inlet, the composite reconnaissance detachment enabled the torpedo cutters to rush in with the amphibious landing force and quickly capture Liinakhamari harbor.[37]

---

[37] The commander of the reconnaissance detachment of Headquarters, Northern Defensive Region, Captain I. P. Barchenko-Yemelyanov, and the commander of the 181st Special Purpose Reconnaissance Detachment of Headquarters, Northern Fleet, Senior Lieutenant V. N. Leonov, were both awarded Hero of the Soviet Union for this action. Two of Viktor Leonov's enlisted subordinates were also

Having seized Liinakhamari port, NDR naval infantry amphibious assault units, along with the composite reconnaissance detachment and 63rd Brigade reconnaissance company, began an attack in the direction of Trifona and Pechenga. The enemy forces around Pechenga faced a genuine possibility of encirclement from the rear.

During the interrogation of prisoners captured by the composite detachment on Cape Krestovyy, valuable information was acquired about the defensive system of Kirkenes harbor and Varanger Peninsula. This information (after confirmation through other sources) was used to correct data on objectives in Kirkenes, Vardo, Vadso, and so on.

The activities of Northern Defensive Region intelligence organs in the Sredniy Peninsula sector were completely directed at support of 12th Naval Infantry Brigade units.

A reconnaissance aircraft sortied from Pummanki airfield at dawn on 10 October with the goal of gathering more information on the situation on the battlefield after the breakthrough of the enemy's first belt of defenses on Sredniy Peninsula. It established that the enemy, under pressure from our forces, was withdrawing from the isthmus of Sredniy Peninsula toward the south. The movement toward the west of 120 enemy vehicles and carts was noted along the road from Titovka to Porovaara River. The greatest collection of enemy vehicles, carts, and troops was found on the road between Lakes Suormusyarvi and Ustoyarvi. Northern Fleet Air Forces launched five air strikes against these targets on the afternoon of 10 October.

By 0700 on 11 October, NDR scouts had confirmed that the enemy had abandoned all of their positions on Sredniy Peninsula during the night. Considering the information from the scouts, 12th Brigade units quickly continued their offensive, not meeting enemy resistance.

Reconnaissance data was fully confirmed.

In subsequent days, air reconnaissance systematically monitored the front line and the enemy road net leading away from it. On the afternoon of 11 October, reconnaissance aircraft detected a large concentration of vehicles, carts, and troops on the road sector in the area of Lakes Suormusyarvi and Mutka-yarvi. Northern Fleet Air Forces conducted several air strikes on these targets that same day, inflicting heavy losses on the enemy.

Air reconnaissance established the movement of main enemy forces west from Pechenga on 12 October. An increase in the movement of truck columns of supplies and personnel was noted from Lake Mutka-yarvi to Porovaara. Movement to the east was not noted.

On 13 October, when our units were approaching Porovaara, air reconnaissance established that the enemy had left up to a battalion of infantry on the high ground southeast of Porovaara. With this information, the command made the decision to launch air strikes against this enemy force, guided to the target by reconnaissance aircraft. These strikes destroyed a significant number of enemy troops and disrupted their defenses. Our ground units launched their attack immediately after the air attacks and occupied the high ground on the way to Porovaara.

The Northern Fleet command devoted much time during the Pechenga operation to actions of its forces to disrupt enemy sea lines of communication. It was believed that as our ground offensive unfolded, the enemy, lacking a developed system of ground transportation, would be forced to give more attention to sea transport. Only by sea could they conduct a massive and rapid reintroduction of reserves to the front line or carry out the evacuation of their retreating troops and valuable cargo from the mainland.

It has already been mentioned that the mission for interrupting enemy sea lines of communication had been assigned to the Surface Squadron, Torpedo Cutter Brigade, individual aviation commands, and Submarine Brigade. Along with their combat operations to disrupt enemy sea lines of communication, these commands also carried out intelligence collection missions, for their own needs as well as for the needs of the overall operation. This was especially true of aviation and submarines.

Fleet aviation conducted 243 reconnaissance sorties on enemy sea lines of communication during the operation, detecting 54 enemy convoys. Reconnaissance of enemy sea lines of communication was conducted continuously along the northern coast of Norway, as far as Hammerfest. Each day of the operation, the nature and intensity of shipping, movement of principal naval forces, and concentration of enemy transports and small ships were known. As a rule, reconnaissance was conducted three times a day—in the morning, in the

---

awarded HSU—Seaman Semyon Agafonov and Seaman Andrey Pshenichnykh.

middle of the day, and before last light. In addition to reconnaissance aircraft, strike aviation units were also frequently used, mainly for reconnoitering close-in lines of communication and pre-strike reconnaissance of enemy convoys and single ships. Air reconnaissance generally preceded the actions of strike aviation on enemy convoys and ships. All this to a significant degree facilitated the successful accomplishment of missions for interrupting enemy sea lines of communication. Crews that flew air strikes knew the exact location of the convoy, its composition, formation, and the presence of covering and escorting forces.

We will review the most typical examples of air reconnaissance support to the combat activities of Fleet Air Forces strike aviation.

1. Air reconnaissance detected four transports, a fast amphibious barge, and nine patrol vessels in Kirkenes harbor on 10 October. A reconnaissance aircraft observed an enemy convoy of three transports and 12 escort vessels moving toward Bekfjord at a speed of 7–8 knots at 0755 on 11 October.

   Having received these reconnaissance reports, the command made the decision to launch a quick air strike on the ships in Kirkenes harbor and on the convoy at sea. This attack sank five transports, three escort vessels, three barges, and six motor launches. Three transports, two escort cutters, and one motor launch were damaged. Six enemy aircraft were shot down in air combat.

   Fifty-six bombers and strike aircraft and 92 fighters participated in attacks on enemy convoys and ships in Kirkenes harbor on 11 October.

2. Air reconnaissance detected an enemy convoy of two transports, a destroyer escort, a minesweeper, and two escort vessels in the area of Persfjord, moving toward the northwest at 0810 on 12 October.

   Four torpedo bombers from Fifth Torpedo Aviation Division sortied to attack the convoy.

   They detected the convoy at 1334 and attacked it, sinking the minesweeper, and heavily damaging a 4,000-ton transport.

   Utilizing air reconnaissance reports, Northern Fleet Air Forces conducted 200 air sorties against Kirkenes harbor and enemy convoys at sea on 12 October. These attacks sank one transport, a destroyer escort, a minesweeper, an escort vessel, three escort cutters, two self-propelled barges, three motorized launches, and one unidentified ship. Three transports and three motorized launches were damaged.

3. A reconnaissance aircraft detected an enemy convoy in the Porsangerfjord area at 0925 on 14 October. It consisted of two large transports, two destroyer escorts, four escort vessels, five escort cutters, and one minesweeper.

   Five torpedo bombers sortied to attack the convoy. They sank both transports, with a combined displacement of 14,000 tons, and one enemy escort cutter in a sudden and bold attack.

4. Air reconnaissance detected a large enemy convoy moving north from Kirkenes on the morning of 16 October. It contained three transports, two destroyer escorts, six escort vessels, a minesweeper, two self-propelled barges, and 13 escort cutters. Three fighter aircraft flew air cover over the convoy.

   Northern Fleet Air Forces flew 116 sorties in five successive attacks on the convoy that day.

Air reconnaissance conducted continuous observation of the convoy, which to a large degree made the actions of the strike groups possible.

Air reconnaissance also played a large role in the actions of the Northern Fleet's submarines, torpedo cutters, and surface ships.

Submarines operating on enemy sea lines of communication maintained continuous communications with reconnaissance aircraft throughout the operation. During daylight hours, submarines withdrew from visual observation of the coastline to receive timely reports from air reconnaissance. They maneuvered on the surface and maintained continuous radio watch on the air reconnaissance frequency. When it was impossible to remain surfaced, the submarines came up to periscope antenna depth 10 minutes of every hour and received summarized air reconnaissance data from their base communications center.

Submarines conducted a significant number of successful attacks on enemy convoys based on data from air reconnaissance and other sources between 10 and 31 October. In addition to vectoring submarines to enemy convoys, in a number of cases reconnaissance aircraft remained positioned over the convoy and assessed the results of submarine attacks.

Carrying out their combat missions on enemy sea lines of communication, submarines also conducted intelligence collection. They detected 10 convoys and 16 individual enemy ships and transports during the operation. They rapidly reported their findings to fleet command, and when the situation permitted, these same submarines attacked the convoys they had detected.

Operating in Varangerfjord, torpedo cutters conducted 23 combat sorties from 7 to 31 October, nine of which resulted from air reconnaissance data and four of which were coordinated with night reconnaissance aircraft.

In addition to operations against enemy sea lines of communication, torpedo cutters were employed to reconnoiter enemy shore defenses. Thus, for example, on the night of 13 October, two torpedo cutters reconnoitered enemy shore batteries on the western shore of Petsamovuono Inlet. They used the demonstration method of reconnaissance, with the goal of drawing fire on themselves from the batteries. However, the enemy batteries that were of interest to the command did not open fire—the enemy had already withdrawn. During their transit along the coastline to the west, the cutters received fire from both small- and large-caliber cannons. This permitted them to establish the new defensive position to which the enemy had withdrawn after the fall of Pechenga.

The actions of fleet staff intelligence department during the operation were totally directed toward the most rapid processing of captured documents. Daily intelligence summaries that included supplementary and clarifying information were delivered to operation participants.

Captured documents taken in the seizure of Liinakhamari harbor were quickly processed and utilized for the landings in Kirkenes harbor, Holmengerfjord, and Kobbholmfjord.

After the capture of Kirkenes harbor, individual enemy units continued to defend on Varanger Peninsula. The scouts of 181st Reconnaissance Detachment made a parachute assault in the latter days of October to ascertain the situation in this region, and especially in the area of the ports Vardo and Vadso. Their radio was destroyed during the landing as a result of strong winds, and the scouts were unable to establish communications with the fleet staff intelligence department.[38] Another group of 52 scouts from 181st Reconnaissance Detachment was landed by torpedo cutters to search for the parachutists and evaluate the situation. The landed detachment accomplished its assigned mission, despite the extremely difficult conditions. The scouts systematically reported information concerning the situation by radio over the course of 10 days in the enemy's rear. In addition, they captured and delivered to base prisoners and extremely valuable documents of the German command.

The beginning of the Pechenga operation called for increased radio traffic between the enemy command and its major formations and units. At the same time, supplementary radio nets were opened. All this required the implementation of a series of countermeasures by the communications intelligence service of the fleet staff intelligence department.

Supplementary monitoring shifts were activated to intercept radio traffic of newly detected enemy communications nets. A special radio intelligence group with the necessary equipment was sent to Sredniy Peninsula. This group's mission was to monitor radio traffic of enemy base stations at Kirkenes, Vardo, Vadso, and Pechenga, and of shore defense radio stations on the Varangerfjord coastline; of enemy fighter, bomber, and reconnaissance aviation operating from airfields at Luostari, Kirkenes, Banak, Salmiyarvi, and Nautsi; and of torpedo and escort cutters based in Varangerfjord harbors. During the operation, the group reported all information gathered about the enemy to the chief of the intelligence department of fleet staff and maintained continuous communications with the operations duty officer of their own shore radio detachment staff.

With the goal of constantly focusing the work of shore radio detachment shift radio operators and operations duty officers, information about the activities of enemy forces was disseminated and specific missions were assigned that flowed from the situation before the new shift came on duty.

Communications intelligence collection paperwork was abbreviated to ease the work of operations duty officers and accelerate the processing of enemy data. In addition, not only the operations duty officers but also officers of communications intelligence service were assigned to process the data that was collected.

During specific battles, the enemy frequently resorted to radio transmissions in clear text. A 24-hour shift of translators was organized for the most rapid translation of these transmissions.

These measures taken to organize the work of communications intelligence service of the fleet staff intelligence department permitted continuous monitoring

---

38 Members of the detachment were also killed and injured in the jump. Leonov discusses this mission in the latter portion of chapter 8 of *Blood on the Shores*.—Translator

of the enemy over the course of the Pechenga operation, and systematic receipt of critical information on the disposition of their naval forces and the combat activities of his individual units and major commands.

Communications intelligence monitored 447 enemy naval and naval transport ships at sea, more than 400 aircraft, and on seven occasions the evacuation by the Germans of their own communications centers during the period from 7 to 15 October.

The intelligence department of fleet staff was the single place where data was collected from all intelligence collection forces and means that were operating in the theater. After processing and verification by comparison of data across various sources, the results were reported to the command and then distributed to interested units and fleet major commands. During the operation, the chief of the fleet intelligence department and the chief of his surface intelligence section were continuously located at the Northern Defensive Region forward command post, exercising leadership and control of all fleet intelligence collection forces and means.

Evaluating the activities of functions in the Pechenga operation, the fleet command noted that "intelligence data available to Northern Fleet was confirmed in its authenticity and completeness in the absolute majority of cases."[39]

The successful combat actions of the Northern Fleet major commands and units in the Pechenga operation were supported to a significant degree by well-organized and purposeful intelligence collection work in the theater. All the activity of intelligence forces and means, both in the period of preparation for the operation and during its conduct, was fully directed at support of the missions assigned to Northern Fleet major commands and units. By the beginning of the operation, fleet command had been provided with detailed information concerning the disposition and activities of enemy forces. Intelligence disclosed the beginning of the enemy's evacuation from the Kandalaksha and Kestenga axes in a timely manner. Intelligence established the moment of reinforcement of defenses on the Murmansk axis and in the Pechenga–Kirkenes area. In the course of the operation, intelligence continuously monitored the enemy's withdrawal routes on land, the points where the enemy uploaded troops and equipment in northeastern Norwegian ports, and the movement of convoys at sea. The availability of this data, completely and correctly reflecting the situation in the theater, had important significance for the development of success in all phases of the operation.

Several positive aspects are to be noted concerning intelligence support of combat activities of fleet major commands and units in the Pechenga operation:

- the rational exploitation of all intelligence collection forces and means in the interests of supporting combat activities of the units participating in the operation;
- the good organization of mutual coordination of fleet intelligence collection forces and means between themselves, and of fleet intelligence collection organs with analogous organs of the Karelian *Front*;
- and the precise organization of leadership of intelligence forces and means in the theater, through which all information concerning the enemy was concentrated in a single place.

All this permitted the continuous monitoring of enemy activities and the provision of necessary intelligence data to the command during the entire course of the operation.

The experience of the Pechenga operation has shown that the success of intelligence support to fleet major commands and units participating in a combined operation with ground forces depends to a significant degree on the appropriate daily coordination of fleet intelligence collection functions with *Front* intelligence. Besides supporting continuous communications between the chiefs of fleet and army intelligence by radio (telephone and telegraph), it was necessary to exchange intelligence liaison officers and through them conduct all necessary coordination of intelligence data, foremost of all concerning the situation on the ground sector of the front.

Considering that a portion of fleet forces, such as naval infantry, will operate on land during the conduct of similar combined operations with ground forces, it is necessary to define carefully the responsibility for the conduct of intelligence collection on the land and sea axes during the allocation of intelligence collection forces and means in the theater.

---

39 *Northern Fleet Summary on Operation West for the Period 7–31 October 1944*, book 1, page 44.—Translator

TRANSLATOR'S APPENDIX 2

Excerpted from *Frontovyye bydni Rybachevo* (Frontline life on the Rybachyy Peninsula) by I. P. Barchenko-Emelyanov and *Litsom k litsu: Vospominaniya morskogo razvedchika* (Face to face: Recollections of a naval scout) by Viktor Leonov

Text extracted and translated from I. P. Barchenko-Emelyanov, *Frontovyye bydni Rybachevo* (Frontline life on the Rybachyy Peninsula) (Murmansk: Knizhnoye Izadtelstvo, 1984), pp. 136–152.

[PAGE 136] [25 August 1944. Barchenko-Emelyanov was informed by unnamed general officer (commander of Northern Defensive Region—SOR—General Yefim Timofeevich Dubovtsev) that an especially important mission was being assigned that involved actions in the enemy's deep rear. It would require from his men physical endurance, high combat capabilities, presence of mind, decisiveness, and self-control.]

[PAGE 137] [The general advised him to keep these things in mind in his daily training, with greater attention on night movement, and development of coordination with other subunits. He gave him a month for preparation.]

[PAGE 138] [11 September, Barchenko-Emelyanov was informed that Cape Krestovyy was the objective, that his combined force would be approximately 200 men, including artillerymen, sappers, and communications personnel. He was instructed to maintain operational secrecy (do not inform his men), study the map and the mission, and come back in four days with his impressions. Viktor Leonov arrived with approximately 50 of his fleet scouts. Barchenko-Emelyanov's senior NCO was responsible for organizing equipment, provisions, and other logistical requirements.]

Raid on Krestovyy

The fall of 1944 on Rybachyy was unusually dry and warm. September was particularly nice. Morning fog, which enveloped both the sea and land, quickly dissipated. I could not remember such a fall season.

Utilizing the lovely days, we conducted intensive preparation. The detachment was supplemented by subunits [attachments] that had special purposes: a combat crew of artillerymen from 113th Separate Artillery Battalion under the command of firing platoon commander Sh. L. Rozenfeld; a group of sappers from 388th Separate Sapper Battalion; radio operators; and medics. The combined strength of the detachment grew to 195 personnel.

133

Recalling the commander's guidance, we worked diligently in developing supporting tasks for the various attachments, including marches on terrain both in day and night conditions. Twice I met with our aviators at Pummanki [airstrip on northeast corner of Rybachyy Peninsula] in order to coordinate issues of communications and signals if we needed their support. It was very touching to me that several of the pilots knew and remembered my brother Michael [who apparently had been killed some time before this].

As an officer, to whom it was a high honor to command a combined detachment, I recognized my responsibility for accomplishing the mission that was an important element in the larger fleet operation. I also understood the complexity of this mission: the detachment was to execute a 40 km concealed approach march into the enemy's deep rear on extremely complex terrain, characterized by deep ravines, steep slopes, and countless mountain streams.

The order for execution of the combat mission was being withheld. Caught up in guessing, putting forth various suppositions, with difficulty we suppressed our tortured sense of insecurity. Finally, on 7 October, the deep echo of a relatively distant artillery preparation reached Rybachyy. Our spirits were immediately lifted: "It has begun!"

I recall the heretofore unseen enthusiasm with which the detachment greeted the long-awaited order. Assemblies of the communists and *Komsomolists*, which were conducted in the subunits on the eve of the departure, resulted in vibrant meetings, at which scouts assured the Communist Party, the fleet Military Council, and the command element of *SOR*, that they would not spare their effort and their very lives for the accomplishment of the assigned mission.

[Brief discussion of political effort follows—not translated.]

On 9 October, an hour prior to embarking on the cutters, a member of the fleet Military Council, Vice Admiral A. A. Nikolaev, came to visit us. He was in the traditional travel uniform—sailor's pea jacket. He gave a brief, rousing talk, greeting the scouts with enthusiasm. He was an experienced organizer and clever propagandist, and with his simple and plain talk was able to reinforce in the hearts of our men to fight the enemy decisively to the last drop of their blood.

By 2100, the detachment had been fully loaded onto the cutters. Battalions of 63rd Brigade of Colonel A. M. Krylov were also embarking at the adjacent pier. Their mission was to land to our left and attack the enemy on the Mustatunturi Ridge from the west. At approximately 2130, Small Subchasers [*MO*] 429 and 430 and torpedo cutter [*TKA*] 211, under the overall command of Senior Lieutenant B. M. Lyakh, set a course for our landing site. The enemy coastline met us with the illuminating beams of searchlights and heavy artillery fires. Having established a smoke screen, the cutters approached the shore. The landing was conducted quickly and in an organized manner. With a hurried rush, the detachment occupied the coastal heights and, without personnel losses, moved out of the enemy's zone of fire, having lost one of the five radios we were carrying.

Having reported to the command regarding our landing, I gave the order to get into march formation and begin movement toward the target—Cape Krestovyy. The lead patrols, equipped special strip maps, precisely held to the selected march route, closely monitored by my chief of staff, A. N. Sintsov.

Having left the coastal zone of Malaya Volokovaya Inlet far behind and reaching an open snow-covered plateau, we saw far in the distance to our east the enormous glow of fires. We heard the thunder of an artillery cannonade, which tore through the air and echoed in the ravines. This was our own artillery on the peninsula, lighting up the long-prepared defense of the Germans on Mustatunturi Ridge, clearing a pathway for the attack of the naval infantry of Colonel V. V. Rasokhin's 12th Brigade and the machine gunners of two machine-gun battalions.

We moved, not stopping, behind the advance patrols, which were carefully following the slopes of the hills. By the middle of the night, the weather had worsened, a strong wind came up, and we were peppered by a snowstorm. We had to slow down our movement: in such a situation, it is not difficult to lose contact along the march file, which in turn could have led to separation of the column into segments.

By morning, the snow had turned into rain, and the entire landscape was quickly again turned into a brownish-gray color. The scouts had to remove their white camouflage capes. For the purposes of maintaining march security in the daytime, we halted movement, spread the men out among the rocks in fighting positions, oriented for the possibility of engagement. All day on 10 October, single enemy aircraft flying at low level followed the depressions, water courses, and rocky hills, covered with countless boulders. Apparently, the enemy command suspected something. But all attempts to detect us from the air turned out to be fruitless.

In the evening, a radio message arrived from the command post of SOR: "Mustatunturi has been captured. Accelerate your movement." With the onset of dusk, the detachment set out again. We had not gone a kilometer, when the sky grew so dark that we had simply to grope our way forward. It was not easy for the scouts to carry the additional ammunition supply, five days of rations, their weapons, and other equipment. But despite it all, we had trained so long to overcome physical hardship, developing endurance, calmness, and steadfastness.

By morning of 11 October, exhausted by the night movement, we reached the area of Lake Syasiyarvi. The men had to rest. We had absolutely no information about the enemy in this area; therefore, I debated for some time before I made the decision. Observers, sent to the nearest elevations from where they could well inspect the close-lying terrain, did not observe any enemy.

I consulted with Sintsov [his chief of staff]. We decided to make a stop here and conceal the detachment in a grove of small willows. Having been bolstered by meat warmed in glasses of alcohol and tea, the men regained their will and dropped into a brief, uneasy sleep. Suddenly, a German *jaeger*, who had appeared from the direction of the sea, somehow failed to notice us. Fortunately, he was in such a rush that he was not looking around. Therefore, we had no reason to give our position away and left him to go on his way.

Having waited for first light, we departed and were already not far from our objective, in the hills overlooking Cape Krestovyy, when an unfortunate incident occurred. Somehow, a grenade belonging to scout Panteleev, from Petrov's platoon, detonated on his equipment belt. It was unfortunate to not know precisely how this happened (we had to bury Panteleev at the spot where he died), and were concerned that the enemy, if they were nearby, had been able to hear the explosion. Nothing good could have come of that.

By the onset of darkness, we reached the coastal outcropping at Petsamovuono Inlet, from which we could see the contours of the black formation that was Cape Krestovyy. Beyond it on the far shore of the inlet could be seen the port Liinakhamari—after our air raids had set it on fire.

Taking advantage of the semi-darkened panorama of this immense, cup-shaped bay, which lay before our feet, and having recalled from my memory the features of the particular local landmarks studied earlier on the map, I glanced down to where our intended path of travel was to reach Cape Krestovyy and, recognizing it, shuddered. Ahead of us was an almost vertical cliff, to climb down from which only alpinists would have the strength.

In this moment, once again, the opportunity presented itself to rely upon the foresight and planning of our detachment senior NCO, Sergey Getman. In a few moments, from somewhere he took out whole bundles of rigging, which he had brought along "just in case," and from them made belts, rope lines, and other devices for use with the equipment. We spent about six hours descending the vertical walls.

During my service in reconnaissance, I had developed a professional habit—on the march—to periodically confirm the presence of my men. While walking in file, I would issue the oral command, "Report your personnel status." Here, when we had descended to the base of the cape, the first thing that I required was to confirm the presence there of all our men. To my great surprise, Lieutenant Kubarev was unable to confirm the presence in his platoon of scout Provotorov. The soldier was gone without a trace. This was at the very moment when only 200 meters remained to the enemy objective that we were supposed to attack. My head was spinning.

I looked at my watch and saw that not more than an hour remained until dawn (it was already the morning of 12 October). Time was running out. I summoned the group commanders and in half-voice directed a halt, assigned them their missions, and issued an oral order. Led by their commanders, the scout subunits immediately hurriedly moved onto the cape. The scouts of Viktor Leonov, with a group of artillerymen, rushed toward the 88 mm antiaircraft battery; the platoon of Aleksandr Petrov, with a group of demolitions men, moved to the area of the 150 mm battery, deployed on the [north] end of the cape at the very edge of the water; scouts Anatoliy Kubarev and Yuriy Pivovarov went to the fortified position that provided cover for the approaches to the batteries.

The sudden appearance of our scouts shocked the enemy. The encircled-by-barbed-wire-obstacles strongpoint, on the slopes of which were positioned firing points, including hardened bunkers with heavy machine guns, immediately came to life. In the path of our attacking men stood a bunker from which the Germans were conducting fierce fire. Rockets [flares] shot up from the enemy's observation posts, which illuminated the moving line of our scouts. But nothing was able to stop them now.

Having thrown their pea jackets onto the barbed wire, scouts Afanasev, Sidorov, Lukyanchenko, and Arteev quickly overcame this obstacle and attacked the enemy firing point. A grenade, thrown by the skilled hand of Anatoliy Sidorov, silenced the enemy bunker. The remaining assaulting sailors acted decisively.

Unable to halt our rapid attack, the *jaegers* began to withdraw in fragmented groups to the area of the 150 mm battery. We occupied one of the bunkers taken from the enemy for the command post of our detachment staff, from which Sintsov, with his now protected radio, quickly established contact with the *SOR* command, which was closely monitoring our situation.

In this fast-flowing engagement, we suffered our first (if one does not count the unfortunate incident with Panteleev) loss. Shrapnel from a closely detonating shell seriously wounded scout Orlov. The medics hurried forward and carried him into cover, but his wounds turned out to be so critical that he lost consciousness and then died.

At the very height of the battle, Lesha Provotorov appeared in front of me and in a rapid-fire voice reported: departing from the last halt, his comrades forgot to wake him, and he . . . But I cut him off. "Go to the firing line!" I ordered the confessing soldier.

Scouts Kubarev and Pivovarov continued to press the Germans in the area of the heavy battery, the approaches to which were covered by several rows of barbed wire and trenches, which were anchored in the granite. Taking cover behind the rock outcroppings, huddled in engineer-prepared fortifications, the fascist soldiers conducted intensive automatic fire and launched spasmodic grenade [not clear whether this is hand grenade or mortar fire, since *granata* is also the Russian word for "mortar round"] barrages. But this could not stop the scouts.

Senior sailors A. Ya. Rozaev and A. I. Sidorov managed to burst into the positions of the 150 mm battery and disable one of the guns with grenades. In this unequal engagement, communist Rozaev was seriously wounded, but just the same continued to probe forward, while he still had remaining strength. Seeing that the life of his comrade was in danger, *Komsomolets* Anatoliy Sidorov took hold of him and dragged him behind cover, firing from his automatic rifle and tossing grenades. But an enemy bullet also found him. Losing blood, the wounded Anatoliy continued to crawl from cover to cover and to drag the now weakened, unconscious Rozaev. An enemy grenade took the lives of both brave scouts.

At this same time, the scouts of Viktor Leonov were attacking the 88 mm antiaircraft battery, which was positioned on the downhill slope 300 meters south of the enemy strongpoint. They had approached it undetected and surrounded it from three sides. [This does not comport with Leonov's account, which describes losing the element of surprise at the top of the hill.] Groups under the command of Lieutenant F. K. Zmeev, Chief Petty Officer A. A. Barinov [one of Leonov's platoon leaders], and the commander himself of the scouts, V. N. Leonov, having hastily overcome the barbed wire, quickly unleashed automatic fire and grenades on the enemy's bunkers and barracks.

Two battery positions opened intense machine-gun fire on the attacking scouts. The scouts had to penetrate to the gun platforms, while overcoming the fires of the gun crews that were scurrying out of their sleeping bunkers. Anatoliy Barinov, Vladimir Fatkin, and Aleksandr Manin died bravely in this heavy exchange. Fending off enemy counterattacks, Leonov's men silenced the bunkers with grenades, and continued to move toward the flak guns. Particularly outstanding during this fight were Boris Guguev, Ivan Lysenko, and Semyon Agafonov. The group of artillerymen under the command of Rosenfeld turned the captured guns against the enemy nodes of resistance and his anti-cutter artillery, which was conducting fire on Krestovyy from Liinakhamari port.

Lieutenant Petrov's platoon, which had been sent with a group of sappers along the shoreline to the location of the 150 mm heavy battery, because of the incoming tide was not able to reach it. An attempt by the scouts from Viktor Sharonov's squad to overcome the last sloping soil, beyond which the battery was located, was unsuccessful. Several men who had scrambled along the edge of the shoreline could not hold on and ended up in the icy water. [In neither case does the text indicate whether these attempts were made on the west side of the German position or the east side.]

The predawn attack we had undertaken on Krestovyy and voluntary commotion in the enemy garrison did not remain unnoticed by the Hitlerites that were sitting in Liinakhamari port. All the combat forces and anti-cutter artillery that were located there, as well as a 210 mm shore battery located on Cape Devkin [the shoulder of land opposite Cape Krestovyy that defines the northwest opening out to the open sea] were quickly brought up to combat readiness. In addition, the Germans had large caliber artillery batteries on Capes Numeroniemi and Nurmensetti [the shoulders of land where the throat of the inlet reaches the open sea], intended for blocking the entrance to Petsamovuono Inlet. All this weight of gun barrels was turned in our direction. Our detachment suffered serious losses from this massed fire support. Emboldened by the fire support of their artillery, the enemy began to regain their senses and to undertake periodic counterattacks.

In the middle of the day, groups of soldiers began to cross the fjord to reinforce the [German] garrison. Fighting reached a fever pitch. Attacks followed one after another. Groups of enemy soldiers began to appear even in the vicinity of the detachment's command post. Lieutenant Sintsov and I were forced to crawl to a German machine gun that had been captured that morning and defeat these attacks. The Hitlerites managed to clear the 88 mm antiaircraft battery. We had no place to retreat to: to our rear were vertical cliffs; the fascists, their backs to the water, fought with the despair of the doomed.

The tempo of the battle grew. Our detachment began to run low on ammunition. We had to request air support and resupply of ammunition. The fleet command immediately responded to our request. Northern Fleet aviation appeared in the sky. A group of *Il-2 Shturmoviks*, under the cover of fighters, having received target designations given by signal rockets, struck a powerful ground attack on the enemy dispositions. Our situation significantly improved.

The appearance of the aircraft delivering us ammunition and provisions greatly encouraged our men. Even though all the parachutes did not open, we were no longer threatened by ammunition "starvation."

At midday, when we had been forced to give up the 88 mm battery, a disheveled Leonov arrived at my command post. Briefly having described the extremely difficult situation which by that time had developed in his sector, he requested assistance. More and more reinforcements were being hurled across the bay, and the enemy was attacking with great ferocity. I sent Petrov's platoon to him, which had been unable to penetrate to the area of the 150 mm battery and was being kept in reserve. Two squads of scouts from Pivovarov's platoon reinforced a sector as well directly adjacent to the 88 mm battery.

Having regrouped our men in the face of the resistance and replenished our ammunition supply, we again began to attack, and by the end of the day had once again captured the 88 mm battery, taken the shoreline under our complete control, and deprived the enemy of the possibility of hurling reinforcements across the water, as well as driving the remaining Hitlerites into the area of the 150 mm battery. Those [Germans] who did not manage to withdraw to the inescapable position began to surrender singly and in small groups. At nightfall, the battle quieted down, and firing occurred only in isolated locations.

From among the fleet headquarters' scouts, Aleksandr Nikandrov, Pavel Baryshev, and Andrey Pshenichnykh distinguished themselves during this engagement. Though wounded, Lieutenant Zmeev and party organizer Tarashinin remained in the formation. While fending off the enemy landing, the scouts from Petrov's platoon acted bravely. Senior sailor and *Komsomolist* Said Abdulbaleev, sailors Ioin and Malakhov went around the enemy's flank and killed several enemy soldiers with a trophy machine gun, during the process capturing a Hitlerite corporal.

Senior Sailors Nikolay Baranov and Anatoliy Leshukov, with a light machine gun positioned on the left flank, with their fires were covering our scouts who were counterattacking the enemy battery. During the approach of one of the boats with an enemy assault force, they destroyed approximately 10 Germans soldiers, thus preventing them from approaching the detachment's rear.

On the night of 12–13 October, the *SOR* chief of staff, Captain First Rank D. A. Tuz, transmitted to the detachment the report that on this night it was intended to land an amphibious assault force in Liinakhamari port. It was approximately 0300 when three groups of cutters with the assault force burst into the fjord. As it later became clear to me, officers Shabalin, Korsunovich, and Zyuzin commanded these groups. The Hitlerites greeted them with dense artillery fires. It was as light as day. The actions of the cutters were clearly visible in the illuminated shell bursts, and we admired "their work" in our spirits. The 88 mm gun battery we had captured did not remain silent and was being used to suppress enemy firing points.

All night long and the following day, the machine gunners of Major I. A. Timofeev and naval infantry of Lieutenant B. F. Peterburgskiy were engaged in heavy combat in the capture of Liinakhamari port.

Early on the morning of 13 October, before daylight, we made several additional attempts to penetrate the area of the remaining node of enemy resistance—the Germans' 150 mm battery. But the steep slopes and dense fire of defensive fortifications that covered the approaches to it prevented us from accomplishing our task. I considered it a senseless waste of casualties to attack it during daylight. But the desire to be done with the besieged remnants of the garrison concerned me.

Our force on Krestovyy had grown by this time. A company of 63rd Brigade scouts under the command of Captain Ilyasov had arrived. A platoon of Captain Sledin had also been attached to us. This platoon was supposed to have landed in Liinakhamari, but because the cutter delivering the assault force had been damaged during the rush into the inlet, it went to ground toward the northern shoreline of the fjord. Sledin put his men ashore and, marching along the east shore of the inlet, arrived at Krestovyy. Thus, we had sufficient force to capture the battery at night.

By this time we had rounded up approximately 20 prisoners, among them a first lieutenant. Having consulted with A. N. Sintsov, I decided to recommend to the Hitlerite that he serve in the role of parliamentarian—to deliver a surrender ultimatum to the leader of the besieged garrison.

Our interpreter, Aleksey Ivanovich Kashtanov, a charming, energetic scout from Leonov's group, translated our suggestion to the German officer. He initially balked, but then, having thought it over, agreed to the suggestion.

The amusing incident with our "parliamentarian" comes to mind. When the German officer approached within several meters of his own men with two of my soldiers, the Germans, without seeing a German uniform, opened fire. Immediately pressing himself to the granite, the officer crawled backward on his belly and begged me not to send him back up there. Digging around in the equipment of the medical point, deployed near the cliff, we pulled out a light-colored rag and handed it to the German officer to use as a white flag.

When he again approached his own troops, waving this panel, they did not fire on him.

Casting aside all caution, we stood up at full height at the edge of the gap and with unusual interest looked over this entire scene. We observed a group of officers engaging the first lieutenant. Then they disappeared. A half hour passed, while this procedure went on, and still there was no resolution. It was time to give the signal for the final assault of the encircled battery, when suddenly everything began to move. The soldiers, singly and in groups, began to assemble in one place and, quickly forming a column, with the head of the garrison himself at the front, headed in our direction; they had accepted our ultimatum.

The registration of the POWs was conducted in the dugout barracks of the 88 mm battery.

One-by-one, the soldiers walked up to the table, calmly clicked their heels, curtly reported, and handed over [their] soldiers' identification booklet. The list, which Misha Illarionov compiled with the assistance of interpreter A. I. Kashtanov, contained 78 last names.

The registration of the prisoners and processing of the trophies was completed by 1800. A. N. Sintsov prepared and sent to the command a detailed report, the response to which was issued without delay. The fleet commander, A. G. Golovko, and commander of SOR, Ye. T. Dubovtsev, thanked all the participants in the successful accomplishment of the combat mission.

At this time, when the remnants of the German garrison were brought into our positions, I sent a group of scouts with their veteran soldier [literally, *order bearer*] I. K. Meletyev, in order that they do a detailed examination and inspect the dugout barracks, depots, and gun positions of the 150 mm battery. Upon their return, Meletyev reported that the battery was entirely deserted, and that they had encountered one officer who was "dead drunk," and they had been unable to rouse.

On the night from 13 to 14 October, they transported us SOR scouts, minus the fleet headquarters scouts [Leonov's men] to Liinakhamari to reinforce Major Timofeev's amphibious landing force. At dawn we conducted several attacks, in the process losing several men to wounds, including some radio operators. By midday, Liinakhamari port was completely cleared of the enemy. Units of Colonel Rassokhin's brigade, which had broken through the defenses on Mustatunturi Ridge and fought their way toward Liinakhamari, began to arrive.

Here, on liberated soil, occurred the unforgettable meeting with combat comrades, with whom we had previously served. [Names and recollections follow, untranslated here.]

The cutter of the commander of SOR soon arrived. Dubovtsev and Tuz disembarked and headed in our direction. I had to assemble my men quickly and form them up for meeting these high commanders. When I looked out over my "young achievers," I involuntarily froze. In front of me stood men dressed in every possible way—my eyes stopped on forbidden head coverings, *jaeger* high-top boots, German ponchos, and every other kind of overgarment that could be construed as clothing. The general cursed us out as one would expect, basically. Then, smiling, he praised the men and thanked them for successful accomplishment of the mission.

Days later, we returned to our Rybachyy "motherland." We had to get ourselves back in order and be prepared for the assault on Kirkenes. But all our anticipation turned out for naught. The 14th Army and our 12th Brigade had quickly reached the Norwegian border and captured the town [25 October]. The German-fascist forces were driven from the boundaries of the Motherland, and our Soviet flag once again waved over the from-time-immemorial Russian earth of Pechenga.

[FROM PAGE 152, THIRD FULL PARAGRAPH] In the three-day battle for Krestovyy and in Liinakhamari port, we lost 53 men killed and wounded. [This text does not distinguish the distribution of these casualties between the cape and the port. End of relevant text.]

※ ※ ※

From the memoir of Viktor Leonov, *Litsom k litsu: Vospominaniya morskogo razvedchika* (Face to face: Recollections of a Naval scout) (Moscow: Molodaya gvardiya, 1957). Translated by James F. Gebhardt and retitled in English to *Blood on the Shores: Soviet Naval Commandos in World War II* (Annapolis: Naval Institute Press, 1993), pp. 108–119.

The wind grew stronger, savagely lashed our faces with sleet and salty spray, and howled threateningly. Gigantic daggers of light from the searchlights crisscrossed and impotently ripped at the curtain of the sky. The storm clouds came lower and hung over our heads.

The rumble of battle was growing clearer.

Sailors ran along the cutter's deck. They picked up the gangplank. This meant that we soon would be leaving the deck. The cutter would depart. Lyakh's boat would not come for us, because this time the assault force of naval scouts would walk from one seashore to another, from the bay to the cape, and not return to base. After we seized Krestovyy, we would join in the general flow of the offensive. There would be new raids, terrible new battles. But through it all, as the poet wrote, "Wait for me! I will return despite everyone else's death!"[40]

No, I had to think about something else! In the first place, about communications between the three groups, about observation and reporting. Did I act correctly, dividing the detachment into three groups? [Political officer] Guznenkov was a good comrade, but what would he be like heading a group in battle?

"We're coming to the shore," Lyakh said to me.

The shore was not visible in the pitch darkness. The cutter slowed, then stopped.

One after another, the scouts came up out of the cabin onto the deck. They looked suspiciously toward the shore and waited for the sailors to throw off long gangplanks made especially for the landing. We listened as the gangplank slapped the water. The cutter crewmen jumped down and picked up the end of it. Standing up to their waists in freezing water, they provided us a dry path to the shore.

"Your men are good to us!" I said to Lyakh. "Thank them."

Lyakh held my hand in his longer than usual. The cutter commander knew where and why we were going. The day before he had joked, "And why, Viktor, do they give you such happy march routes: Mogilnyy? Krestovyy?"

"Because from Lyakh's cutter you can take the devil by the horns!" I said.

Now Boris Lyakh was silent; his long and firm handshake replaced the words he wanted to say.

---

40 From the poem by Konstantin Simonov, "Wait for Me," which appears in its entirety on the previous page of this memoir. Simonov (1914–1979) was a famous Soviet writer and poet, who as a war correspondent traveled from one sector of the Soviet–German front to the other, writing both poetry and prose for the troops as well as the civilian population. He spent several weeks in the Murmansk area in October–November 1941, including time with the Northern Fleet Reconnaissance Detachment.—Translator

"Say hello to Shabalin for me," I said to Lyakh on parting.[41] "Tell him that we'll meet him there."

"Of course, you'll meet him. I'm worried for you. Do you know what the words Viktor and Viktoriya stand for?"[42]

"No, you can tell me later, when we meet."

Satisfied with such an innocent lie and naïve symbol (if there are grounds for a meeting, then a meeting *will* take place), I ran along the gangplank and jumped onto the slippery rocks of the shore.

The motor of the withdrawing cutter started up. I did not turn around but hurried toward the scouts. They were setting up a defense just in case.

Judging by the time, Barchenko's detachment already had begun to negotiate the hills and rocks. Our path to Cape Krestovyy was shorter and more difficult.[43]

At midnight, we were scaling a steep hill. Standing on Semyon Agafonov's shoulders and leaning against the cliff, the detachment *partorg* [party organizer] Arkady Tarashinin was cutting steps in the almost vertical granite wall. Others followed his example. With the aid of these steps and rope we made it to the top of the hill and saw new, even steeper mountains ahead. It was a difficult path to the "key to Liinakhamari!"

The wind had subsided a bit, but sleet was falling. We came into a valley, which led to the next checkpoint of the march route. Covered with a flat layer of snow, the valley was very dangerous. It might seem to the newcomers that it would be easier here. But Fatkin, the point man, raised his arm, and the file of scouts froze. Fatkin tied one end of the rope around himself, gave the other end to Andrey Pshenichnykh, then lay in the snow and crawled. He crawled slowly, feeling each meter with his hands to detect any crevasses hidden under the snow. Fatkin cleared a safe path for us on this mountain plateau.

The sky was getting lighter when we scaled another peak, and the battle that had erupted during the night on the crest of Mustatunturi seemed closer. The searchlight beams from the direction of Liinakhamari still probed the cliffs. I stopped and let the file of scouts move past me, walking with long strides, moving their legs with difficulty in the darkness. The men needed a rest. It would be better to sleep a bit so that we could move more safely during the day. The snow continued to fall, covering our tracks.

We organized a break under a rock overhang, and in a half hour the figures of curled-up scouts were transformed into white mounds. Everyone fell asleep. Only my runner, Boris Guguev, and my radio operator, Dmitriy Kazhaev, kept watch. I closed my eyes and, already falling asleep, heard Kazhaev repeat headquarters' call sign, then switch over to receive.

"Jupiter, Jupiter, how to you hear me?" "I hear you loud and clear."

I instantly tuned in. The radio operator, having pressed his palms to the headset, gave me an expressive look and nodded in affirmation.

"Jupiter, I understood you! I understood you," Kazhaev distinctly repeated. "Earth is nearby. Earth is right next to me. Everything will be passed to him immediately. How do you read me? Over."

The fleet commander was informing us that Mount Mustatunturi had been cleared of the enemy and that units of the Karelian *Front* had reached the road to Petsamo from the south. He ordered us to speed up our movement.

I ordered the men to get up. The snow mounds began to move as they came to life.

Guznenkov, Tarashinin, and Manin, the group agitators, informed the scouts about the successes of the attacking forces and about the upcoming day's march.[44] They encouraged the tired scouts. Once again, we were on our way.

It was getting dark when we saw the outline of Cape Krestovyy ahead of us, a rocky, black cape hanging over the sea. The *jaegers* had positioned their guns in a high location. From there, they could see the bay of Petsamovuono and the sea, and, if the weather were clear, our Rybachyy Peninsula, on which they trained the barrels of their guns. Tomorrow at this time our assault cutters

---

41 Boris Lyakh and Aleksander Shabalin were *PT* boat captains with whom Leonov had a close personal relationship, based on their frequent missions to insert or extract Leonov's men from an enemy-held shore. Their awarding of Hero of the Soviet Union subsequent to this operation is footnoted in the main text.

42 In the Russian text these two words have the accent marks shown on the second syllable, indicating the English names Victor and Victoria, from the Latin root *vincere*, past participle of the verb meaning "to conquer."

43 The implication of the text here is that Leonov's and Barchenko-Emelyanov's detachments moved by different routes from the landing site to the objective area. Makar Babikov, in *Voyna v Arktika*, 280, confirms this, saying that two routes were used to present less of target for German detection. The two detachments were close enough to each other to provide mutual support.—Translator

44 An agitator in this context was a Communist Party propagandist or activist, whose duty it was to inspire and motivate the men.—Translator

would begin their raid past Cape Krestovyy into Liinakhamari. But there was still a night ahead of us, a long autumn polar night.

When they saw the cape, the scouts picked up their pace. We scaled down the last and steepest rocky face into the rear of the firing positions on Cape Krestovyy. Night was falling, and we crawled closer but did not climb up onto the rock-strewn plateau of the gun positions. We divided into three groups to form a semicircle around the first battery [the antiaircraft battery, the objective assigned to Leonov's group]. The second battery [the objective of Barchenko-Emelyanov's group] was below, at the very edge of the water.

It was quiet all around. At times it seemed that there was no one on Krestovyy, and if there were any batteries there, the artillerymen, feeling safe, in their rear, slept soundly.

We crawled noiselessly between large and small boulders, approaching closer and closer to the center of the cape; Boris Guguev crawling ahead was wriggling across the ground like a lizard.

Then suddenly, having touched a barbed wire point with his hand, Guguev jerked back. But it was too late. One small bell jingled, and a series of colored flares arched up into the sky. Their blinding light pressed us to the ground. Straight ahead of us was a barbed wire fence. A barrack, half buried in the earth, was visible on the other side. The figure of a sentry, who was guarding the entrance to the earthen barrack, loomed above the roof. We also spotted two guns with elevated barrels, which now were slowly being lowered in our direction, and a guard running from the barbed wire toward the barrack. All of this was 20–40 meters from us.

The guard did not make it to the guns—Guguev cut him down with a burst from his submachine gun. But the second guard managed to scamper into the revetment.

"Move out," I commanded.

"Forward, Northern Fleet sailors!" Ivan Guznenkov echoed my call.

Barinov's platoon was the closest to the obstacle. Taking off his quilted jacket, Bapvel Baryshev threw it onto the barbed wire and then crossed over it. Tall Guznenkov vaulted across the barbed wire, crawled forward, and then opened fire on the barrack doors.

The scouts began to pull their jackets and ponchos off as they approached the wire. But Ivan Lysenko ran up to the iron stanchions on which the wire was hung, bent down, and with a powerful jerk hoisted the stanchion to his shoulders. He slowly raised himself up to his full height and, spreading his legs wide apart, shouted frantically: "Forward, brothers! Dive under!

"Atta-boy, Lysenko!"

I charged through the breach that had been created in the fence. Rushing past me, the scouts ran toward the barrack and cannons, toward the shelters and positions.

Semyon Agafonov climbed onto the roof of a dugout, near a cannon. Why did he do that? I wondered. Two officers rushed out from the dugout. Agafonov shot the first (later it was determined that he was the battery commander) and knocked out the second with a buttstroke of his submachine gun. Jumping down, Agafonov caught up with Andrey Pshenichnykh, and they began to clear the path to the guns with grenades.

Agafonov and Pshenichnykh were still fighting in hand-to-hand combat with the gun crew, while Guznenkov and two scouts, Kolosov and Ryabchinskiy, were turning a cannon in the direction of Liinakhamari. *Jaegers* were streaming out of the barrack to meet the scouts, who were running toward them. They opened fire on our men from the run.

Wounded in the chest, Ivan Lysenko fell on his side but did not drop the stanchion. Scouts were still crawling under wire, which Lysenko held up. When no one remained behind Lysenko, he began to sway and, breathing heavily, fell face forward on the ground, dropping the stanchion.

Cover Guznenkov! Cut the *jaegers'* path from the barrack to the guns! I ordered Barinov. I led a group of scouts to suppress the bunkers from which machine guns were banging away. We blinded the machine gunners with aimed fire at the embrasures from submachine guns and rifles and closed in with short rushes to throw grenades.

Scouts from Barinov's squad were in heavy fighting with the jaegers, who were desperately seeking to reach their firing positions. Badly wounded, sailor Smirnov fell at the very door of the barrack. The detachment doctor, Lieutenant Luppov, crawled over to Smirnov and lifted him to his shoulder. A machine gun fired from the barrack window, and our doctor fell motionless with the dead sailor on his back.

Fatkin and Sobolev, Kolosov and Kalaganskiy ran toward the barrack window and hurled grenades into the room. The machine gun fell silent amid the dying *jaegers'* cries and groans.

"Don't slow down!" Anatoliy Barinov shouted. He was getting up to lead the scout in the seizure of the third cannon. But at that moment he saw a large group of *jaegers*, reinforcements from the gun crews of the second battery, going around toward our rear.[45]

"Watch out!" Volodya Fatkin shouted behind us. I turned and saw Barinov's scouts dashing into the attack. The Germans wavered and went to [the] ground, but did not fall back, and opened heavy fire.

A runner came over from [Makar] Babikov, who had replaced the wounded Barinov, and informed me that the *jaegers* were pressing in. I hurried over to help. The Germans withdrew toward their battery, but platoon commander Barinov and Volodya Fatkin, the youngest scout in the detachment, were already dead. They died heroes' deaths. Kolosov and Kalaganskiy were wounded.

Having lost control of the battle, the enemy artillerymen were rushing from dugout to dugout, from shelter to shelter. There were many of them. Although the *jaegers* had suffered enormous losses, centers of resistance sprang up first in one place and then another.

"We've captured the second gun!" Zmeev's runner reported to me. "But the lieutenant is wounded. And Tarashinin wounded in the hand. And also . . ."

"Well, speak!"

"Sasha Manin, our *komsorg* [Komsomol organizer], is dead."

The firing died down. By dawn the last center of resistance was suppressed. The first battery on the crest of the hill was in our hands. But difficult trials still lay ahead of us.

Guns and mortars were firing at us from the opposite shore—long-range artillery fired from Liinakhamari. We lay pressed to the ground, and fragments of rock and shell shrapnel flew above us in a cloud of snow spray.

I ordered the men to remove the breech blocks from the cannons and crawl toward the nearest ridge, from which we could overwatch the destroyed battery.[46] When the artillery barrage lifted and the air cleared over the high cliff of Cape Krestovyy, we could see the stretch of Devkin drainage. Two enemy cutters and three launches came out into the bay, skirting the cape.

"That's why they fired an artillery preparation!" Guznenkov said to me. "Now they will land an assault party."

"That's to be expected. An assault against an assault!" I turned toward the scouts. We'd never been in this kind of battle before.

"Get down close to the shore. It's a pity that they'll catch it from submachine guns."

After dividing the detachment into several assault groups, I ordered the commanders: "Attack the landing force! Don't let the *jaegers* land; don't allow them to get a toehold on shore!"

The first enemy assault force did not know our strength. One cutter had already succeeded in landing two squads of soldiers, but they were forced to withdraw after attacking us. Guguev, Agafonov, and Pshenichnykh, positioned in ambush, completely wiped out the Germans who had landed.

Then the enemy changed its tactic. Their assault boats now went along the bay across a broad front, forcing us to spread out our defense and create several small assault groups. The battle flared up across an expanse of 3–4 kilometers, and the outcome hung on the initiative and independent actions of the separate groups. Experienced scouts commanded them—Nikandrov, Babikov, and Agafonov. The wounded Zmeev and Tarashinin did not fall out. Zmeev, Guznenkov, and I were on the most dangerous axes.

The *jaegers'* second attempt to land an assault force also yielded no results, so they deceived us. Still another assault force came out of Liinakhamari port and took a course southward deep into the bay, away from the cape. One of the young scouts shouted, "Hey, they've given up!"

"They aren't up to an assault landing against an assault!" "Don't rejoice!"

Warrant Officer Nikandrov, looking at the departing cutters, worriedly shook his head, then came over to me and said, "Comrade Lieutenant, I think the Germans will land farther into the bay. They'll skirt the hill and try to take the cape by the same cliff that we used."

"You mean go along our march route?" Guznenkov asked. "That's possible." Opinions differed.

Not more than a half an hour had passed when Babikov, who was watching the water, reported that

---

45 The crews from the second battery—the shore battery—were housed near their guns several hundred meters away and were at this very moment fighting off the attacks of Barchenko-Emelyanov's detachment. The men referred to by Leonov were probably antiaircraft gun crews or support personnel.—Translator

46 Attachments to the composite detachment included an unspecified number of artillerymen. Leonov may have had a few with him who were familiar with the workings of these German guns.—Translator

another two cutters had entered the bay. The new assault force turned sharply toward the shore, toward us.

What was the enemy planning? Was this only a demonstration landing to distract us from the main attack? I ordered Babikov to organize a defense on the slope of the hill that overlooked the water and, no matter what happened, to keep a reserve of 20 scouts near him.

Guznenkov went with Babikov's platoon. I sat down to write a radio message. The detachment needed ammunition and provisions. Headquarters had promised to drop us food and ammunition from airplanes and, in case we needed it, to provide fire support from the air. The way events were unfolding, that support might quickly become necessary.

I had just given the radio message to Kazhaev when I saw running toward us sailor Maltsev, a guard who was watching over the wounded lying in the rocks not far from the edge of the hill. Maltsev himself was wounded in the cheek. Completely exhausted, he fell at my feet and gasped—"There... Germans... crawling!" Maltsev pointed in the direction of the cliff.

"Should we recover Babikov's group?" "It's too late! Follow me!"

We ran past the wounded, who by this time had guessed what danger threatened them. We hurried toward the rocks in which we had hidden ourselves the previous night and from which the *jaegers* were already firing, trying to get a toehold on the hill. Bent over, hiding behind the rocks, we crawled closer to the Germans. Still unable to see each other in the tight labyrinth of rocks and boulders, we clashed, face to face.

An unusual battle flared up, rare for its intensity and suddenness. There were warlike cries and desperate howls, the clatter of submachine gun bursts and the metallic clash of barrels.

Scouts and *jaegers* darted between the rocks. There were buttstrokes and short-dagger thrusts. It was the kind of struggle in which fists, cold steel, and a rock picked up off the ground went into motion, as well as violent thrusts and grappling, kicks in the stomachs, and trips.

A few short meters separated the Germans from the edge of the steep hill they had climbed. We knew that other *jaegers* were climbing this same incline, step by step, foothold by foothold. Those who had made it to the top were awaiting help. They had nowhere to which to retreat, and they fought with the savage fury of men who had only one chance—to hold on in the rocks at the edge of the hill.

But we pushed forward to the edge with even greater determination. Behind us were our wounded comrades. Still farther behind us, Babikov's group was fighting along the shoreline. Everyone would perish—the entire operation would collapse—if we did not throw the first group of *jaegers* that had clambered up the cliff into the abyss.

Andrey Pshenichnykh cleared himself a path quicker than the others. Thin, wiry, strong and agile, he lunged, fell, disappeared, and then reappeared in another place. Two *jaegers* waited for him to appear on the other side of the rock. A short thrust forward, then a feinting movement, and one German collapsed, knocked down with a buttstroke. But in falling, he hacked at Andrey, who then sprawled on the slippery rock. Another *jaeger* immediately hurried toward him. I raised my submachine gun but fired the burst into the air because I saw Tarashinin and Guguev behind the German. Tarashinin swung his submachine gun with his uninjured right hand.

Grenades flew toward him. Tarashinin and Guguev dropped flat.

"Hold on, Andrey!" I shouted, rushing to help Pshenichnykh. Two bayonets blocked my path. I dove to the side and one bayonet, slicking toward my head, damaged my helmet.

"Andrey, watch out! Hey—"

A tall *jaeger* was holding a rifle over the scout sprawled on the ground. I did not see how Andrew got out of harm's way, but I heard the clatter of the buttstock on the rock. Then the rifle was falling out of the German's hands, and he was bending over to pick it up. At that instant I jumped over the rock and knocked him out with a buttstroke of my submachine gun.

"Hey, behind you!" Pshenichnykh shouted.

I turned around and fired a burst from my submachine gun. The *jaeger* who had followed me did not get off a shot.

"How are the other men doing?" Andrey asked, getting up, and calmly glancing around. We surged far forward.

"I'm here! Here I am!" little Pavel Baryshev cried out, as he made his way toward us. But we couldn't see him behind the large rocks. Then Tarashinin and Guguev ran up, and Nikandrov showed up with his group.

We closed in on the enemy. With the edge of the cliff yawning behind them, they themselves forward in a last counterattack. We beat it with desperate cries.

Everyone was in awe of Andrey Pshenichnykh and was congratulating him. They were comparing Andrey with the best master of hand-to-hand combat, Semyon Agafonov, who was then in Babikov's group. But when nothing any longer threatened him, the hero of the battle trembled, looked at me with frightened eyes, and smiled guiltily. "How could I stumble like that?" "Ooh, they were evil! Death looked me in the eye, but the commander saved me. Honestly speaking, brother."

"It's all right, Pshenichnykh, calm down! You fought remarkably well. It's easy to slip here."

We got ourselves back in order. Our losses were four lightly and two seriously wounded. We left guards at the edge of the cliff and we heard increasing fire to the left and right of the hill that our scouts were defending.

While we were fighting near the edge of the cliff, the *jaegers* had managed to land two more small assault groups near the hill and were closing in on Babikov. They also forced us to go to ground and then to pull back.

Once again there were wounded behind us, and still farther. If the enemy held on to the shore and brought in reinforcements, then the same fate awaited us as those whom we had not long ago thrown into the abyss.

We pinned the landing force to the ground with dense fire and at the same time fired on the cutter that was approaching the shore. But several launches came out into the bay. The situation worsened.

I thought about our ammunition supply with alarm. Not much remained. In the din of the battle, I forgot about the radio message. But the howl of the red-starred *Shturmoviks* over the cape reminded me of it.

"They're ours!" Guguev cried, and he shook his uninjured arm. "Give us a hand, flyboys!"

Three Ilyushins made the first pass and began to dive on the cutter and the launches, which now were quickly leaving the bay. The pilots radioed us for orientation. We marked our positions with flares, then directed the aircraft onto the enemy positions. They dropped us ammunition and provisions by parachute. The first three aircraft circled over the cape, continuously raking the *jaegers* with fire, preventing them from renewing the attack until another flight of *Shturmoviks* arrived. The pilots helped us to hold on until darkness.

The enemy brought reinforcements in by boat at night. We beat off several attacks, but nonetheless were forced to withdraw to a hill occupied by the naval infantrymen from Barchenko's detachment.[47] With an advance group, Barchenko himself had penetrated along the shore toward the second battery and pinned it down. We maintained communication with his group.

"Comrade Lieutenant, they are leaving!" I heard the voice of runner Kashtanov, who had clambered up the hill. "The Germans are dragging some kind of cargo along the shore toward the dock."

I led the detachment toward the sea. We caught up to the withdrawing *jaegers* and fell upon the column, which was moving along the shore and was already close to the dock, from the march. Here, too, the *jaegers* counterattacked, leaving boxes with cargo on the shore. New groups of Germans hurried from the dock to the aid of their beleaguered column. Returning fire, we began to withdraw toward our hill. But the *jaegers* were all around, stubbornly crawling upward despite their losses. It seemed they had decided to finish us off.

I shouted that we had the strength: "Help will come soon! Hold on!" The words resounded along the crest of the hill.

Then searchlights came on in Liinakhamari and on the heights of the opposite shore of the bay. We saw *jaegers* quite near to us and threw our last grenades on the move. Illuminated by their own searchlights, the enemy pulled back. But the beams of the searchlights, picking the folds of the cliffs and the ridges of the hills out of the darkness, concentrated toward the bay. I will never forget that moment—in the light beam was a stretch of bay along which small vessels were moving quickly.

They were our assault cutters. One, a second, a third. They moved, maneuvering and firing from cannon and machine guns along the right shoulder of Devkin drainage. Now they were approaching Cape Krestovyy. The cape was silent. Guns from Liinakhamari were firing randomly. There was a duel between the cannons on the right shoreline and the guns of the cutters. Cape Krestovyy was silent! The breechblocks of the first battery's guns were in our hands, and the gun crews of the second battery were defending themselves against

---

47 Leonov withdrew his men to the center of the cape, toward the strongpoint that was by this time controlled by Barchenko-Emelyanov's men.—Translator

the infantrymen of Captain Barchenko's detachment, which was besieging them.

"Ura!" Guznenkov stood up to his full height and greeted the cutters coming into the bay. "U-rra-a!" The shouts rolled along the crest of the hill.

Not waiting for a command, the scouts dashed into battle. Even the wounded who could still walk and fire joined us.

Their morale broken, overcome by panic and fear, the *jaegers* wavered and, not able to withstand our charge, ran toward the sea. But they couldn't run far. By morning, the battle was being fought along a narrow strip of shoreline. Only the most desperate Germans from the Krestovyy garrison were resisting. At one point, Semyon Agafonov fought with two Germans. Having cut one down, he threw the other man into the water and shouted, "Give up, you son of a bitch! I'll kill you! Hands up!"

The German threw his rifle down, raised his left hand, and squatted down. With his right hand he picked up a rock, waved it threateningly, and then fell, cut down by a short submachine gun burst.

Agafonov went to the shoreline of the bay, squatted down, and rinsed his hands. "Well, it's done, it seems, everyone!"

Guznenkov was now back at the first battery with his group. The scouts replaced the breechblocks in the weapons, loaded the guns, and fired a salvo into Liinakhamari port. We were not great marksmen, but we had plenty of shells, and we finally managed to set fire to a petroleum storage tank and a wooden warehouse near the dock.

Fires burned in Liinakhamari, where naval infantrymen landed from the cutters were moving into the town. Fighting was also going on along the eastern shore of the bay, from which the bypass of the port had begun. Only on Cape Krestovyy was it quiet. Then the second battery capitulated, and the prisoners were gathered in one place. Seventy defeated and disarmed *jaegers* sat, guarded by a single, light wounded scout.

Soon Shabalin's torpedo cutter came over to Cape Krestovyy. "So here we meet," Aleksandr Osipovich said to me calmly. Only the gleam in his eyes betrayed his joy. "Thank you, brother! I was pressed close to the left shore. I put my trust in you. If the guns on Krestovyy had spoken, we'd have been fish food by now. But there's no time to think about that now." Shabalin relayed Major General Dubovtsev's order that we come to the aid of the naval infantrymen who were storming Liinakhamari.

Admiral Golovko was already in Liinakhamari. On his order, we established security patrols and posts for guarding the most important facilities. I asked permission from the admiral to return to Krestovyy for the burial of our dead scouts.

"The detachment fought heroically!" the admiral said. "Put everyone in for an award. Don't be bashful! We are recommending you for the award Hero."

"I thank you, Comrade Admiral! Only, how about Agafonov and Pshenichnykh! They broke into the battery first and captured it. And how they fought later! All the detachment's scouts consider them to be heroes."

"Well, if everyone feels that way"—the admiral smiled a bit—"then there will be no mistakes. Write the reports."

I returned to Krestovyy toward the end of the day and recounted my conversation with the admiral. It turned out that the admiral had already met with the wounded scouts and asked them about the battles on Krestovyy.

"After the conversation with the admiral," Guznenkov said to me, "Kilosov and Kalaganskiy immediately asked him for a favor."

That worried me, but Guznenkov calmed down. "They said to the fleet commander, 'We are lightly wounded. Therefore, Comrade Admiral, order them not to send us far into the rear. We'll quickly heal in the base, by the sea, near the detachment.'" And the admiral promised to intercede for them.

TRANSLATOR'S APPENDIX 3

Higgins and Vosper Patrol Torpedo Boat Deliveries to Northern Fleet Through Lend-Lease, 1943-1945

Extracted and compiled from S. S. Berezhnoy, *Flot SSSR: Korabli i Suda Lendliza: Spravochnik* (Soviet Navy: Vessels and Ships of Lend-Lease: Handbook) (Saint Petersburg: "Belen," 1994), pp. 58–82.

TABLE TA3.1. Higgins patrol torpedo boats

How to read this table:

First column (unnumbered) is for reference only
COLUMN 1: Numerator—*VMF* hull #; denominator—USN hull #
COLUMN 2: Date [day.month.year format for all columns with dates] accepted by Soviet Receiving Commission, place (if known)
COLUMN 3: Soviet port to which delivered
COLUMN 4: Date of arrival in Soviet port
COLUMN 5: Date of acceptance to *VMF* ship list
COLUMN 6: Fleet or flotilla of final delivery: *SF*—Northern Fleet
COLUMN 7: Participation in Petsamo–Kirkenes Operation (Y = yes)
COLUMN 8: Notes (loss, victories, transfer means, etc.)

	1	2	3	4	5	6	7	8
1	202/265	09.11.43 NY	M	29.12.43	14.01.44	SF	Y	25.09.44, with other *TKA*, sunk V-6105 "Holstein"
2	204/267	09.11.43 NY	M	29.12.43	14.01.44	SF	Y	Damaged enemy transport and minesweeper
3	205/268	09.11.43 NY	M	29.12.43	14.01.44	SF	Y	19.08.44, V6102 "Keln," "*RT* 496"; "Colmar"; 12.10.44, minesweeper "M-303"
4	206/269	09.11.43 NY	M	29.12.43	14.01.44	SF	Y	19.08.44, "Colmar"
5	207/270	09.11.43 NY	M	29.12.43	14.01.44	SF	Y	1 patrol vessel
6	208/271	17.11.43 NY	M	29.12.43	14.01.44	SF	Y	1 enemy minesweeper
7	210/273	17.11.43 NY	M	29.12.43	14.01.44	SF	Y	
8	211/274	17.11.43 NY	M	29.12.43	14.01.44	SF	Y	14.09.44, sunk minesweeper "M252" and transport
9	213/276	17.11.43 NY	M	29.12.43	14.01.44	SF	Y	Sunk 2 enemy fast assault barges
10	215/289	3.12.43	M	01.02.44	20.02.44	SF	Y	07.05.44, "Modor 2"; 21.10.4, minesweeper "M31"
11	216/290	3.12.43	M	01.02.44	20.02.44	SF	Y	09.04.44, tanker "Ster"; 23.03.44, V 6109 "Nordwind"
12	218/292	3.12.43	M	01.02.44	20.02.44	SF	Y	2 patrol vessels, 1 transport; 07.05.44, "Modor 2"
13	219/294	3.12.43	M	01.02.44	20.02.44	SF	Y	1 transport, 1 patrol vessel; 07.05.44, "Modor 2"
14	222/293	3.12.43	M	29.02.44	01.04.44	SF	Y	1 guard vessel; 25.09.04, sunk V6105 "Holstein"

Translator's note: While a total of 52 Higgins-constructed patrol torpedo boats were delivered to the Soviet Navy, 20 were shipped to Murmansk, of which these 14 are shown in Berezhnoy as having participated in the Petsamo–Kirkenes Operation. The remaining 32 were shipped to the Soviet Far East ports of Vladivostok and Petropavlovsk-Kamchatka.

The Higgins design was 78 ft in length, with a 20 ft. beam and a draught of 5.2 feet, and displaced 49–55 tons. Powered by three 1315 h.p. Packard liquid-cooled, supercharged V-12 gasoline engines, it had a top speed of 41.5 knots and an economical speed of 21.4 knots. Equipped with four 750-gallon rubber-sealed fuel cells, the boat had an economical range of 450 miles. In Soviet use, it was crewed by 11 men. The armament included two side-launched torpedoes, twin-mounted 12.7 mm machine guns, and two 20 mm cannons. From 1943 on, it also featured a Raytheon-manufactured radar, with a range of 25 nautical miles. Northern Fleet retained 20 of the Higgins boats.

TABLE TA3.2. Vosper patrol torpedo Boats

How to read this table:

First column (unnumbered) is for reference only

COLUMN 1: Numerator—*VMF* hull #; denominator—USN hull #
COLUMN 2: Shipyard: F—Fiff's NY; AY—Annapolis Yacht; BH—Herreshoff–Bristol, RI
COLUMN 3: Date [day.month.year format for all columns with dates] accepted by Soviet Receiving Commission, place (if known)
COLUMN 4: Soviet port to which delivered: M—Murmansk
COLUMN 5: Date of arrival in Soviet port
COLUMN 6: Date of acceptance to *VMF* ship list
COLUMN 7: Fleet or flotilla of final delivery: *SF*—Northern Fleet, *KBF*—Red Banner Baltic Fleet
COLUMN 8: Participation in Petsamo–Kirkenes Operation (Y = yes)
COLUMN 9: Notes (loss, victories, transfer means, etc.)

	1	2	3	4	5	6	7	8	9
1	226/366	F	15.02.44	M	04.04.44	27.04.44	KBF	Y	Initially slated for Royal Navy. Conducted actions on enemy lines of communication in Varanger Fjord, 06.10.44. 24.05.45, moved by White Sea–Baltic Canal to Kronshtadt.
2	228/368	F	16.02.44	M	04.04.44	27.04.44	KBF	Y	Initially slated for Royal Navy. Conducted actions on enemy lines of communication in Varanger Fjord, 06.10.44. 24.05.45, moved by White Sea–Baltic Canal to Kronshtadt.
3	230/370	F	16.02.44	M	04.04.44	27.04.44	KBF	Y	Conducted actions on enemy lines of communication in Varanger Fjord, 06.10.44. Sunk 1 patrol vessel, 1 transport. 24.05.45, moved by White Sea–Baltic Canal to Kronshtadt.
4	237/410	F	22.02.44	M	04.04.44	27.04.44	KBF	Y	Conducted actions on enemy lines of communication in Varanger Fjord, 06.10.44. In *SF*, sunk 2 minesweepers, 1 transport. 24.05.45 moved by White Sea–Baltic Canal to Kronshtadt.
5	238/411	F	22.02.44	M	04.04.44	27.04.44	SF	Y	Conducted actions on enemy lines of communication in Varanger Fjord, 06.10.44. Sunk 2 patrol vessels; 12.10.44 transport "Lumme."
6	240/413	F	05.03.44	M	04.04.44	27.04.44	KBF	Y	Conducted actions on enemy lines of communication in Varanger Fjord, 07.10.44. During P-K Operation, together with other TKA, sunk 2 enemy vessels. 24.05.45, moved by White Sea–Baltic Canal to Kronshtadt.
7	241/430	F	25.02.44	M	04.04.44	27.04.44	KBF	Y	Conducted actions on enemy lines of communication in Varanger Fjord, 07.10.44. During P-K Operation, sunk 2 and damaged 2 enemy vessels. Used as training vessel from 15.01 to 12.03.45, then on 24.05.45, moved by White Sea–Baltic Canal to Kronshtadt.
8	242/431	F	04.03.44	M	04.04.44	27.04.44	KBF	Y	Conducted actions on enemy lines of communication in Varanger Fjord, 07.10.44. During P-K Operation, together with other *TKA*, sunk 4 enemy vessels. 24.05.45, moved by White Sea–Baltic Canal to Kronshtadt.

continued on next page

TABLE TA3.2—*continued*

	1	2	3	4	5	6	7	8	9
9	243/432	F	05.03.44	M	04.04.44	27.04.44	KBF	Y	Conducted actions on enemy lines of communication in Varanger Fjord, 07.10.44. During P-K Operation, together with other *TKA*, sunk two enemy vessels and 1 transport. 24.05.45, moved by White-Sea Baltic Canal to Kronshtadt.
10	244/406	F	24.02.44	M	26.08.44	18.09.44	KBF	Y	During P-K Operation, sunk 1 transport. 31.07.45; from 15.01 to 12.03.45 used as training vessel. Moved by White-Sea Baltic Canal by White Sea Canal to Kronshtadt.
11	245/407	F	24.02.44	M	26.08.44	18.09.44	KBF	Y	After participation in P-K Operation, from 15.01 to 12.03.45, used as training vessel from 15.01 to 12.03.45. On 24.05.45, moved by White Sea–Baltic Canal to Kronshtadt.
12	246/448	F	09.07.44	M	26.08.44	18.09.44	KBF	Y	After participation in P-K Operation, on 24.05.45, moved by White Sea–Baltic Canal to Kronshtadt

Source: Extracted and compiled by from S. S. Berezhnoy, *Flot SSSR: Korabli i Suda Lendliza: Spravochnik* (Soviet Navy: Vessels and Ships of Lend-Lease: Handbook) (Saint Petersburg: "Belen," 1994), pp. 20–58.

Translator's note: Of the 90 total Vosper hulls that were shipped to the USSR, 41 of 58 went to Murmansk, 17 additional were shipped to Arkhangelsk (a majority crated, to be later assembled at a plant in Leningrad), and the remaining 32 were shipped to Soviet Far East ports of Vladivostok and Petropavlovsk-Kamchatka. As this table indicates, a large number of *TKA* that began their Soviet Navy service in Northern Fleet later went to the Red Banner Baltic Fleet.

The Vosper PT boat was 72.5 ft. in length, with 20 ft. beam and 5.1 ft. of draught. It displaced 43.5–45 tons. It was also powered by three 1200 h.p. Packard liquid-cooled, supercharged V-12 engines, which gave it a maximum speed of 40 knots, economical speed of 21.8 knots, and economical range of 525 miles. Its armament was two torpedoes: two paired .50 caliber machine guns, one 20 mm cannon. It was also crewed by 11 men. Northern Fleet retained 14 of the Vosper boats.

TABLE TA3.3. Large submarine chasers delivered to USSR through Lend-Lease, participated in Petsamo–Kirkenes Operation

How to read this table:

First column (unnumbered) is for reference only.

COLUMN 1: Numerator—Soviet Navy *BO* (*bolshoy okhotnik za podvodnykh lodak*) (large hunter for submarines) hull #; denominator–USN SC (submarine chaser) hull #.

COLUMN 2: Shipyard:
  EC—Elizabeth City, NC
  FB—Fisher Boat Works, Detroit, MI
  HP—Harris & Parsons, Greenwich, RI
  QA—Quincy Adams, Quincy, MA
  RB—Rice Brothers, East Boothby, ME
  TK—Thomas Knutson Shipbuilding, Halesite, NY
  VY—Vinyard Shipyard, Milford, DE

COLUMN 3: Date accepted by Soviet crew [day.month.year format for all columns with dates], place (if known)[1]

COLUMN 4: Soviet port to which delivered: P—Polyarnoye (Northern Fleet main base north and across Kola Bay from Murmansk); A–Arkhangelsk, V–Vladivostok, PP-K–Petropavlovsk-Kamchatka

COLUMN 5: Date of arrival in Soviet port (if known)

COLUMN 6: Date of acceptance to *VMF* ship list

COLUMN 7: Fleet or flotilla of both first employment and final destination: *SF*—Northern Fleet; *KBF*—Red Banner Baltic Fleet; *ChF*—Black Sea Fleet; *TOF*—Pacific Fleet; *KF*—Kamchatka Flotilla; *STF*—Northern Pacific Flotilla (the latter two flotillas were subsets of the Pacific Fleet)

COLUMN 8: Participation in Petsamo–Kirkenes Operation (PK=yes)

COLUMN 9: Notes (loss, victories, transfer means, etc.)

	1	2	3	4	5	6	7	8	9
1	212/721	FB	27.09.43		18.08.43		SF, ChF	PK	05.10.43, moved from Leningrad to Polyarnoye (*SF*), arriving 24.11.43, where it defended internal and external lines of communication in the Barents, Karsk, and White Seas from 12.43 to 05.45
2	213/1484	EC	05.07.43	P	05.07.43	25.08.44	SF	PK	05.07.43, departed Mayport (Jacksonville, FL),[a] arriving in Polyarnoye 25.08.43. There it operated in the Barents, Karsk, and White Seas for 14 months; conducted sweeping operations in Varnager Fjord from autumn 1944 to spring 1945.
3	214/1480	RB	05.07.44	P	25.08.44	05.07.44	SF	PK	05.07.43, departed Mayport (Jacksonville, FL), arriving in Polyarnoye 25.08.43. There it operated in the Barents, Karsk, and White Seas for 9 months; conducted sweeping operations in Varnager Fjord from autumn 1944 to spring 1945.
4	215/1496	VY	05.07.44	P	25.08.44	05.07.44	SF	PK	05.07.43, departed Mayport (Jacksonville, FL), arriving in Polyarnoye 25.08.43. There it operated in the Barents, Karsk, and White Seas for 9 months; conducted sweeping operations in Varnager Fjord from autumn 1944 to spring 1945
5	216/1488	RB	05.07.44	P	25.08.44	05.07.44	SF	PK	05.07.43, departed Mayport (Jacksonville, FL), arriving in Polyarnoye 25.08.43. There it operated in the Barents, Karsk, and White Seas for 9 months; conducted sweeping operations in Varnager Fjord from autumn 1944 to spring 1945.

continued on next page

---

1 Berezhnoy is not always clear here. From a linguistic perspective, it appears that for many vessels, the Soviet crew was brought to the United States to accept their delivery. This has significant logistic implications for transporting the crews, providing adequate quarters, messing, familiarization training, and then planning for the return voyage to the USSR, within regularly scheduled convoys or in relatively small packages of submarine chasers from various ports on both East and West Coasts of the United States. On the US side, given the geographical dispersion of the ship builders shown, how were these vessels moved from shipyard to port? Contract crews? US Navy crews? Rail and internal waterways? There is much yet to be researched regarding these and other issues of Lend-Lease, of this and several other classes of vessels.—Translator

TABLE TA3.3—continued

	1	2	3	4	5	6	7	8	9
6	217/1489	EC	05.07.44	P	23.09.44	05.07.44	SF	PK	05.07.43, departed Mayport (Jacksonville, FL), arriving in Polyarnoye 25.08.43. There it operated in the Barents, Karsk, and White Seas for 14 months; conducted sweeping operations in Varnager Fjord from autumn 1944 to spring 1945.
7	218/1492	SB	05.07.44	P	25.08.44	05.07.44	SF	PK	05.07.43, departed Mayport (Jacksonville, FL), arriving in Polyarnoye 25.08.43. There it operated in the Barents, Karsk, and White Seas for 9 months; conducted sweeping operations in Varnager Fjord from autumn 1944 to spring 1945.
8	219/1475	QA	05.07.44	P	25.08.44		SF, KBF	PK	05.07.44, departed Mayport (Jacksonville, FL), arriving in Polyarnoye 25.08.44. There it operated in the Barents, Karsk, and White Seas for 9 months. Moved by White Sea–Baltic Canal to Pillau (Baltiysk) on 23.05.45.
9	220/1490	EC	05.07.44	P	25.08.44	18.07.44	SF	PK	05.07.43, departed Mayport (Jacksonville, FL), arriving in Polyarnoye 25.08.43. There it operated in the Barents, Karsk, and White Seas for 5 months, after which it was used for training purposes. Moved by White Sea–Baltic Canal to Pillau on 23.05.45.
10	221/1481	RB	05.07.44	P	25.08.44	25.08.44	SF	PK	18.07.44, departed Mayport, arriving in Polyarnoye on 25.08.44. There it operated in the Barents, Karsk, and White Seas for 9 months. Moved by White Sea–Baltic Canal to Pillau on 23.05.45.
11	222/1498	TK	05.07.44	P	25.08.44		SF	PK	18.07.44, departed Mayport, arriving in Polyarnoye on 25.08.44. There it defended internal and external lines of communication in the Barents, Karsk, and White Seas for 9 months, after which it was used for training purposes from 15.01.45 to 12.03.45.
12	223/1476	QA	05.07.44	P	25.08.44		SF	PK	18.07.44, departed Mayport, arriving in Polyarnoye on 25.08.44. There it defended internal and external lines of communication in the Barents, Karsk, and White Seas for 9 months.
13	224/1507	HP	05.07.44	P	25.08.44		SF	PK	18.07.44, departed Mayport, arriving in Polyarnoye on 25.08.44. There it defended internal and external lines of communication in the Barents, Karsk, and White Seas from 08.44 to 01.45, after which it was used for training purposes. 02.03.45, torpedoed and sunk by U-995 while conducting combat training with SF submarine M-200.

Sources: Extracted and compiled by translator from S. S. Berezhnoy, *Flot SSSR: Korabli i Suda Lendliza: Spravochnik* (Soviet Navy: Vessels and Ships of Lend-Lease: Handbook) (Saint Petersburg: "Belen," 1994), pp. 120–152. Additional clarification and amplification of ship building firm identifications and locations were taken from the website http://shipbuildinghistory.com/

Basic Data: Full displacement—126.4 t; length—34.2 m; beam—5.47 m; draught—1.87 m; propulsion—2 × 980 h.p. diesels; maximum speed—17 kts.; economic—12 kts.; economic range—1,450 mi. Armament: 1 × 40 mm and 3 × 20 mm guns; 2 × .50 cal. machine guns; four depth-charge dispensers and 10 "Hedgehog" or Mark-20 "Mousetrap" launchers.[b] Crew—32. The sketch on p. 152 of the Berezhnoy text shows an SC-497 class submarine chaser, which has a wooden hull.

a. Naval Station Mayport, located along the Atlantic coast just east of Jacksonville, Florida. This entry lends credence to supposition that in this case, as well as in others, Soviet Navy crews were being brought to the United States for some minimal period of on-vessel familiarization, then sailing some or all of these subchasers back to Soviet ports.—Translator

b. The Russian terms used here are *bombomyot* and *bombosbrasyvatel* respectively. Descriptions and photographs of this vessel class (SC-497), show it with depth charge launchers on both sides of the stern and either a British-designed "Hedgehog" or a US Navy Mark-20 "Mousetrap" system at the bow, both of which launched mortar-like projectiles forward of the vessel in a patterned salvo. The depth charges were launched individually and triggered barometrically at a preset depth, while the projectiles launched from the bow-mounted spigots detonated upon contact with the enemy submarine's hull.—Translator

Recommended Bibliography

Barchenko-Emelianov, I. P. *Frontovyye bydnyi Rybachevo* (Frontline life on the Rybachyy Peninsula). Murmansk: Knizhnoye Izdatelstvo, 1984.

Berezhnoy, S. S. *Flot SSSR: Korabli i Suda Lendliza: Spravochnik* (Soviet Navy: Vessels and ships of Lend-Lease: Handbook). Saint Petersburg: "Belen," 1994.

Gebhardt, James F. *The Petsamo-Kirkenes Operation: Soviet Breakthrough and Pursuit in the Arctic, October 1944*. Leavenworth Papers Number 17. Fort Leavenworth, KS: Combat Studies Institute, 1989. This is the companion piece to this work and should be read for comprehension of the primary ground offensive.

Greentree, David. *Petsamo and Kirkenes 1944: The Soviet Offensive in the Northern Arctic*. Oxford: Osprey Publishing, 2019. Book draws heavily from Gebhardt's work and has excellent maps.

Intelligence Support of the Northern Fleet in the Great Patriotic War (1941–1945). Study no. 38. Moscow: Naval Press of the Ministry of the Navy of the USSR, Moscow, 1950.

Leonov, Victor. *Разведчик Морской Пехоты* (Naval infantry scout). Moscow: Yauza, 2009. Memoirs of twice Hero of the Soviet Union Loza, who led the capture of the German battery on Cape Krestovoy during the Petsamo–Kirkenes Operation and captured thousands of Japanese soldiers during the subsequent Manchurian campaign. First published in 1951 after severe redaction by the Stalinist government.

Leonov, Victor. *Лицом к Лицу: Мемуары Морской Пехоты* (Face to face: Recollections of a naval scout). Moscow: Tsentrizdat, 2005. Leonov's memoir of his Northern Fleet special detachment from 1941 to 1945 including rewrite of above work and is the basis for Jim Gebhardt's translation. First published in 1957.

Leonov, Victor. Translated by James F. Gebhardt. *Blood on the Shores: Soviet Naval Commandos in World War II*. Annapolis: Naval Institute Press, 1993. Jim used the expanded 1957 work and added detail from personal interviews with Leonov and a chapter on Soviet Naval Scouts and Commandos.

Northern Fleet Summary on Operation West for the Period 7–31 October 1944, book 1.

Voss, Johann. *Black Edelweiss: A Memoir of Combat and Conscience by a Soldier of the Waffen SS*. Bedford, UK: Aberjona Press, 2002. Author was a machine gunner in the Sixth "Viking" SS Division who fought in Finland, the Petsamo-Kirkenes Operation, and the Vosges Mountains of France.

Other Soviet/Russian works translated and published by James Gebhardt

Antipov, Vlad. and Igor Utkin. *Dragons on Bird Wings: The Combat History of the 812th Fighter Regiment*. Vol. 1: *Liberation of the Motherland*. Kitchener, ON: Aviaeology, 2006.

Dmitry Loza. *Attack of the Airacobras: Soviet Aces, American P-39s and the Air War Against Germany*. Lawrence: University Press of Kansas, 2002.

Dmitry Loza. *Commanding the Red Army's Sherman Tanks: The World War II Memoirs of Hero of the Soviet Union Dmitry Loza*. Lincoln: University Press of Nebraska, 1996.

Dmitry Loza. *Fighting for the Soviet Motherland: Recollections from the Eastern Front*. Lincoln: University Press of Nebraska, 1988.

Ministry of Defense of the USSR. *The Official Soviet SVD Manual*. Boulder, CO: Paladin Press: Operating Instructions for the 7.62 mm Dragunov Sniper Rifle, 1997.

Ministry of Defense of the USSR. *The Official Soviet 7.62 mm Handgun Manual: Instructions for Use and Maintenance of the Nagant 7.62 Revolver Type 1895 and the Tokarev 7.62 mm Semi-automatic Pistol Type 1933*. Boulder, CO: Paladin Press, 1997.

Ministry of Defense of the USSR. *The Official SKS Manual: Instructions for Use and Maintenance of the 7.62 mm Simonov Self-loading Carbine (SKS)*. Boulder: Paladin Press, 1997.

Ministry of Defense of the USSR. *The Official Soviet AKM Manual: Operating Instructions for the 7.62 mm Modernized Kalashnikov Rifle (AKM and AKMS)*. Boulder, CO: Paladin Press, 1999.

Ministry of Defense of the USSR. *The Official Soviet Mosin-Nagant Rifle Manual: Operating Instructions for the Model 1891/30 Rifle and Model 1938 and Model 1944 Carbines*. Boulder, CO: Paladin Press, 2000.

Ministry of Defense of the USSR. *The Official Soviet AK-74 Manual: Operating Instructions for the 5.45 mm Kalashnikov Assault Rifle (AK-74 and AKS-74) and Kalashnikov Light Machine Gun (RPK-74 and RPKS-74)*. Boulder, CO: Paladin Press, 2006.

Ministry of Defense of the USSR. *The Official Soviet Stechkin Pistol Manual: Instructions for Use and Maintenance of the Stechkin 9 mm Automatic Pistol (APS)*. Boulder, CO: Paladin Press, 2007.

Ministry of Defense of the USSR. *The Official Soviet RPG Manual: Operating Instructions for the RPG-2 and RPG-7 Shoulder-Fired Antitank Rocket Launchers*. Boulder, CO: Paladin Press, 2007.

Ministry of Defense of the USSR. *The Official Soviet Mosin-Nagant Sniper Rifle Manual: Operating Instructions for the Model 1891/30 7.62 mm Sniper Rifle with PU Scope and Observation Instructions*. Boulder, CO: Paladin Press, 2010.

People's Commissariat of Defense and the Ministry of Defense of the USSR. *The Official Soviet Army Hand Grenade Manual*. Boulder: Paladin Press 1998.

Strekhnin, Yuriy Fedorovich. *Commandos from the Sea: Soviet Naval Spetsnaz in World War II*. Annapolis: Naval Institute Press, 1996.

About the Translator

James Gebhardt began his formal foreign language study with four semesters of Latin in a North Dakota public high school (1964–1966). His first exposure to the Russian language came during his undergraduate education at the University of Idaho (1972–1974), with continued graduate-level study at the University of Washington, Seattle (1974–1976). After designation as a Soviet foreign area officer in 1983, he completed the 47-week Basic Russian Course at the Defense Language Institute, Presidio of Monterey, followed by two additional years of immersion study in language as an element of a broad Soviet studies curriculum at the US Army Russian Institute in Garmisch-Partenkirchen, Germany, graduating in 1986.

His military experience includes three years as an enlisted infantryman, which included a Vietnam tour; commissioning in Armor Branch through the ROTC program; and several years of duty in armor billets in the continental United States and Germany, culminating in command of an M60A3 thermal-sight-equipped tank company. After designation as a Soviet foreign area officer, he performed duties as a history instructor and unclassified sources military analyst at Fort Leavenworth and, in his final year on active duty, as the Deputy Field Office Chief, San Francisco (Travis AFB), for the On-Site Inspection Agency, escorting Soviet military and scientific personnel throughout the western United States in the implementation of several disarmament treaties.

His seminal historical work, Leavenworth Papers No. 17, *The Petsamo-Kirkenes Operation: Soviet Breakthrough and Pursuit in the Arctic, October 1944*, published in 1990 under the auspices of the Combat Studies Institute, US Army Command, and General Staff College, continues to be recognized internationally as authoritative 30 years later. This monograph has been translated and published in derivative form in both Sweden (2001 and again in 2020) and Norway (2016), and the Swedish version translated into Polish (2011). His subsequent efforts include works published by the US Army's Combat Studies Institute (two titles as a contract historian); Naval Institute Press (two titles); University of Nebraska Press (two titles); University Press of Kansas (one title); Paladin Press (11 titles—translations of Soviet Army small arms technical manuals); the National Park Service in Anchorage (two titles); and publishers in Canada and Australia (one title each). His primary fields of study were Lend-Lease to the USSR and Soviet Navy special operations force structure and combat experience in World War II. Over the past two decades, he translated 9 of the 10 studies currently available in English from the 40-volume collection represented here.

His most recent efforts were to translate from German microfilmed war records a large collection of documents (90 in all, comprising approximately 240 pages of text) of the Twentieth Mountain Army and subordinate units that describe the detection, apprehension, and elimination of small Soviet–Norwegian covert agent teams inserted into German-occupied northern Norway from September 1941 to December 1943. He also translated three significant Soviet Navy doctrinal documents, promulgated by the Soviet Main Naval Staff in 1937, 1940, and 1945. This "trifecta" totals almost 400 pages in English of the prewar, early-war, and postwar doctrine that guided the actions of the Soviet Navy in those critical time periods and beyond.

About the Contributors

Charles K. Bartles, Lieutenant-Colonel, is an analyst and Russian linguist at the Foreign Military Studies Office at Fort Leavenworth, Kansas. His specific research areas include Russian and Central Asian military force structure, modernization, tactics, officer and enlisted professional development, and security assistance programs. Chuck is a lieutenant colonel in the United States Army Reserve who is imagery (35A1D) and space operations (FA40) qualified. He has deployed to Afghanistan and Iraq and has served as a security assistance officer at embassies in Kyrgyzstan, Uzbekistan, and Kazakhstan. Chuck has a BA in Russian from the University of Nebraska–Lincoln, an MA in Russian and Eastern European studies from the University of Kansas, and a PhD from the University of Missouri–Kansas City. He designed and redrafted the maps for this volume.

David M. Glantz, Colonel, US Army, Retired, was a founding member and director of the Soviet Army Studies Office 1986–1993 and is considered the West's leading scholar and historian on the Soviet military in World War II. He was the Mark M. Clark Visiting Professor of History at the Citadel Military College of South Carolina. Among his honors are the 2000 Samuel Eliot Morrison Prize for lifetime achievement given by the Society for Military History and the 2020 Pritzker Literature Award for lifetime achievement.

Lester W. Grau, Lieutenant-Colonel, Retired, is an analyst and Russian linguist at the Foreign Military Studies Office at Fort Leavenworth, Kansas. His specific research areas include Russian military tactics, the Soviet-Afghan War and the ongoing Russian-Ukraine conflict. He fought and carries a limp from combat in Vietnam. He served 27 years in the US Army, retiring as a Lieutenant Colonel and deployed as a civilian to Afghanistan and Iraq. He holds a BA from Texas Western College, a MA from Kent State University and a PhD in Russian and Central Asian History from the University of Kansas. He is the author of 20 books and more than 250 articles and book chapters.